Arts Therapies and New Challenges in Psychiatry

Despite their increasing popularity and reported effectiveness, there is a dearth of evidence-based research on the practices that fall under the umbrella of "the arts therapies". The successful treatment of a variety of psychiatric illnesses through the application of the arts therapies has long been recognized in many countries around the world, including psychosis, schizophrenia, depression and borderline symptoms.

Providing valuable data on the effectiveness of the arts therapies, *Arts Therapies and New Challenges in Psychiatry* fills an important gap in the literature on psychiatric illnesses. Contributors to this impressive volume have carried out research in psychiatry and mental health with patients diagnosed with a variety of illnesses. The international focus of the book shows the global, cross-cultural relevance of the arts therapies, whilst quantitative and qualitative evidence is used to demonstrate the need for art, music-, drama- and dance therapy in a wide variety of contexts. This book shows that research in these fields can be carried out convincingly using a broad range of approaches, including each field's own professional matrix.

Providing a much-needed assessment of the arts therapies, this book will appeal to art therapists, music therapists, dance therapists and drama therapists, as well as psychiatrists, psychologists, psychoanalysts and educators of arts therapy training.

Karin Dannecker has been the Director of the MA in Art Therapy programme at the Weissensee Art Academy Berlin since 2000. Her research interests include the effectiveness of art therapy, the role of aesthetics in art therapy, and the psychology of the artist. Professor Dannecker has also worked with psychiatric and psychosomatic patients since 1987. Her clinical work includes art therapy with children, adolescents, rheumatology patients and art therapy with adult psychiatric and psychosomatic patients.

International Research in the Arts Therapies

A Routledge Book Series

Series Editors: Diane Waller and Sarah Scoble

This series consists of high-level monographs identifying areas of importance across all arts therapy modalities and highlighting international developments and concerns. It presents recent research from countries across the world and contributes to the evidence-base of the arts therapies. Papers which discuss and analyse current innovations and approaches in the arts therapies and arts therapy education are also included.

This series is accessible to practitioners of the arts therapies and to colleagues in a broad range of related professions, including those in countries where arts therapies are still emerging. The monographs should also provide a valuable source of reference to government departments and health services.

For more information about the series, please visit www.routledge.com.

Titles in the series

1 **Intercultural Arts Therapies Research**
Edited by Ditty Dokter and Margaret Hills de Zárate

2 **Arts Therapies and New Challenges in Psychiatry**
Edited by Karin Dannecker

Arts Therapies and New Challenges in Psychiatry

Edited by Karin Dannecker

Routledge
Taylor & Francis Group
LONDON AND NEW YORK

ICRA
INTERNATIONAL CENTRE FOR RESEARCH IN ARTS THERAPIES

ECArTE
EUROPEAN CONSORTIUM FOR ARTS THERAPIES EDUCATION

First published 2018 by Routledge

2 Park Square, Milton Park, Abingdon, Oxfordshire OX14 4RN
52 Vanderbilt Avenue, New York, NY 10017

Routledge is an imprint of the Taylor & Francis Group, an informa business

First issued in paperback 2019

British Library Cataloguing in Publication Data
A catalogue record for this book is available from the British Library

Library of Congress Cataloguing in Publication Data
A catalog record for this book has been requested

ISBN: 978-1-138-67197-3 (hbk)
ISBN: 978-0-367-36896-8 (pbk)

Typeset in Bembo
by Wearset Ltd, Boldon, Tyne and Wear

Contents

Contributors

Susanne Bauer, Prof. Dr, is a psychologist and a music therapist certified by the German Association for Music Therapy (DMtG). She received her PhD in Ulm, Germany, where her research focused on the perception and expression of emotions in patients who suffer from schizophrenia. Susanne Bauer lived in Chile for almost 20 years, where she cofounded and directed the first post-graduate music therapy programme at the University of Chile in Santiago. She is now professor of music therapy and director of the master's programme in music therapy at the University of the Arts in Berlin. In addition to her scientific and training activities, Susanne Bauer is involved in the treatment of adults in a psychosomatic clinic. She is a member of the Asociación Chilena de Musicoterapia (AChiM) and the Society for Psychotherapy Research (SPR).

Karin Dannecker, Prof. Dr, has been the director of the MA art therapy programme at the Weissensee Art Academy, Berlin, since 2000. She has worked with psychiatric and psychosomatic patients since 1987 and has published two monographs and edited three books and numerous articles on art therapy. Her Habilitation was published under the title *Psyche und Ästhetik: Die Transformationen der Kunsttherapie*. Her academic interests are research into the effectiveness of art therapy, the role of aesthetics in art therapy, and psychology of the artist. Her clinical work includes art therapy with children, adolescents and rheumatology patients and art therapy with adult psychiatric and psychosomatic patients.

Christine Falquet-Clin, Dr, is a psychiatrist, hospital practitioner and musico-therapist in activity in the adult day care of the Centre Hospitalier Annecy Genevois's (CHANGE) mental health centre, and a doctoral student in art therapy at the Paris Descartes University under the supervision of Prof. E. Lecourt and Prof. A. Boissière.

Thomas Fuchs, Prof. Dr, is Karl Jaspers Professor for Philosophical Foundations of Psychiatry and Psychotherapy, Head of Section "Phenomenological Psychopathology and Psychiatry" at the Centre of Psychosocial Medicine, University of Heidelberg.

Johannes Junker, Prof., studied theology and philosophy in Germany and drama therapy in the Netherlands, where he also completed his supervision and coaching training. Besides his 21 years' professional experience as a drama therapist and head of department in a psychiatric and forensic hospital in Germany (1990–2011), he was for many years dean of the part-time BA course "Music, Art and Drama Therapy" (2004–2009) and dean of the international MA course "Artistic Therapies" at the Hogeschool van Arnhem en Nijmegen, Netherlands (2009–2011). From 2011 to 2016 he was professor and rector at the Hochschule für Kunsttherapie Nürtingen in Germany. Since 2016 this private university has been integrated in a state university, Hochschule für Umwelt und Wirtschaft Nürtingen Geislingen, where he is now vice dean of art therapies. He has published numerous papers in Dutch, German and English in the areas of professional development and drama therapy for specific conditions.

Iveta Koblic Zedková, MD (Czech Republic), is general adult psychiatrist, trained in Gestalt psychotherapy and dance movement therapy. During her clinical practice she gained rich experience in therapeutic work, mainly in schizophrenia spectrum disorders, and psychosomatic and neurotic disorder patients. With the support of DAAD scholarship, she took part in the TESIS Project ("Towards Embodied Intersubjectivity") at the section for phenomenology and psychopathology (Prof. Fuchs, Heidelberg). As a PhD student at the 1st Medical Faculty, Charles University, Prague, her main areas of research interest are early-onset schizophrenia and the role of body/movement in the implicit, nonverbal dimension of the psychotherapeutic encounter. Currently, she is the president of the dance movement therapy association, CR TANTER, and works in the outpatient neuropsychiatric facility, INEP Medical. She has lectured on projects in psychosocial competencies in medical students and creative arts therapies in institutional upbringing. She is the editor and co-author of the book *Dance Movement Therapy: Theory and Practice*.

Sabine C. Koch, Prof. Dr, psychologist and dance/movement therapist, is the head of the dance movement therapy department at SRH University of Heidelberg, Germany. She has more than 100 publications and runs national and international projects in the area of arts therapies, addressing aspects of theoretical, methodological, qualitative and evidence-based nature. Her most recent book focuses on *Body Memory, Metaphor and Movement* (2012) and her most recent articles include a meta-analysis of the effects of dance and dance therapy on psychological outcomes, a paper on indications and contra-indications of dance movement therapy (DMT), factors of effectiveness in DMT, as well as an evidence-based study on the effects of mirroring-based DMT on young adults with autism.

Alexander Kopytin, PhD, is a professor in the Department of Psychology at the St Petersburg (Russia) Academy for Post-Graduate Pedagogical

Training, and in the Department of Psychotherapy at the St Petersburg Medical Academy for Post-Graduate Training.

Alexey Lebedev, MD, is a trained psychiatrist and art psychotherapist in the Department of Psychotherapy, Hospital for War Veterans, Volgograd, Russia. Correspondence concerning the chapter may be addressed to the first author at alkopytin@rambler.ru.

Edith Lecourt, Prof. Dr, is full professor of clinical and pathological psychology at the University of Paris Descartes/Sorbonne Paris Cité, laboratories PCPP EA 4056 and TEC EA 3625. She is a psychologist, psychoanalyst and music therapist. She was co-founder of the first French music therapy association (1972), and organizer of the first world congress of music therapy (Paris, 1974). She is the director of the first MA and PhD in arts therapies at the Sorbonne Paris Cité (with four specializations in arts therapies), created in 2011. She has also developed group psychoanalysis at the university and is president of the French Federation of Groupanalysis. She has published many articles and books on these subjects.

Christiane Montag, PD Dr med., works as a consultant in clinical psychiatry and psychotherapy at the Psychiatric University Clinic of the Charité at St Hedwigs Hospital in Berlin. She is head of the research group "Empathy and Interpersonal Processes" in the schizophrenia research division of the Department of Psychiatry and Psychotherapy of the Charité University. Her research interests involve social cognition, emotional processing and psychotherapy in patients with psychotic disorders.

Valerie Pohlmann is a clinical psychologist (MSc.) who graduated from the University of Bremen in 2015. She was involved in the Heidelberg node of the Marie Curie TESIS project by writing her thesis on the effects of movement therapy in schizophrenia and attending movement therapy with schizophrenic patients as a co-therapist. She has a BSc. degree in psychology from Heidelberg University. In her bachelor's dissertation she investigated correlations between metaphors in movement and language following the conceptual metaphor theory.

Alice Reid is a Franco-British psychologist who has recently graduated with a master's degree from the Ecole de Psychologues Practiciens in Lyon, France. During her training she worked in a psychiatric clinic for female patients, in homes for mentally disabled people and in different types of psychosocial rehabilitation units. She has always been interested in training to become an art therapist. Alice Reid currently runs courses for caregivers and hospital employees to help them cope with stress at work and has plans to continue working with psychiatric patients using the squiggle technique. In spring 2016 she published her first article entitled, "Psychogenealogy and its history", in the French periodical *Soins Psychiatrie.*

Elizabeth Stone, MA, ATR-BC, LP, LCAT, is a licensed art therapist and psychoanalyst in private practice in Grenoble, France, working with adults, children and adolescents. She has been on the faculty of the Ecole des Psychologues Practiciens de l'Université Catholique de Lyon. She also consults through the Association Grenobloise d'Aide à la Recherche en Oncology (AGARO) at the Centre Hospitalier Universitaire (CHU) de Grenoble. Formerly on the faculty of New York University where she did her graduate studies, she has been involved in the training and supervision of art therapists in Italy, Switzerland, France and the United States. A graduate of the New York School of Psychoanalytic Psychotherapy and Psychoanalysis, she lectures and publishes widely on creative expression in art therapy in Europe and the United States.

Zuzana Vasičáková Očenášová, Mgr., MSc., is a dance movement therapist and mediator based in Bratislava. She is a founding president of the Slovak Association of Dance Movement Therapy and a founding member of Laban Atelier Bratislava. She has been working with people in psychiatric care, with dyads of parents and children with autism and with combined physical and mental disabilities, with seniors, with people experiencing eating disorders, with survivors of domestic violence and with people with physical challenges, as well as in the area of personal and professional development and conflict resolution. Currently she works as a dance movement therapist in cooperation with psychiatric day care and is developing her own practice. She is conducting her PhD research on dance movement therapy and Laban movement analyses within the theme of work with dyads at the Institute of Clinical Psychology, Masaryk University in Brno. She is a student of long-term training in process-oriented psychology.

Lambros Yotis, MD, PhD, trained as a psychiatrist (Athens University), dramatherapist (PGDip, University of Hertfordshire, UK) and theatre actor (Athens Drama School). He has worked for over 20 years in psychiatric institutions in Greece (Athens University Day Hospital), in psychiatric rehabilitation and for the international programme of the World Health Organization against the stigma of mental illness (Athens University Mental Health Research Institute). He completed a PhD in "Dramatherapy Performance and Schizophrenia" at the University of Hertfordshire, UK (2002). He is a founding member of the Association of Dramatic Expression and Therapy "Palmos" in Athens; there he works as a dramatherapist, group leader, tutor and supervisor. He has also trained in playback theatre and is an accredited trainer (International School of Playback Theatre, New York – Jonathan Fox). In 2004 he founded the first professional playback theatre group in Greece, namely "Playback Ψ", of which he is the artistic director. In addition, he works as a theatre director and teaches improvisation in schools of acting.

Preface

For several decades, the arts therapies have been vital components in the treatment of patients with psychiatric disorders. Art, music, dance and drama therapists are members of psychiatric teams and generally their work is highly valued. Often the well-being of patients is based on what they have experienced in the arts therapies.

Professionals and other interested persons know that psychiatric illnesses are accompanied by restricted abilities to communicate verbally or in other comprehensible ways, as well as with altered perception of reality and affect behaviour. This increases patients' level of suffering and feelings of being socially isolated. Here the arts have long been used to help overcome barriers of conventional communication and enhance the development of self-awareness and self-expression.

Any artistic process fosters integrative processes of feeling, acting, thinking, cognition and introspection. Because the arts media and the artistic process relate directly to sense perception, they can be applied even when logical thinking is impaired or when emotions dominate or seem to be buried. Creating art means to work with another, an outer sensually perceptive medium, to slow down impulses, to apply physical motor control and mental structuring, to find rhythm and form. An artwork always contains something of the inner as well as the outer world of its creator. It symbolizes the artist's way of feeling and perceiving his/her world, his/her hopes and fears, his/her fantasies and how he/she deals with relationships. The symbolic process fosters intersubjective experiences.

Creating an image, a dance movement, music or a drama or piece of theatre requires tolerance for what becomes visible or audible. Any artist, and the artistically working patient as well, knows or senses that the work feeds back to him/her what was formerly part of his/her inner world.

The introduction of a third element into the therapeutic relationship – the work of art, the music, dance or drama – signifies for most psychiatric patients a great relief. As their lives often have been characterized by failing and disappointing relationships with others, it is generally much easier for them to tolerate being with someone like the arts therapist, in a situation in which the main focus of attention is on creating an expressive form. In this therapeutic alliance patients do not have to deal with the potentially threatening aspects of mainly verbally relating to a therapist. With the art therapist the use of words is directed towards working with the medium, understanding the artistic expression, the symbolic meaning and the metaphor.

Artists who become therapists bring with them specific experiences that designate them as having deep empathy for people who suffer from verbal communication problems.

Each art process requires the artist to allow him/herself access to his/her inner life. He/she must get in touch with his/her fantasies, with illogical, fragmented, unresolved themes, before he/she actively starts creating. Bearing this tension and relying on these personal experiences is what an artist as well as an art therapist is especially familiar with. Thus, these states of mind as part of the creative process are the premises the arts therapist applies when he/she encourages patients to create, to use artistic media to express themselves and communicate feelings and thoughts. Symbolic communication is what he/she particularly understands. His/her artistic as well as therapeutic abilities make him or her suited to supporting the psychiatric patient to find form in what until then has been formless, fragmented or uncontrollable, hidden or repressed.

The main goals of the arts therapies with psychiatric patients are the retrieval of self and reality, the development of a healthy body image, gaining or regaining an appropriate perception of the environment and other people, and the improvement of cognitive functions and autonomy. Above all it is the capacity to symbolize and to express feelings in communicative form, to build and maintain substantial relationships and to increase self-confidence which constitutes the specific efficacy of the arts therapies.

Despite the widely and successfully applied treatment strategies of the arts therapies for people with severe mental illness, there is only a limited number of studies providing relevant significant evidence that the use of the arts therapies reduces the appearance of negative symptoms of psychiatric patients. Internationally, the research done can be found in various databases such as the *Cochrane Library* (Wiley), *Medline* (EBESCO), *PsyInfo* (ProQuest) and *Scopus* (Elsevier). The authors of the NICE Clinical Guidelines (82, 2009) on the treatment of schizophrenia score the results of the treatment of schizophrenic patients as highly positive and they recommend the arts therapies for such patients. Yet the need for further studies in all the arts therapies is strongly emphasized by representatives of health care institutions and health insurance providers. Generally, the recommendation of treatment guidelines is to rely on a high level of scientific evidence-based studies, such as the findings of meta-analyses and large randomized control trials (RCT). However, arts therapists tend to prefer research which is based on their own professional matrix.

Today the debates reflect a wide range of approaches. Most discussions focus on the necessity to apply regular evidence-based models of measuring the efficacy of arts therapies on the basis of empirically gained data, fulfilling the requirement to produce comprehensible data according to medical models, whereas others critically question these methods because they are not capable of gathering together the complex processes of the therapeutic relationship in the arts therapies, where the arts define the method and the quality of therapy.

The main suggestion is to investigate why arts therapies interventions are effective. This means examining each artistic medium with regard to the qualitative and healing potential it carries intrinsically. Research may also focus on the specific quality of the therapeutic relationship between patient and art therapist. The dual relationship is determinately extended by the art medium. As in modern psychotherapy, the relational processes are considered crucial to processes of change in art therapy.

In psychotherapy, research treatment outcomes cannot be fully comprehended via questionnaires because such self-assessments by patients are subjective and changing and the results therefore are unreliable in respect of the evidence of the treatment method. These observations seriously question the empirical medical models of RCT-based research. As in the psychotherapy sciences, arts therapists complain about a lack of attention to researching the specifically defined quality characteristics of their treatment modalities.

Despite controversial debates, there remains an overall need to implement research with substantiated scientific methods. Today the arts therapies are on the way to utilizing evidence-based models developed out of their own matrix. Research moves between investigating the art mode as the third element in the therapeutic relationship, the qualitative characteristics of the media and the collection of qualitative data on the therapeutic relationship. Likewise, parallel research based on quantitative, empirically medical RCT methods is applied in all arts therapies. This happens mainly and naturally in interdisciplinary collaboration with the medical and/or other departments according to the research questions. Psychiatrists are involved in and often enthusiastically support such projects. The arts therapists and the medical staff learn from and enrich each other, knowing that their engagement will help their patients to improve the quality of their lives.

This book aims to contribute to the knowledge of and insight into why arts interventions with patients with a variety of psychiatric disorders are effective. Since the core psychiatric illness requiring more intense research is schizophrenia, the contributions mainly focus on these symptoms. Many arts therapists have a wealth of therapeutic experiences with patients suffering from schizophrenia and they are inspired to do and follow an in-depth investigation about why and how their work is successful. The chapters emphasize new challenges arising from the demands of clinical work, health politics and new theoretical, social and cultural issues.

The authors work and live in six European countries. This variety of backgrounds reflects a unique collection of viewpoints in arts therapies research, demonstrating that art therapy is not a "one-size-fits-all" approach in psychiatry. Although the contributions contain much that can be considered common denominators for the efficacy of the arts in therapy in this field, there are nevertheless some specific social and cultural influences that reflect the background of the authors. This is part of the challenge and it is the most enriching one in terms of demonstrating that collaboration in the arts therapies across borders leads to an exchange and increase of knowledge.

The book is structured according to the alphabetical order of the contributors' names.

In the first chapter **Susanne Bauer**, from Berlin, Germany, provides an introduction with an extensive overview on the musical representation of emotions of schizophrenic patients, considering the question of whether they present particularities in their perception of music, musical representation of emotions and musical dialogue behaviour. Her randomized study of schizophrenic patients investigated the question of whether schizophrenia is an illness which inhibits the appraisal and processing emotions, and whether music therapy can contribute to the hypothesis that schizophrenic patients play and perceive more irregularly and feel different from healthy people. Subjects were asked to represent sadness, joy and anger on musical instruments, classify three expressly composed piano pieces, and participate in a musical dialogue.

Christine Falquet-Clin and **Edith Lecourt**, in Chapter 2, present a clinical qualitative research on the place of aesthetic emotion in music therapy with adult psychiatric patients (PCPP and TEC laboratories of the Paris Descartes University). The research has two principal objects: the development of a theoretical background on the psychic processes involved in receptive music therapy through the clinical relationship; the study of these emotional moments through the methodology of the analysis of individual case studies in a French psychiatric hospital. It focuses on the questions of whether aesthetic emotion could be both the witness to and the impetus encouraging the work of symbolizations, of the transformations of the hypercomplex and enigmatic psychic raw material that are vital to the psyche, and whether aesthetic emotion reveals the fecundity of the interaction between the material used in artistic and in clinical practice. These questions are studied through case studies on receptive music therapy with adult patients. One of these case studies illustrates the place of aesthetic emotion in the therapeutic process.

In the next contribution, **Johannes Junker** from Nürtingen, Germany, gives an overview of dramatherapy work in the treatment of schizophrenic psychoses. The focus lies on specific treatment options, on the one hand, and on previous publications on this topic with special emphasis on research, on the other. Research results to date are collated and assessed as to their proven effectiveness and methodic relevance. As far as the effectiveness of dramatherapy treatment is concerned, supporting evidence as required by the German health system as a starting point for possible and necessary future research is included. Several examples of dramatherapy methods that have been tested in a research project are introduced and their relevance to different aspects of this condition discussed.

In Chapter 4, the psychiatrist and art therapist **Alexander Kopytin**, from St Petersburg, Russia, and the psychiatrist **Alexey Lebedev**, from Volgograd, Russia, present findings from a study of the therapeutic effects of a group art therapy used in the form of a brief intervention in the psychotherapy unit of a Russian hospital for war veterans. An experimental group (art therapy) and a control group were composed of 112 patients being treated for stress-related disorders. A suite of assessment tools to measure the dynamics of patients' symptomatic status, personality and quality of life revealed the multifaceted effects of interactive group art therapy. Though certain positive effects were also observed in the control group, these effects were less evident than in the experimental group.

Chapter 5 presents the results of a pilot study carried out by **Christiane Montag** and **Karin Dannecker** with acute schizophrenic patients in a university hospital in Berlin. The Psychiatric University Clinic of the Charité at St Hedwigs Hospital and the Art Therapy Department at the Weissensee Art School Berlin collaboratively conducted the research with 54 acute schizophrenic patients. In this randomized controlled study, the question was whether art therapy leads to symptom reduction in acute schizophrenic states. The empirical findings are presented in this chapter. Parallel qualitative approaches were applied: the art therapy sessions were filmed, the artworks were photographed. The qualitative approach to evaluating the project, including the series of artworks, is introduced.

Valerie Pohlmann, **Sabine C. Koch** and **Thomas Fuchs** from Heidelberg, Germany, then present an investigation of changes in the well-being of schizophrenic patients after 20 sessions of body-oriented psychotherapy provided by three dance movement therapists in a multicentre study. Results are discussed from an embodiment perspective. Schizophrenia is a self-disorder characterized by positive and negative symptoms. While medication can successfully address positive symptoms, it cannot change negative symptoms. Schizophrenia can, furthermore, be conceptualized as a disturbance of the embodied self or a *disembodiment*, suggesting that body-oriented psychotherapy/dance movement therapy as nonverbal body-oriented methods can address the challenges of the disorder. There is evidence that body-oriented psychotherapy/dance movement therapy effectively reduces negative symptoms of schizophrenia.

The aim of the pilot study from **Alice Reid**, from Lyon, France (Chapter 7), was to explore the way in which the squiggle technique might be relevant when it is adapted to a group activity organized for schizophrenic patients undergoing a psychosocial rehabilitation programme. The results suggested that the use of the squiggle could increase a patient's flexibility. On average, patients practically doubled their answers in the divergent thinking tasks and began to use new strategies to adapt their inner world to the squiggle. The medium facilitated the creation of secure relationships within the group. The participants gradually took more interest in each other's work, thereby increasing and developing their questions and comments. The different parts of the squiggle were used to make a unified object or several objects interacting together or to build a full context or story. An increasing number of links being made between their production and their own story provided evidence of the emergence of a stronger narrative self.

In her explorative study in Chapter 8, **Elizabeth Stone**, who lives and works in Grenoble, France, offers a reflection from clinical practice based upon the premise that the role of the "borrowed" image advances the therapeutic action of art therapy with psychiatric patients. A series of case vignettes illustrates how the level of fragility in the individual's psychic structure influences the way the outside image is internalized and functions in strengthening the ego. The author posits the argument that the theoretical roots of "borrowing" or copying originate in the intrapsychic internalization process, through which self and object relations develop. Winnicott's concept of the transitional object (and transitional phenomena) stands as the prototype for the borrowed image in art therapy. The author's use of the term "borrowed image" refers to a range of outside images that include art reproductions, the live model, the landscape, photos or the artwork of other patients, and serve as a basis for creating painting, drawing and sculpture.

Zuzana Vasičáková Očenášová from the Slovak Republic and **Iveta Koblic Zedková** from the Czech Republic explore the challenges of using Slovak folk dances as a potential therapeutic substrate in dance movement therapy working with clients experiencing psychiatric disorders. Representing and expressing cultural and social contexts of the bodily self, folk dances can be seen as a valuable resource for therapeutic interventions. In Slovakia, a pilot research study using Laban movement analysis of five selected Slovak folk dances was conducted in order to be used as a base for further exploration. The analysis brought up typical movement patterns, shadow movement qualities, movement shifts, as well as differences in movement choices of men and women. The prevailing common movement choices were identified in order to explore further therapeutic potential. For psychiatric patients therapeutically highly relevant clusters were identified in the data material. The authors conclude that the complex dance forms of Slovak folk dances can provide a rich source for dance movement therapy in psychiatry, both in the overall setting and for particular interventions, on three important levels, mostly in impaired psychiatric patients.

Psychiatrist and dramatherapist **Lambros Yotis**, living in Athens, Greece, relates to Aristotle's "Poetics" as the first sign system in theatre theory, a doctrine written by Aristotle (384–322 BC) to describe the core elements of the performance of ancient Greek tragedy. Contemporary practice in dramatherapy usually deals with the clients' material within a group and does not include performance before an audience. Chapter 10 presents a tool for the assessment and evaluation of a dramatherapy project with clients with schizophrenia that took place at the Eginition Day Hospital of the National and Kapodistrian University of Athens, Medical School, Department of Psychiatry. "Dramatherapy Performance Evaluation" is inspired by Aristotle's "Poetics" and gives the opportunity to assess both the performance process and the event, as well as the clients' symptoms during the construction of the performance. It also shows the change in the clients' "negative symptoms" of schizophrenia after a dramatherapy performance project.

Concluding this Preface, I would like to remark that editing this book was an exciting project in many ways. First because it reflects how rewarding international collaboration in doing research can be. In the arts therapies we generally share a high level of enthusiasm for our fields as well as concerns for further developing the profession. Those concerns may address issues coming from one's own country and culture, as some of the chapters in the book clearly reflect. Themes and questions stemming from one's own cultural and social background and political region arise in the arts therapies.

Psychiatric patients especially are sensitive to these. They express feelings of alienation in their society and they long to be understood, which often is reflected in their art. Some of the authors emphasize this qualitative aspect and prove that the arts therapies provide a special space and possibilities for patients with schizophrenia and other psychiatric diagnoses to investigate their conflicts with cultural and personal identity and relationship issues. Here the investigation of the role of the arts in therapy, which cannot be manifested in numbers but made plausible, is crucial in these qualitative approaches to research.

Second, we know, on the other hand, that there are common and cross-cultural issues which scientifically grounded research in the arts therapies needs to take into consideration. Generating evidence-based results requires following the research methods of the natural sciences. Hence some contributions are based on randomized controlled studies and provide data as the results of the investigations.

The authors of the chapters have devoted themselves greatly to contributing to the aim of the book, which is to extend the knowledge of and insights into the efficacy of the arts therapies. As the editor of the book, I want to thank them all for the profound results of their meeting these challenges.

Karin Dannecker

Reference

NICE (National Institute for Clinical Excellence). (2009). Schizophrenia: Core interventions in the treatment and management of schizophrenia in adults in primary and secondary care. *NICE Clinical Guideline 82*. London: NICE.

Chapter 1

Music therapy

Differentiation of emotions in schizophrenia

Susanne Bauer

Background

This chapter presents a study of relationships between music and disease, more specifically between the perception, expression and representation[1] of music by schizophrenic persons.

Many contemporary scientific disciplines deal with questions concerning "music and mankind", how music and sound affect the body, intellect and soul of healthy and mentally ill people: such disciplines include developmental psychology and emotional psychology, the musicological sciences and music psychology, neurobiology and neurosciences, medicine and psychoanalysis. Some of these studies were considered relevant for understanding the basis of our experimental research. For example, musicologists and music and perception psychologists address the question of *how* people perceive music and exactly *what* they perceive, the emotional and physiological effects of music, and the psychic processes involved during musical representation and the musical expression of healthy people (Böttcher & Kerner, 1978; Frank, 1975; Harrer, 1975; Pekrun, 1985; Revers, 1975). Further, developmental psychologists explain the basics of normal affective interpersonal behaviour and early preverbal dialogue (Jörg et al., 1994; Papousek & Papousek, 1988; Stern, 1991; Trevarthen, 2002). On the other hand, psychologists and psychiatrists investigate the affective behaviour of schizophrenic persons in order to verify whether and how the illness influences perception and expression of feelings (Hufnagel, Steimer-Krause & Krause, 1991; Krause, Steimer-Krause & Ullrich, 1992; Steimer-Krause, 1996; Steimer-Krause, Krause & Wagner, 1990). Many of these findings converge in the discipline of music therapy, which forms the basis of this study. For music therapists in Germany, treatment of people with schizophrenia has been part of the everyday clinical routine for decades. Early publications on the subject appeared in the 1980s (Kneutgen, 1980; Meschede, Bender & Pfeiffer, 1983; Ostertag, 1985; Strobel, 1985). Musical behaviour patterns of schizophrenic persons described in case analyses lead to the conclusion that there are probably some repeating musical expression methods related to the clinical picture and that these may be disorder-specific (discussed in more detail later). Regarding research, it has been repeatedly demonstrated that music therapeutic treatment can positively influence so-called "negative symptoms" and improve social competence (Gold, Heldal, Dahle & Wigram, 2005; Gold, Solli, Krüger & Lie, 2009; Ulrich, Houtmans & Gold, 2007). The following section will present results which refer to perception, representation and experiencing of feelings and music in healthy and schizophrenic persons, as well as their significance for dialogue behaviour.

Perception psychology and musicology

Wellek (1982) provided an important contribution when he posed the question of "how" and "what" a person hears upon being subjected to musical stimuli. He established that "for the child and the childlike person in general, a picture or a musical piece has points of attraction or repulsion, which lead to immediate replies of attraction and rejection" (p. 250). In his opinion, a child cannot yet understand the gestalt as a whole, and understands just as little the gestalt depth of a musical piece (ibid.). Other gestalt psychological studies of music perception implied that the perception occurs through a focused identification and tracking of a "figure" on a "ground". A melody can certainly be perceived as a figure or "good gestalt" even if it does not fit into the harmonic framework (Büchler, 1987, p. 53). Identification of ground and figure in music is related to previous learning and cultural processes. Every experience leaves an imprint in the brain, and new perceptions connect with existing "imprint gestalts" ("*Spurgestalten*") (Thomas, 1990). According to Büchler (1987), the brain is aware of a logical and reliable continuation of a presented piece of music. If the expectation is fulfilled, the entirety acquires a meaning, but the result of an unfulfilled expectation is meaninglessness (ibid.). De la Motte-Haber (1996) conjectured that the perception of musical relationships occurs through assimilation of categorical structures, thereby creating not only regimes but also meanings, and that this process was "a fundamental form of information processing" (p. 156). Jourdain (1998) assumes that the brain seeks familiar indices and patterns: "We recognize musical stylistic devices, that is, we remember them from previous experiences. Memory is therefore a determining factor for musical perception" (p. 304). People select dominant or central features of a musical piece and generalise these to an overall impression, i.e. they interpret the part as the whole ("inductive process"). De la Motte-Haber (1996) determined that tempo is considered a typical dominant feature behind which other musical features recede in importance (pp. 158ff.). Jourdain (1998) also speaks of selective perception and generalisations in the evaluation (of music), particularly by untrained listeners (p. 320).

Developmental psychology

With reference to dialogue configuration, developmental psychologists were able to determine that affective-cognitive development is promoted by vocal stimulation (Altmann de Litvan et al., 2001; Beebe & Lachmann, 1994; Malloch, 1999; Papousek, 1981; Papousek & Papousek, 1988; Stern, 1991; Trevarthen, 2002). Papousek (1995) describes how learning of dialogue structure (turn-taking) takes place before learning of speech; mothers answer the tones or gestures of their infants, stimulate them to new action, wait again for their reactions and react anew. Motherly responses initially take the form of imitation, with increasing variations appearing later (Papousek, 1981; Stern, 1991). The quality and quantity of vocalisation behaviour in children change so greatly during the first months of life that by the 18th month they can carry on an actively structured and coordinated dialogue. Jörg et al. (1994) describe three early interaction schemes: (a) synchronicity: simultaneous occurrence of identical behaviour or feeling states with simultaneous eye contact; (b) reciprocity: reciprocal influencing through new stimuli; (c) elicitation: occurrence of behaviours which lead the communication in a new direction. A faulty interaction results when answers are inconsistent and when reactions are illogical or rigid, when a child's negative signs and new stimuli go unperceived or disregarded, and when elicitations are not answered. Mutual lack and rejection of eye contact are also characteristic of an unsuccessful interaction.

Thus the healthy newborn child has a multitude of hereditary cognitive abilities such as perception, storage, organisation, differentiation and recognition of stimuli; these make it possible for the infant to undertake high-level communication with its environment. To make an appropriately weighted response to its early needs, the child requires an adequate system of affect understanding and affect coding (Osofsky & Eberhart-Wright, 1988), whereby the intensity of its affect utterances is linked to the cultural, familial and historical context (Hochschild, 1996; Krause, 1983). In addition to all of the pre-speech phase possibilities such as gesture, mimicry and voice, musical expression plays an increasingly important role in the early development of humans, particularly with respect to identity building and socio-cultural affiliation. The intersubjective relationship and interaction behaviours acquired in the early stages of development are reflected in adult dialogue behaviour and can be observed and altered in a therapeutic context (Stern, 2010).

Psychiatry and emotion psychology: affect and emotional behaviours

Scientific studies of psychiatry show that perception, affect behaviour and interaction are altered in people with schizophrenia. Numerous studies of persons with primarily negative symptomatology have found a constant tone of voice as well as facial expression which are independent of the spoken content, likewise an increased social withdrawal and abandonment of social relationships. Blunted affect and impoverishment of emotional life were also observed (Creer & Wing, 1989; Kanas, 1996; Katschnig, 1989; Wygotski, 1985). Other studies asked schizophrenic patients and healthy controls to identify feelings in facial expressions presented in photographs or pictures (Lewis & Garver, 1995; Toomey & Schuldberg, 1995; Walker, McGuire & Bettes, 1984). The schizophrenic patients identified feelings represented in the facial expressions significantly less accurately than did persons in the control group. Paranoid patients did have significantly better results than non-paranoid schizophrenic patients (Lewis & Garver, 1995). Other investigations measured facial expression and mimicry changes in schizophrenic patients and healthy controls during presentation of differently emotionally charged cinematic scenes (Kring, Kerr, Smith & Neale, 1993; Kring & Neale, 1996). The results showed distinctly reduced mimicry in persons with schizophrenia compared to the controls. Nevertheless, schizophrenic persons perceived positive and negative emotions just as well as the healthy controls. Krause et al. (1992) obtained similar results in their studies. They determined that the barrenness of mimic expression in schizophrenic persons was often accompanied by very intense experience-based and verbalised negative affects. Investigations of interactive behaviour of schizophrenic and healthy partners (Hufnagel et al., 1991; Steimer-Krause, 1996; Steimer-Krause et al., 1990) captured facial movements using the EMFACS coding system developed by Friesen and Ekman. The results showed that healthy partners adapted themselves to the mimic expression behaviour of their schizophrenic partners and conducted themselves with less expressiveness than partners of a healthy control group. On the other hand, schizophrenic patients tended to emotionally identify with the expressive behaviour of the healthy partner. In their investigation of subjective emotional activity of persons with schizophrenia in the year 2000, Myin-Germeys, Delespaul and deVries adopted the experience sampling method (ESM) to capture the emotional effect of everyday experiences; they found that the illness as such does not present an impediment to feeling emotions. Compared to a healthy control group, the experimental subjects even showed *greater variability* in negative emotions than the control group, though for positive emotions it was significantly lower. The *intensity of feeling* of positive emotions in members of the experimental group was thus significantly lower, whereas for negative emotions it was significantly higher. No significant differences in schizophrenic patients "with flat affect" and "without flat affect" were found in the subjective experiencing of emotions. The "flat affect" classified by the external raters using the Brief Psychiatric Rating Scale (BPRS) could not be confirmed by the experimental subjects themselves. Correlations were poor to non-existent. With respect to therapeutic procedure, the authors consider these results to be relevant, and they see it as a therapeutic responsibility to find a method which promotes the integration of emotions (Myin-Germeys et al., 2000, p. 851). The title of the study by Myin-Germeys and colleagues speaks for itself: "Schizophrenia patients are more emotionally active than is assumed based on their behaviour."

In his meta-analysis of some 55 English-language studies on the subject of schizophrenia and emotions, Trémeau (2006) found that schizophrenic persons express their emotions via verbal, facial and acoustic channels more poorly than healthy controls, but that their behaviour does not clearly and significantly differ from that of depressive persons. On the other hand, the studies which he reviewed showed that schizophrenic persons suffer from a deficit in the identification, expression and experiencing of emotions. With respect to the experiencing of emotions, his conclusion contradicts the findings of Myin-Germeys. Trémeau explicitly points out the difference between recognition and appraisal of feelings: "recognition is part of emotional intelligence and social perception, whereas appraisal is part of emotion processing" (ibid., p. 60). In order to gain a better understanding of the effects of emotional processing deficits on social functioning, he recommends studies of further and as yet unidentified aspects of emotional processing (ibid., p. 67).

Investigations of the capability to perceive and differentiate vocally expressed emotions in schizophrenic persons have been appearing for several years; among the research groups is that of Petri Laukka and Patrik Juslin at the University of Uppsala in Sweden. One of these studies (Leitman et al., 2010) concerns the researching of prosody and identification of emotions on the basis of vocal acoustic stimuli such as tone pitch, timbre and intensity. This study presented the first evidence that schizophrenic persons, in contrast to healthy controls, are unable to utilise pitch, pitch variability or prosody in the identification of emotions.[2] Likewise, in the estimation of emotional arousal, schizophrenic persons performed significantly more poorly than healthy controls. In contrast to the case of pitch, when volume was related to estimation, there were no significant differences between the two groups. Further studies of schizophrenia, prosody and perception of emotions can only be referenced here (Jahshan, Wynn & Green, 2013; Kantrowitz et al., 2013; Matsumoto et al., 2006).

Music therapy and schizophrenia: clinical aspects and research

Concerning musical expression in people with schizophrenia, Reichelt (1989) describes one of his patients as having a proficiency in imitation which "rigidifies to routine" or, in addition, a "passive drivenness" (p. 69). In another patient he then observed his "endless crotchets (quarter notes)" or "unstructured drumbeats tending toward infinity" (p. 73). Vogt (1991) cites lacking dynamic flexibility of tempo and volume, and lacking dialogue structure in play, among others, as a typical behaviour pattern of his patient (pp. 18–19).

Kunkel (1996) observed in the play of a male patient the continuous repetition of bits of themes (*Motivsplitter*), a back and forth alternation between two tones, impulse-free playing and uninterrupted playing (pp. 17–18). In sessions with a paranoid schizophrenic patient, this author could hear a very loud persevering and excited playing on the drum. The patient could not respond to the musical offerings of the therapist; an interplay was not detectable in the dialogue (Bauer, 1996, p. 107).

One of the most comprehensive systematic studies of musical perception in schizophrenic patients was undertaken by Kneutgen (1980). He developed a self-evaluation form for registering emotional reactions to music (e.g. this music makes me sad: yes/a little/no), and he found no significant differences between healthy persons and persons with schizophrenic illness (p. 1035). In a further test of the intensity of musical experience, Kneutgen also found no differences, i.e. schizophrenic persons went along with the music to the same extent, as did healthy persons in the control group. In contrast, there were significant differences in the continuity of the experience, i.e. the patients slipped out of rhythm more often, only to return again to full synchronisation (p. 1036).

Pavlicevic and Trevarthen (1989) compared the level of musical communication between patients and therapists for 15 chronically schizophrenic patients, 15 unipolar depressive patients and 15 non-psychiatric persons. The result showed a clearly identifiable difficulty in contact initiation by schizophrenic patients in comparison to the other groups on a scale of 1 ("no contact") to 6 ("established mutuality"). Calculation of the resulting Musical Improvisation Rating score indicated significant differences. In a further study (Pavlicevic, Trevarthen & Duncan, 1994) to ascertain the interactive behaviour of schizophrenic patients, the authors developed a scale, the Music Interaction Rating for Schizophrenia, and compared two groups of schizophrenic patients with each other. The scale classifies musical behaviour in musical dialogue according to nine levels, where level 1 means "no musical contact" and level 9 means "musical partnership". In the group of patients treated with music therapy over a period of 10 weeks, a significant improvement of average values was achieved; in particular, an improvement of musical quality and length of musical responses could be demonstrated.

For her doctoral thesis, Claußnitzer (1996) developed a test to evaluate the perception and expression of music comparing a group of 13 schizophrenics, a group of 17 with mixed diagnosis, and a matched control group ($N=30$). The results could not confirm the hypothesis of a diagnosis-specific behaviour in schizophrenics. Compared to the other two groups, schizophrenics had significantly better results in recognising melodic sequences. Furthermore, the rater could not differentiate the music of the schizophrenic subjects from that of the mixed diagnosis group. The expected "typical musical patterns" did not appear, or only partially so, during the improvisation. The author concluded that besides the fact that typical ways of expression exist, many others are possibly depending on psychic factors such as mood, emotional tension and/or others (pp. 75–81).

A completely different picture was presented by Ulrich et al. (2007). They examined the additional therapeutic effect of group music therapy for acute care psychiatric inpatients. Some 37 patients, of whom 27 were diagnosed with schizophrenia, were randomly divided into two groups; for a period of five weeks the experimental group received standard treatment plus music therapy, and the control group only standard treatment. A pre/post-test design was used. The principal focus of the music therapy was interpersonal contact, the aim being a reduction of negative symptoms and an enhanced quality of life. Questionnaires for patients and nurses (two raters for each subject) were filled out before and after the music therapy sessions. The results showed that music therapy had significant effects on negative symptoms (diminished) and interpersonal contact (improved). No differences between the two groups were found in quality of life. In the self-assessment scale, music therapy was perceived by the patients as having positive effects on their contact with other people. The rater assessment did not correlate with these results. Apparently, nurses did not recognise the changes. The authors presume that changes are very subtle and they recommend that music therapists "listen carefully to the patients" (p. 368).

Dialogue behaviour in music therapy

Musical partner play relies upon psychic capabilities; Schmölz (1988) lists listening, assimilating, empathising, processing, understanding, reflecting, assessing, delimiting, retracting, repelling, countering and wanting to dispute something, among others (p. 10). The music therapist Katja Loos (1986) believed the imitating of the therapist's musical play patterns to be a behaviour pattern from the infantile imitation stage, while the discovering of one's own play patterns corresponded with a more mature phase of development (p. 59). In this respect the dialogue of music therapy can be of diagnostic value. It helps to establish mutual understanding in that it facilitates musical "give and take". It offers musical support and reinforcement through imitation and adoption of musical patterns of one's counterpart, repetition and emphasis of one's own patterns, and connection of musical elements of both participants or introduction of new musical ideas, as shown in the examples of Pavlicevic and Trevarthen (1989) and Pavlicevic et al. (1994).

Investigation

This investigation was carried out in 1998 in a public psychiatric hospital in Santiago de Chile and served as a doctoral thesis (Bauer, 2000). It considered the question of whether schizophrenic patients present particularities in their perception of music, musical representation of emotions, and musical dialogue behaviour. Fundamental assumptions and hypotheses were based upon the above described observations and research results from music therapy available to that date. The most important findings from my investigation, which I was requested to present here, will be compared with current recent research results.

Aims of the study

The experimental investigation was meant to compare musical representation, interaction and perception of paranoid schizophrenic patients (SP) with that of healthy controls (CP). One was to determine whether there were any significant differences in music-emotional behaviour, i.e. the presentation, expression and perception of music in the two groups. This would provide a contribution to basic research in music therapy, the results of which would be relevant for applied music therapy.

Sampling and subjects

The investigation was conducted in the Istituto Psiquiátrico Dr José Horwitz Barrak, a psychiatric facility with *c*.800 beds in Santiago de Chile. Permission for the investigation was issued by the director of the hospital, and ethical clearance was granted by the Ethics Committee of the Sociedad Chilena de Salud Mental. There were 24 participants with a schizophrenic diagnosis, 12 women and 12 men; average age was 34.5 years (control group (CG) 31.2 years). All patients were inpatients, and 13% (CG 17%) had finished elementary school, 71% (CG 62%) had finished secondary school and 17% (CG 21%) had entered higher education. Most patients were stabilised on antipsychotic medication. Aside from paranoid schizophrenia, study subjects could not have any other diagnoses such as epilepsy, alcohol or drug abuse, mental retardation or other organ damage. The lower age limit was set at 18 years and the upper limit at 48 years. Patients with only an initial psychiatric diagnosis were excluded. The determining factor for participation in the study was the most recent diagnosis. Pre-selection was made by the ward nurse. Potential study subjects were asked whether they would like to participate in a musical test, and no one refused. One or two patients could be tested per week in a *c*.20 m^2 common room. The investigation took place over a period of about four months. At the time of their examination, patients were in stable clinical condition, they had weekend passes, and were nearing their date of discharge.

Among the 24 participants in the study diagnosed according to the DSM-IV (APA, 1995) as schizophrenic persons, 19 were classified as paranoid, three as paranoid hebephrenic and two as paranoid catatonic schizophrenia types. The last two patients displayed primarily paranoid symptoms.

The 24 persons in the control group were recruited via advertisements and personal contacts. Both groups were matched in age, educational level and social background; for control purposes and optimal socio-cultural group adaptation, the Graffar test (Graffar, 1956) was applied to both groups. Requirements for participation in the control group were: (a) occupational involvement, i.e. stability in execution of everyday activities; (b) affective stability within the family; and (c) no psychiatric medication treatment – all applicable to the previous three years. Drug use and alcohol dependence were exclusion criteria. This information was recorded in a partially structured preliminary interview. Some 35 persons were pre-tested, of whom 11 were classified as unsuitable. Individuals from poorer socio-economic backgrounds received a financial remuneration for their participation. Examination of the controls took place either in a musical therapy practice or in a community centre.

Experimental design

The investigation procedure consisted of four parts, experimental unit (EU) numbers 1 to 4 – EU1: musical instrumental representation of sadness, anger and joy; EU2: listening to, describing and classifying music according to emotions in three original piano compositions; EU3: instrumental dialogue play with a female music therapist on prescribed instruments, a bar chime (*Stabglockenspiel*) and a metallophone; EU4: repetition of EU1.[3]

The musical representations (EU1 and EU4) and the dialogue (EU3) were audio recorded; the verbal descriptions (EU2) were transcribed in minutes. Evaluation of the results was performed by two different rater groups (R1 and R2), each consisting of three raters. Group R1 was involved in the development of the musical evaluation scale, was familiar with the investigation and was trained to identify congruence. This group analysed and evaluated the music examples from EU1 and EU4 as well as the dialogue examples from EU3 in a group-independent random sequence. Group R2 was an independent group of raters, not familiar with the investigation, who classified the musical examples represented in EU4 with respect to their intended feeling categories (sadness, anger, joy). All 144 musical examples (48 persons × 3 feeling categories) were presented in a group-independent random sequence, so that the raters could not know whether a person belonged to the patient group or the control group.

Data analysis

Psychometric analysis of the results utilised the following procedures: Interrater reliabilities (EU2 and EU3) were calculated with Spearman's rank correlation coefficient; determination of the musical representation results (EU1 and EU4) of the separate groups utilised the non-parametric paired sample Wilcoxon signed rank test; comparison of the two groups was made with the Mann–Whitney U test for independent samples. Statistical analysis of frequency comparisons (EU1 and EU4) was done with the one-sided Fisher's exact test; in case of instrumental variability the statistical analysis used the generalised Fisher's exact test. The calculation was made with the StatXact package (Mehta, 1991). Comparison of nominal scaled data between the groups (interaction behaviour in EU3 and musical changes between EU1 and EU4) utilised the Kruskal–Wallis chi-square test. For comparison of two correlations, the test for equality of two correlation matrices was applied based upon Fisher's z-transform. The significance value was set at the 5% level for all analyses.

Results

EU1 and EU4: tests of hypotheses regarding differentiated musical representation (R1 group)

Hypothesis H1a that schizophrenic patients play less melodically for the representation of "joyful" and "sad" than healthy controls could not be confirmed. However, hypothesis H1b, which says that schizophrenic patients play the "joyful", "sad" and "angry" feelings more loudly, more irregularly and faster than healthy controls was partly confirmed, namely in the representation of "sad". Study group persons played significantly louder in "sad" than persons in the control group (average of EU1 and EU4: $p = .002^{**}$, statistical calculation with Mann-Whitney U test for independent samples) and significantly faster than persons in the control group.[4] The average of EU1 and EU4 here had a significance value of $p = .045$.

EU1: test of musical variability among "joyful", "sad" and "angry" (R1 group)

We wished to know how differently the four variables "volume", "melody", "rhythm" and "movement" were treated in the representation of the three feeling categories. A test of the hypothesis (H1c) that the study group played in a less differentiated manner than the control group produced the following results: There was a significant difference ($p = .037$) for "volume" in the pooled results (EU1 and EU4). Controls differentiated better in volume between the three feeling qualities, played with more variation and used more sounds between *pp* (very soft) and *ff* (very loud). A similar result was observed for "melody". Pooling both results (EU1 and EU4) led to a highly significant difference ($p = .003$). Here also, the controls represented the three emotions melodically more differentiated on a scale from 1 to 4 than schizophrenic patients. On the other hand, the "rhythm" variable was varied significantly more strongly by the study group persons than by persons in the healthy control group. The pooled values for EU1 and EU4 gave a significance value of $p = .018$. No significant differences were found for the "tempo" variable. Both groups utilised "slow", "pacing" and "fast" to the same extent.

EU1 and EU4: test of instrumental variability in the representation of different feeling categories

Hypothesis H1d, that for the representation of "joyful", "sad" and "angry" music, schizophrenic persons use one instrument rather than two or three, in contrast to healthy controls, could not be confirmed. Statistical analysis with the generalised Fisher's exact test revealed no statistically significant differences between the investigated groups. EU1: $p=.662$ ns, EU4: $p=.824$ ns. Both groups were most likely to use two rather than three instruments in EU1 (study group: one = 2, two = 12, three = 10; control group: one = 1, two = 15, three = 8), and three instruments in EU4 (study group: one = 2, two = 8, three = 14; control group: one = 1, two = 10, three = 13).

EU4: evaluation of the represented feeling qualities in EU4 (R2 group)

Rater group R2 evaluated the represented feeling qualities of all 48 experimental subjects. The following hypothesis was examined: The feeling qualities "joyful", "sad" and "angry" represented by the schizophrenic patients were more poorly identified by the non-pre-informed raters than were those of the control group. With respect to the examination of emotional characteristics in all three music pieces, significant differences appeared between the study group and the control group in the evaluation of "joyful" and "angry" elements. The raters felt the music of the control group to be significantly more "joyful" ($p=.009$) and music of the study group to be significantly more "angry" ($p=.003$). The represented musical pieces were then examined to determine if the prescribed feeling qualities were identified as such by the raters. The music intended as "joyful" showed a significant difference ($p=.014$); it was more clearly represented by the control group. The music intended as "angry" showed a tendency towards the study group ($p=.099$), i.e. representation of this emotion was clearer in the study group and was better identified as such by the raters. Sad elements in the "sad" music were perceived equally well by both groups. In summary, a significantly higher detectability of "joyful" was shown in the control group music, a tendentially higher detectability of "angry" in the study group music, and no significant differences in the detectability of "sad".

EU2: examination of differentiated perception with auditive test material

The null hypothesis was assumed for both the study group and control group. The Mann–Whitney U test was used to determine whether the detection rate in the study group was lower than in the control group. This test showed no significant group differences with respect to "differentiated perception" of the presented music pieces (independent U test, perception, $p = .597$, ns). Schizophrenic persons as well as healthy controls identified the emotions intended by the composed piano pieces to the same extent. The detectability rate for the "sad" music lay at 92% in both groups, for the "joyful" music at 96% in the study group and 88% in the control group, and for the "angry" music at 58% in the study group and 71% in the control group.

EU3: appraisal of expressiveness in interactive behaviour in musical dialogue (RI group)

The following hypothesis (H2a) was tested: In musical dialogue with a female music therapist, schizophrenic study subjects use the interaction forms "imitating", "isolating oneself", "insisting", "dominating", "interrupting" and "fragmenting" more often than healthy controls, and the interaction forms "offering" and "repeating" less often than healthy controls. Statistical evaluation was performed using Kruskal–Wallis. The results based on the consensus scale Item (a), "offering", show a significance of $p = .012$** in favour of the control group, which offers new musical material more often than the study group. For Item (g), "isolating oneself", the significance value is $p = .05$*.[5] Here, the study group "outdoes" the control group, i.e. schizophrenic study subjects isolate themselves more often than healthy controls during the dialogue. In all other test items there are no significant differences between the groups.

Dialogue behaviour considering the gender variable

No hypothesis addressing this question was presented. To examine the confounding "gender" variable, dialogue behaviour was analysed for significant differences between men and women. The significance value was calculated with the Mann–Whitney U test. Statistically significant differences existed in Item (g), "isolating oneself" and Item (h), "fragmenting". The difference in Item (g) was highly significant ($p = .003$). This behaviour occurred significantly more frequently in the women than in the men. The difference in Item (h) was also significant ($p = .019$), and this behaviour also appeared more often in women than in men.

Discussion

The "volume" variable

In summary, with respect to the "volume" variable it could be shown that for all three emotions the schizophrenic patients tend to play at the same volume. For "sad", this gave a significant difference in comparison to the healthy control group. For "angry", the value in EU1 lay almost in the significance range; in EU4 it was highly significant, but in this case in favour of the study group, which played "quite loudly". These results may be due to a reduced motor control in the patients, but possibly also due to reduced differentiation of emotional expression itself. The significantly higher volume in EU4 may also be related to emotional strain of the patients at the end of the investigation. Through the repeated request to play "angry", some of the patients fell into a sort of regressive condition and had to be stopped. Here, the "representation" of feelings passed into a sort of "expression" of feelings (see note 1; Wellek, 1982). Healthy controls were clearly more reserved, more controlled and more careful in dealing with "angry", and felt themselves to be rather in a defence mode. One person played three strokes on the drum and then broke off immediately, another repeated a typical rhythm and avoided any sort of authentic playing. It would have been interesting to have the same person later listen to the music which he/she had played and then classify it; this would serve to distinguish between self-perception and external perception in both the study group and the control group among other things to reassess the lack of agreement of self-perception and external perception in schizophrenia found by Myin-Germeys and colleagues (2000).

The "melody" variable

It was found that overall both schizophrenic patients and healthy controls rarely played melodically, thus to almost the same extent not employing this element of music. Nonetheless, in the examination of differentiation of musical expression between feeling qualities, healthy controls performed significantly better than schizophrenic patients. In EU4 and in the overall results there were significant differences: Healthy controls played melodically in a more differentiated fashion; in the representation of the three feeling qualities they alternated back and forth between the evaluation criteria "no melody" ("angry music") and "melodic regular repetitions" ("sad music") more than the schizophrenic patients did. Since melody creation is related to the type of instrument used, the choice of instrument would need to be limited for the purpose of comparing the two groups; a suitable instrument would have to be provided. This was not the case in this investigation. As a result, if the person chose a drum, a priori limitation of melodic expression possibilities was indicated.

The "tempo" variable

For the "tempo" variable, i.e. the use of "slow", "pacing" or "fast", a significant difference was found for the "sad" feeling in group EU1 ($p = .025$) as well as in the combined values of EU1 and EU4 ($p = .045$). Both times the persons in the study group played significantly faster than persons in the control group. Here also, the results might be related to motoric limitations or pharmacologically induced motoric anomalies. On the other hand, rapid speaking/playing is associated with fear in phonetics research (Leitman et al., 2010) as well as in the composition guidelines of Beltrán (1984). Should this premise be correct, the rapid playing of schizophrenic persons could possibly be an expression of an emotional state, namely, fear.

The "rhythm" variable

In this investigation, the "rhythm" variable may be considered the musical element showing the least significant differences between the two groups. Schizophrenic patients did not play "more irregularly" than healthy controls. In "complexity" there was a tendency in EU1 ($p=.084$) and a significant difference in the combined results of EU1 and EU4 ($p=.018$), in that schizophrenic study persons differentiated more in their representation of the three feeling qualities than did the healthy controls, who generally played more uniformly rhythmically. The hypothesis that schizophrenic patients play more irregularly than healthy controls could not be confirmed.

Identification of the prescribed feeling qualities by group R2

Due to the sometimes very short representations, the three raters had difficulty committing themselves to an evaluation. Other pieces of music were very long, and the study subjects changed their manner of playing during a presentation, so that various emotional impressions arose in the raters. Based on the average values over all three feeling emotions as calculated by the raters, one can conclude that the average values lie between 2 "very little" and 3 "a bit", i.e. the presence of the desired emotions was by and large felt to be predominantly low.

An interesting result was the significantly better identification of "joyful" music by the control group, without it being clear which features the raters used to establish this. In none of the musical variables (melody, rhythm, tempo and volume) for "joyful" was there a significant difference between the two experimental groups. We should presume that the "whole" consists of more than just these four variables, and that they impact the listener differently in synergy than in isolation. Concerning the representation of "angry music", it was identified better in the study group. The "volume" variable presumably played an important role here, and according to the rating values of R1, it was significantly lower in the control group. As does de la Motte-Haber (1996), I suspect that volume was the dominant feature determining the overall impression of the raters.

Musical interaction behaviour

Our observation scale was drawn up following the interaction schemes compiled by Jörg et al. (1994). In particular, the reciprocal influencing through new stimuli (reciprocity) and the appearance of behaviour patterns which lead the communication in a new direction (elicitation) should be considered as criteria for healthy or limited interactive behaviour. Mutual eye contact was waived, but it should definitely be considered as additional information in future studies. Jörg and colleagues describe an interaction as faulty if answers are inconsistent and reactions are illogical or inflexible, if negative signs and new stimuli go unperceived or are ignored, and if elicitations are not answered.

There were eight operationalised interaction items to be categorised: "offering", "imitating", "interrupting", "isolating oneself", "repeating", "insisting", "fragmenting" and "dominating".[6] The results showed significant differences in only two of the eight items, namely "offering" and "isolating oneself". Concerning the "offering" item, as expected, schizophrenic patients showed new musical elements less frequently than healthy controls, i.e. on a scale from 1 ("never") to 5 ("always") most values of the schizophrenic patients lay at 2; however, there were two exceptions who reached the values 4 and 5 ("almost always" and "always"), i.e. "typically healthy" interactive styles. In the group of healthy persons, "offering" more often brought values 3 and 4. This means that in the course of dialogue, schizophrenic patients also offer new material, but only very rarely or significantly more rarely than healthy persons.

With respect to the "isolating oneself" item, the significant difference between the experimental groups resulted from the large number of healthy persons evaluated with "never" ($n=13$) and the number of schizophrenic persons evaluated with "almost always" ($n=7$). Surprisingly, among the healthy participants the remaining 11 showed positive values; five were evaluated with the frequency 2 ("sometimes"), three with value 3 ("often"), two with value 4 ("almost always") and one with value 5 ("always").

Similarly surprising was the observation that for the "fragmenting" item, only four schizophrenic persons had a measurable value, which moreover was very low ("sometimes"). Equally low values were found for "imitating", "insisting" and "dominating". "Interrupting" was an interaction style never used by the control group; in the study group it was used twice, with frequency 2 ("sometimes"). This may be partly explained by social adaptation accomplishments, but at the same time shows the attention capacity of patients and their ability at formal turn-taking in musical dialogue.

In agreement with Katja Loos (1986, p. 59), one can conclude that those play partners who were able to offer new elements were in an emotionally more mature phase of development; these were the female music therapist, several persons from the control group and a few persons from the study group. Concerning the "isolating oneself" interactive scheme, no music therapeutic and developmental psychological explanations are forthcoming; apparently, a disorder-specific behaviour pattern is involved. Identification of this interactive scheme in healthy controls suggests three new hypotheses: (1) The concept must be the result of a new and less disorder-oriented operationalisation; (2) An occasional "isolating oneself" is part of a healthy mode of behaviour in dialogue; (3) The healthy controls, those with the values "often", "almost always" and "always", were in reality not very healthy.

In addition, there are ancillary results concerning gender differences. Indeed, highly significant differences between male and female study subjects in the "isolating oneself" item could be established. Females isolated themselves significantly more often than males. Given the results of Schmid (1994) from an investigation of depressive female patients, one learns that the musical receptivity of these patients to the play of a female therapist was markedly reduced (monologue rather than dialogue). This leaves the suspicion that at least some of the female participants in our control group either showed a depressive personality structure or suffered from a depressive malaise at the time of the study, without having been under medical or psychological treatment or having reported such information in the interview.

The results furthermore indicate that in the investigated interactive styles we must consider two things: (a) which dialogue behaviour occurred, and (b) with what frequency it occurred. For the "offering" item this is very clear: of 24 schizophrenic persons, 19 are evaluated positively, thus showing this "healthy" behaviour pattern, though at a lower rate. Of these, 17 have the value 2 ("sometimes"), one has the value 4 ("almost always") and one the value 5 ("always"). In the healthy control group there are 21 positive evaluations overall. Nine of these lie at value 2 ("sometimes"), three at value 3 ("often"), but eight at value 4 ("almost always") and even one at value 5 ("always").

Emotional perception of piano pieces

Although no deductive hypothesis was proposed, the results should nonetheless serve as an impulse and information on the subject of "paranoid schizophrenia and musical perception". Three especially composed musical pieces were played on the piano. After listening to them, participants were asked to describe their impressions. Here one noticed sometimes very similar pictorial mental images in the two groups. The music composed to be "sad" was repeatedly connected with "funeral march" and "yearning". Several patients connected the music with their illness and a yearning for "former times". For the music composed to be "joyful", almost archetypical pictures such as "dancing couple", "children's dance", "wild west" and "women in long dresses" emerged in both groups. While these impressions led to feelings of happiness and positive wishful thinking in the schizophrenic patients, and they enjoyed identifying with this music, this was not the case in the control group. The same descriptions led rather to the impression of dealing with banal and superficial music. In the music composed as "angry", several persons from both groups heard "Tom and Jerry", "a chase", "film music" and "excitement". In both groups the decision on a single feeling category was found difficult.

Bizarre or "psychotic" content was not found in the group of paranoid schizophrenic patients, i.e. their associations greatly resembled those of the controls. Nonetheless, some concrete matters did arise in the study group, for example, the description of the pianist or criticism of the pianist "who hadn't practised properly" or "who needs to study more".

"Joyful" was most clearly identified by both groups. Identification of "sad" was likewise very high. "Angry" produced a low and heterogeneous result in both groups. Interpretation of these data was supported by the theoretical basic assumptions of perception psychology and musicology described earlier. The first two pieces of music were based upon simple, sequentially repeating musical features, a melody, a stable rhythm, a continuous key (D major in the case of "joyful" and G minor in the case of "sad") and a comprehensible volume (medium in the case of "joyful" and very soft to soft in the case of "sad"). The listener can easily recognise these structures, anticipate them and identify musical relationships. Culturally considered, we are dealing with established structures, common also to Chilean culture, which had been stored before the appearance of illness and disorder as "imprint gestalts" ("*Spurgestalten*") (Thomas, 1990). Jourdain (1998) also assumes that the brain seeks familiar patterns and connects memory with musical perception. Unambiguous classification, trusted continuation and fulfilment of the expectation of establishing meaning in the sense of de la Motte-Haber (1996) and Büchler (1987) may have played a role in the categorisation of the musical examples. According to de la Motte-Haber, tempo is a dominant factor which to a large extent determines the musical assessment (1996, pp. 158ff.). For "sad", the tempo was set at "slow" and for "joyful" it was set at "pacing" (speed). Both times, except for a few built-in "*rubati*" (hesitations), the music followed an even and predictable cadence. Information processing is a prerequisite for the assignment of music to emotions, which would signify that it also occurs in the assignment of musical impressions by schizophrenic persons.

In the case of "angry" music, the musical offering was far more comprehensive, uncertain and unpredictable. Variations in volume, melody, rhythm and tempo made anticipation more difficult. One can assume that while listening, the study persons "clung" to various musical features which they perceived as dominant or pivotal, that they generalised their impression and that they made their judgement on the strength of this impression. In musicology this process is described as an "inductive process" (de la Motte-Haber, 1996), and it could explain the rather heterogeneous evaluation of this musical piece. The same result arose in the pilot group as it did in the study and control groups.[7] Both times, selective perception could have influenced the evaluation (Jourdain, 1998, p. 320). The fact that in this part of the investigation the paranoid schizophrenic patients did not differ from healthy controls is reminiscent of the results of Kring et al. (1993) and Kring and Neale (1996); they showed that, contrary to their outward appearance of rigid mimicry, schizophrenic persons perceived positive and negative emotions just as well as healthy controls. Something very similar occurred in the investigation of Ulrich et al. (2007): self-assessment and self-perception differed from observer assessment.

Future similarly designed investigations in this field should include very good and intensive training of raters. Optimisation of the technology would also facilitate repeated and concentrated listening to the musical examples. The health status of controls should be verified with supplementary psychometric tests. Indeed, our results raise the question of whether the only partially proven significant differences between the groups were due to the good abilities of the paranoid schizophrenic patients or a poor "health status" of the control group. Also, through questioning the study subjects, it would be interesting to find out which criteria they used to assign the music pieces to the "joyful", "sad" and "angry" categories. This would allow re-examination of the results and hypotheses of Leitman et al. (2010), among others, that in the case of schizophrenia, prosody does not contribute to the differentiation of emotions.

In conclusion, on the basis of our results one cannot unambiguously say whether or not schizophrenia is an illness, which inhibits the appraisal and processing of emotions. Recognition of emotions seems to be possible; representation of emotions less so. Further research is needed to answer at least this question: What do people with schizophrenia feel, and how do they feel it? A patient once answered the question when he said, "We always feel only fear." Could that maybe be the key to determining why expression doesn't succeed? Fear! In any event, music seems to be an appropriate medium to follow up on this possibility.

Notes

1 According to Wellek (1982, p. 193), the word "expression" should be understood as a "direct and unconsidered action" and the word "representation" as a "mentally oriented and guided event".
2 Higher and more variable pitch for joy, fear and anger; lower and less variable pitch for sadness. Faster tempo for fear and joy; slower tempo for sadness (Leitman et al., 2010, p. 546).
3 For detailed instructions on executing the battery of tests, the operationalisation of characteristics of the musical representation of feelings and features of dialogue behaviour, as well as the composition scheme of the piano music especially composed for the study, see Appendix.
4 ** = highly significant.
5 * = significant.

6 For operationalisation, see Appendix.
7 The auditive material was pre-tested in a group of (male and female) students (N=138). Identification values lay at 87.0% ("sad"), 96.4% ("joyful") and 66.0% ("angry").

References

Altmann de Litvan, M., Wigensberg de Perkan, A., González, E., Bauer, M., Angulo, B., Brovetto, E., et al. (2001). Arrullos, ritmos y sincronías en la relación madre-bebé. *Revista IberoAmericana de Psicomotricidad y Técnicas Corporales, 1*, 49–62.

APA (American Psychiatric Association). (1995). *Diagnostic and statistical manual of mental disorders: DSM-IV* (pp. 280–295). Washington, DC: Author.

Argyle, M. (1983). *Análisis de la interacción* (pp. 166–219). Buenos Aires: Amorrortu. (Original work published 1969 as *Social interaction*. London: Methrev)

Bauer, S. (1996). Musicoterapia y esquizofrenia: El tratamiento psicológico específico en una enfermedad mental. *Revista de Psiquiatría, 13*, 107–113.

Bauer, S. (2000). *Schizophrene Patienten und musikalische Verständigung. Eine experimentelle Studie zum Vergleich musikalischer Repräsentation, Interaktion, und Wahrnehmung von paranoid-schizophrenen Patienten und gesunden Kontrollpersonen. Ein Beitrag zur musiktherapeutischen Grundlagenforschung*. Unpublished doctoral thesis, Human Biology, University of Ulm.

Beebe, B. & Lachmann, F. M. (1994). Representation and internalization in infancy: Three principles of salience. *Psychoanal. Psychol, 11*, 127–165.

Beltrán, R. (1984). *La ambientación musical: Selección, montaje y sonorización* (pp. 3–81). Madrid: Instituto oficial de radio y televisión.

Böttcher, F. & Kerner, U. (1978). *Methoden in der Musikpsychologie* (chapters 2–7). Leipzig: Peters.

Büchler, M. (1987). *Musik und ihre Psychologien* (pp. 53–71). Eschborn bei Frankfurt: Fachbuchhandlung für Psychologie, Verl.-Abt.

Claußnitzer, S. (1996). *Musiktherapie in der Psychiatrie: Musikalische Wahrnehmung und musikalischer Ausdruck im Vergleich diagnostischer Gruppen*. Unpublished doctoral thesis (MD), Heinrich Heine University, Düsseldorf.

Creer, C. & Wing, J. K. (1989). Der Alltag mit schizophrenen Patienten. In H. Katschnig (Ed.), *Die andere Seite der Schizophrenie: Patienten zu Hause* (pp. 97–164). Munich: Psychologie Verlags Union.

de la Motte-Haber, H. (1996). *Handbuch der Musikpsychologie* (2nd rev. ed., pp. 150–214). Laaber: Laaber-Verlag.

Frank, C. (1975). Die Auswirkung rhythmischer Elemente auf vegetative Funktionen. In G. Harrer (Ed.), *Grundlagen der Musiktherapie und Musikpsychologie* (pp. 79–90). Stuttgart: Gustav Fischer.

Gold, C., Heldal, T. O., Dahle, T. & Wigram, T. (2005). Music therapy for schizophrenia or schizophrenia-like illnesses. *Cochrane Database Syst. Rev.* CD004025. http://dx.doi.org/10.1002/14651858.CD004025.pub2.

Gold, C., Solli, H. P., Krüger, V. & Lie, S. A. (2009). Dose–response relationship in music therapy for people with serious mental disorders: Systematic review and meta-analysis. *Clin. Psychol. Rev.*, 29, 193–207.

Graffar, M. (1956). Une méthode de classification sociale d'échantillons de population. *Courrier, 6*, 445–459.

Harrer, G. (1975). Das Musikerlebnis im Griff des naturwissenschaftlichen Experiments. In G. Harrer (Ed.), *Grundlagen der Musiktherapie und Musikpsychologie* (pp. 3–47). Stuttgart: Gustav Fischer.

Hochschild, A. (1996). Soziologie der Emotionen. *Z. psychosom. Med., 42*, 222–234.

Hufnagel, H., Steimer-Krause, E. & Krause R. (1991). Mimisches Verhalten und Erleben bei schizophrenen Patienten und bei Gesunden. *Zeitschrift für Klinische Psychologie, 20*, pp. 356–370.

Jahshan, C., Wynn, J. & Green, M. (2013). Relationship between auditory processing and affective prosody in schizophrenia. *Schizophr. Res., 143*(2–3), 348–353.

Jörg, M., et al. (1994). Kategoriensystem zur Mikroanalyse der frühen Mutter-Kind-Interaktion. *Kinder Jungendpsychiatrie, 22*, 97–106.

Jourdain, R. (1998). *Das wohltemperierte Gehirn: Wie Musik im Kopf entsteht und wirkt* (pp. 293–328). Heidelberg, Berlin: Spektrum.

Kanas, N. (1996). *Group therapy for schizophrenic patients* (pp. 1–11). Washington, DC: American Psychiatric Press.

Kantrowitz, J. T., Leitman, D. I., Lehrfeld, J. M., Laukka, P., Juslin, P. N., Butler, P. D., et al. (2013). Reduction in tonal discriminations predicts receptive emotion processing deficits in schizophrenia and schizoaffective disorder. *Schizophrenia Bull., 39*(1), 86–93.

Katschnig, H. (1989). Die vielen Seiten der Schizophrenie. In H. Katschnig (Ed.), *Die andere Seite der Schizophrenie: Patienten zu Hause* (pp. 1–18). Munich: Psychologie Verlags Union.

Kneutgen, J. (1980). Freie Improvisation als eindeutige Kommunikationsmöglichkeit für schizophren Erkrankte. *Therapie der Gegenwart, 119*, 1025–1046.

Krause, R. (1983). Zur Onto- und Phylogenese des Affektsystems und ihre Beziehungen zu psychischen Störungen. *Psyche, 37*, 1016–1043.

Krause, R., Steimer-Krause, E. & Ullrich, B. (1992). Anwendung der Affektforschung auf die psychoanalytisch-psychotherapeutische Praxis. *Forum Psychoanal., 8*, 238–253.

Kring, A. M., Kerr, S. L., Smith, D. A. & Neale, J. M. (1993). Flat affect in schizophrenia does not reflect diminished subjective experience of emotion. *J. Abnorm. Psychol., 102*, 507–517.

Kring, A. & Neale, J. (1996). Do schizophrenic patients show a disjunctive relationship among expressive, experimental, and psychophysiological components of emotion? *J. Abnorm. Psychol., 105*, 249–257.

Kunkel, S. (1996). Sein oder Nicht-Sein: Musiktherapie mit einem schizophrenen Patienten. In R. Tüpker (Ed.), *Konzeptentwicklung musiktherapeutischer Praxis und Forschung* (pp. 61–102). Münster: LIT Verlag.

Leitman, D. I., Laukka, P., Juslin, P. N., Saccente, E., Butler, P. & Javitt, D. C. (2010). Getting the cue: Sensory contributions to auditory emotion recognition impairments in schizophrenia. *Schizophrenia Bull., 36*(3), 545–556.

Lewis, S. & Garver, D. (1995). Treatment and diagnostic subtype in facial affect recognition in schizophrenia. *J. Psychiat. Res., 29*, 5–11.

Loos, G. (1986). *Spiel-Räume: Musiktherapie mit einer Magersüchtigen und anderen frühgestörten Patienten* (pp. 141–190). Stuttgart: Gustav Fischer.

Malloch, S. (1999–2000). Mothers and infants and communicative musicality. *Musicæ Scientiæ*, Special Issue, 29–57.

Matsumoto, K., Samson, G. T., O'Daly, O. D., Tracy, D. K., Patel, A. D. & Shergill, S. S. (2006). Prosodic discrimination in patients with schizophrenia. *Brit. J. Psychiat., 189*, 180–181.

Mehta, C. (1991). *StatXact, Version 2.02*. Cambridge, MA: CYTEL Corp.

Meschede, H. G., Bender, W. & Pfeiffer, H. (1983). Musiktherapie mit psychiatrischen Problempatienten. *Psychother. med. Psychol., 33*, 101–106.

Myin-Germeys, I., Delespaul, P. & DeVries, M. (2000). Schizophrenia patients are more emotionally active than is assumed based on their behavior. *Schizophrenia Bull., 26*(4), 847–854.

Osofsky, J. D. & Eberhart-Wright, A. (1988). Affective exchanges between high risk mothers and infants. *Int. J. Psychoanal., 69*, 221–231.

Ostertag, J. (1985). Der "wilde Mann" und die "sanfte Weise", Musiktherapie mit einem schizophrenen Patienten. *Musiktherapeutische Umschau, 6*, 223–241.

Papousek, M. (1981). Die Bedeutung musikalischer Elemente in der frühen Kommunikation zwischen Eltern und Kind. *Sozialpädiatrie in Praxis und Klinik, 3*, 468–473.

Papousek, M. (1995). Origins of reciprocity and mutuality in prelinguistic parent–infant "dialogues". In I. Marková, C. Graumann & K. Foppa (Eds.), *Mutualities in dialogue* (pp. 58–81). Cambridge: Cambridge University Press.

Papousek, H. & Papousek, M. (1988). Musikalität am Anfang des Lebens. *Üben und Musizieren, 5*, 25–30.

Pavlicevic, M. & Trevarthen, C. (1989). A musical assessment of psychiatric states in adults. *Psychopathology, 22*(6), 325–334. Erratum (1991). *Psychopathology, 24*(2), 120.

Pavlicevic, M., Trevarthen, C. & Duncan, J. (1994). Improvisational music therapy and the rehabilitation of persons suffering from chronic schizophrenia. *J. Music Ther., 31*(2), 86–104.

Pekrun, R. (1985). Musik und Emotion. In H. Bruhn, R. Oerter & H. Rösing (Eds.), *Musikpsychologie: Ein Handbuch in Schlüsselbegriffen* (pp. 180–188). Munich: Urban & Schwarzenberg.

Reichelt, R. (1989). *Aspekte einer kausalen Musiktherapie mit schizophrenen Patienten.* Unpublished dissertation (Diploma), Music Therapy, Hochschule für Musik und Theater, Hamburg.

Revers, W. J. (1975). Das Problem der Interpretation bei polygraphischen Untersuchungen des Musikerlebens. In G. Harrer (Ed.), *Grundlagen der Musiktherapie und Musikpsychologie* (pp. 91–98). Stuttgart: Gustav Fischer.

Schmid, S. (1994). *Der musikalische Dialog mit depressiven Patienten: Die Implementierung zur Dokumentation und Analyse musikalischer Dialoge und deren Validierung an einer klinischen Gruppe.* Unpublished doctoral thesis, Human Biology, University of Ulm.

Schmölz, A. (1988). Entfremdung – Auseinandersetzung – Dialog: Zur Komplexität des musiktherapeutischen Beziehungsgeschehens. Special Issue. In *Musik und Kommunikation, Hamburger Jahrbuch zur Musiktherapie und intermodalen Medientherapie* (Vol. 2, pp. 1–15). Lilienthal/Bremen: Eres.

Steimer-Krause, E. (1996). *Übertragung, Affekt und Beziehung: Theorie und Analyse nonverbaler Interaktionen schizophrener Patienten.* Berlin: Peter Lang.

Steimer-Krause, E., Krause, R. & Wagner, G. (1990). Interaction regulations used by schizophrenic and psychosomatic patients: Studies in facial behavior in dyadic interactions. *Psychiatry, 53*, pp. 209–227.

Stern, D. (1991). *El mundo interpersonal del infante* (pp. 157–199). Buenos Aires: Paidos. (Original work published 1985 as *The interpersonal world of the infant: A view from psychoanalysis and developmental psychology*)

Stern, D. N. (2010). *Der Gegenwartsmoment: Veränderungsprozesse in Psychoanalyse, Psychotherapie und Alltag* (3rd ed., pp. 224ff.). Frankfurt: Brandes & Apsel.

Strobel, W. (1985). Musiktherapie mit schizophrenen Patienten. Erfahrungen und Überlegungen. *Musiktherapeutische Umschau, 6*, 177–208.

Thomas, R. (1990). Der Begriff der Gestalt in der Musik und der Psychologie. In I. Frohne-Hagemann (Ed.), *Musik und Gestalt: Klinische Musiktherapie als Integrative Psychotherapie* (pp. 17–36). Paderborn: Junfermann.

Toomey, R. & Schuldberg, D. (1995). Recognition and judgment of facial stimuli in schizotypal subjects. *J. Commun. Disord., 28*, 193–203.

Trémeau, F. (2006). A review of emotion deficits in schizophrenia. *Dialogues in Clinical Neuroscience, 8*(1), 59–67.

Trevarthen, C. (2002). Origins of musical identity: Evidence from infancy for musical social awareness. In R. MacDonald, D. Hargreaves & D. Miell (Eds.), *Musical identities* (pp. 21–38). Oxford: Oxford University Press.

Ulrich, G., Houtmans, T. & Gold, C. (2007). The additional therapeutic effect of group music therapy for schizophrenic patients: A randomized study. *Acta psychiat. Scand., 116*, 362–370.

Vogt, H. (1991). *Einzelmusiktherapie mit einem schizophrenen Patienten-Voraussetzungen, Entwicklung und Umsetzung von musiktherapeutischen Interventionsstrategien.* Unpublished dissertation, Music Therapy, University of the Arts, Berlin.

Walker, E., McGuire, M. & Bettes, B. (1984). Recognition and identification of stimuli by schizophrenics and patients with affective disorders. *Brit. J. Clin. Psychol., 23*, 37–44.

Wellek, A. (1982). *Musikpsychologie und Musikästhetik: Grundriss der systematischen Musikwissenschaft* (3rd rev./exp. ed., pp. 192–253). Bonn: Bouvier.

Wygotski, L. (1985). *Ausgewählte Schriften* (Vol. 1, pp. 319–382). Cologne: Pfahl-Rugenstein.

Appendix

1 Instructions for conduct of experimental units 1 to 4

EU1

a Please choose one of the three musical instruments in front of you and play some music which seems sad to you.
b Now please choose the same instrument or another one and play some music which seems joyful to you.
c Now play some music which seems angry to you. You may use an instrument you've already played, or an instrument you haven't chosen yet.

EU2

I will now play three pieces of music for you. After each piece we'll talk about it briefly, how it affected you, how you felt about it, if you imagined something while you were hearing it, and what emotion you would assign to the music.

EU3

Now please take this instrument (Glockenspiel). I'll use this one (*arquin*, a uniquely Chilean glockenspiel). We'll have a musical dialogue, that is, an alternating back and forth on the instruments. I'll begin.

EU4

Lastly, I'd like to ask you to repeat Part 1 of this test, that is, to play one sad piece, one joyful piece, and lastly one piece of angry music.

a Please choose one of the three musical instruments in front of you and play some music which sounds sad to you.
b Now please choose the same instrument or another one and play some music which sounds joyful to you.
c Now play some music which sounds angry to you – and you may use an instrument you've already used, or one which you haven't chosen yet.

2 Description and operationalisation of the interaction modes examined in EU3

Repeating, offering, imitating, insisting, dominating, interrupting, isolating oneself and fragmenting.

a Repeating: the study subject repeats individual rhythmic or melodic patterns offered by the music therapist.
b Offering: the study subject develops a new play pattern based upon successful repetition, and introduces this into the dialogue.
c Imitating: the study subject imitates note for note the music passage(s) offered by the music therapist.
d Insisting: the study subject sticks to one of the patterns played by the music therapist, and repeats it.
e Dominating: the study subject plays louder or faster than the music therapist.
f Interrupting: the study subject breaks into the play of the music therapist before she has ended her musical statement.
g Isolating oneself: the study subject sticks to one or more of his/her own play patterns, and repeats it.
h Fragmenting: the study subject plays incoherent musical phrases; no connection can be made to previous phrases, neither one's own nor those of the music therapist.

3 Composition guidelines for emotions in film music according to Rafael Beltrán (1984)

Guidelines originally published in Spanish. Categories and musical characteristics used for the three pieces employed in this study are shown in **bold**.

Subscale I: sorrow (aflicción)

Feeling category	*Musical characteristics*
Melancholy (*melancolía*)	Tone quality: sombre or warm
Despair (*desesperanza*)	Pitch: grave or subgrave
Dismay (*turbación*)	Harmony: minor key or atonal
Sadness (*tristeza*)	**Melody: even or uneven**

Regret (*arrepentimiento*)	**Tempo: slow**
Discouragement (*desaliento*)	**Rhythm: regular, not percussive**
	Volume:[1] piano, pianissimo

Subscale 2: kindness* (bondad*)

Feeling category	*Musical characteristics*
Tranquility (*tranquilidad*)	Tone quality: warm or clear
Joy (*alegría*)	Pitch: medium or high
Cordiality (*cordialidad*)	Harmony: major key
Mercy (*piedad*)	**Melody: melodious, regular repetitions**
Humility (*humilidad*)	**Tempo: pacing**
Love (*amor*)	**Rhythm: regular, not percussve**
Compassion (*compasión*)	**Volume:[1] mezzoforte to forte**
Indulgence (*indulgencia*)	

Subscale 3: excitement* (excitación*)

Feeling category	*Musical characteristics*
Restlessness (*desasosiego*)	Tone quality: clear and shrill
Elation (*exaltación*)	Pitch: medium, high or low
Violence (*violencia*)	Harmony: atonal
Vehemence (*vehemencia*)	**Melody: uneven**
Wrath (*ira*)	**Tempo: fast**
Anger (*rabia*)	**Rhythm: markedly irregular**
Terror (*terror*)	**Volume:[1] forte to fortissimo**
Horror (*horror*)	
Mental disorder (*desorden mental*)	

Derived from the above are:

- Basis for composition of "joyful", "sad" and "angry" music (EU2);
- Evaluation scales for R1 group (EU1 & EU4).

Joyful

Melody:	melodious or regular repetitions
Tempo:	pacing
Rhythm:	regular, not percussive
Volume:	mezzoforte to forte

Sad

Melody:	even or uneven
Tempo:	slow
Rhythm:	irregular, not percussive
Volume:	piano, pianissimo

Angry

Melody:	no melody or uneven melody
Tempo:	fast
Rhythm:	markedly irregular
Volume:	forte to fortissimo

Note

1 Beltrán makes no reference to volume. Considering the information from music therapy and musicology summarised above, we considered volume a very important distinguishing feature, and therefore included it as a parameter in the list of musical characteristics to be evaluated.

Chapter 2

From the "inside feeling" to narration

Symbolisation and aesthetic emotion in music therapy[1]

Christine Falquet-Clin and Edith Lecourt

Introduction: music therapy research in psychiatry in France

The birth of psychiatry in France was also the beginning of a scientific approach to music therapy. In 1801 Philippe Pinel – the founder of French psychiatry – created a programme for the treatment of insanity with the idea that the "insane" were "patients" that could be rehabilitated in society. In this programme he offered a place for musical activities. It was the time, in France, of the development of "Orphéons" (bands and vocal ensembles) in society (from schools to workplaces) as a means of unifying the French nation. The idea was that music was so powerful that it could also reintegrate the insane into society. Pinel and his disciples, the first psychiatrists, developed the first experiments involving receptive and active music therapy in psychiatry (about 1820–1850). From that time on, music therapy and psychiatry in France have been closely linked. Early research was more oriented to receptive applications. Since the 1980s, the development has been more oriented to active techniques.

This chapter will present ongoing research on receptive music therapy in psychiatry in the EA 4056 and EA 3625 laboratories of the Paris Descartes University.

Issues and hypotheses

Whereas the artistic and aesthetic dimension places art therapy practices among the multiple modalities of physical care, the question of aesthetic emotion within clinical practice remains relatively unexplored, notably within music therapy. Although the literature contains early writings acknowledging the aesthetic dimension (Gaston, 1964; Mueller, 1964; Salas, 1990) and the importance of the creative process (Nordoff & Robins, 1977), music therapy practices have not enhanced it, nor have they integrated it as a fundamental and dynamic asset that can bring about change in the therapeutic process.

According to our hypothesis – which agrees with English-speaking writers such as Aigen and Tsiris, for instance – aesthetic emotion plays a part in a subject's psychic construction and in the links created between subjects, and it seems to us that it is indeed useful to the therapeutic dynamics of music therapy. Our current research aims to better grasp and understand the processes at stake that involve aesthetic emotion and the potentialities for representation and transformation of this modality of care. In order to question this forgotten dimension of quantitative evaluation studies, it seemed appropriate to carry out research from intensive case study.

The qualitative exploratory type of research that we describe in this chapter involves a case of individual receptive music therapy on which a window of clinical research for one year has been opened. It was carried out in conjunction with two laboratories of the Paris-Sorbonne University, TEC ("techniques and body issues") and PCPP ("clinical psychology, psychopathology and psychoanalysis") Paris Descartes University, as well as on the clinical premises of the medical-psychological adult centre of Annecy Geneva Hospital Centre (CHANGE). Since 2011 Professor Lecourt has oriented research on arts therapies on the question of the place of aesthetics in the art therapeutic relationship. Christine Falquet-Clin, psychiatric and music therapist, develops her research in attempting to figure out the emergence of processes that can be linked to aesthetic emotion within a therapeutic relationship that establishes in its frame the encounter with a piece of music, and to follow the psychic movements of transformation and meaning creation. Does aesthetic emotion speak to representation and connection? Is it a witness to these processes? Can these processes move forward from the repetition of suffering and destructivity, favour the exploration of other psychic landscapes and open other possible trajectories?

After a brief overview of the assumptions and theories that serve as a framework to these practices and work hypotheses, Christine will deal with the clinical case of a patient whom we will call Sarah. She will pay specific attention to the unfolding of a session with her, in order to try to account more precisely for the complex processes that she is attempting to observe and describe, for these processes are not easily synthesised and schematised.

Assumptions and theoretical framework

Among the current theoretical advances that attempt to account for the complexity of the human psyche, of its suffering and capacity for change, those that concern the processes of symbolisation have gained major importance in contemporary psychoanalysis. René Roussillon and his team have particularly developed this aspect in terms of primary symbolisation for the transformation of the mnestic perceptive traces in thing representation and of secondary symbolisation for the transformation of thing representation into word representation.

This approach through symbolisation processes is particularly interesting as it offers enriching possibilities of interface with other epistemological fields such as the neurosciences, cognitive sciences, linguistics, anthropology, sociology, philosophy and … art.

The effort of symbolisation is necessary to a non-traumatic functioning of the psyche. But the capacity to symbolise is not forever acquired. It can be lost or suspended by defence mechanisms in some areas of psychic life. The complex networking implied by these transformations is mostly carried out unconsciously and effected differently depending on the degree of psychic organisation linked with the quality of primary environment, age, stages of life, impact of traumatic events and dominant pole of psychic organisation. It also depends on the relationship that the subject has with his or her own symbolising activity. In that logic and before any diagnostic categorisation, the troubles of the people who are welcomed in our psychiatric care centres often refer to experiences that lack representation within the psychic system. They are either early traumas that happened at a time preceding verbal language – that is, experiences that could not be transformed in the interrelation with the primary environment – or later events (moments of crisis or of mutation of psychic organisation, awakening of unaccomplished capacity) that remained unthought-of, unthinkable and that were not treated in due course of time. These experiences that lack inscription, that were set aside and that are uncreated within the ego wait to be taken over. They are of the negative type and suggest a "being deficiency". These experiences that could not be inscribed in the framework of psychic life are often expressed in a nonverbal type of language: that of emotional expression, of the mimic-gestural-postural type, that of action. When word representation is deficient, the register of emotional expression is the favoured means of communication and of mobilisation, and that register I find particularly interesting in my art therapy practice.

Experiences that are not inscribed within the psyche tend to be repeated in an often nagging attempt at introjection and physical integration. Yet, this physical integration depends on the production and creation within the self and for oneself of a symbolic representation of these experiences. This places the "need to create" at the core of psychic processes (Roussillon, 2000). D. W. Winnicott has already put forward the fundamental aspect of the need to create. When the subject's internal and environmental conditions have hindered his/her capacity to create symbolic forms that are vital to the psyche or when life offers no place for potential games and integrative creation, care centres need to offer favourable environments, "intermediary spaces" (Winnicott, 1975/1971) between the subject's psyche and perceptive reality in order to try to restart and pursue experiences that lack subjective integration. The aim will be to offer measures to materialise and attract an activity of representation.

Among the arts, music is one that has always had links with care and social life, in all cultures. The communicative value of sound is at the origin of the elaborate codes of human communication: words and sounds. The practice of art therapy is rooted in that cultural and (pre)historic ground level. That fundamental anthropological aspect is coupled with the place taken by sound (silence, noises, sounds) since the foetal stage of life as the primary matter in the building of any human being's psychic life from their sensory-affective-motor and relational anchoring. The works of Maiello (2010) on the foetal period, of Malloch and Trevarthen (2009) and Stern (1998) on the musical dimension of early intersubjective communication, of Anzieu (1985) on the sound envelope and of Lecourt (1987) on the question of the musical–verbal sound envelope are particularly interesting in this respect. Music is a form of symbolisation given by culture in order to transform the sensory excitement of noise and sound. It offers a suitable space for games and their variations.

Listening to a piece of music during a clinical encounter means turning towards sensory-motivity and bodily anchoring. It means opening a potentiality for aesthetic emotion – these terms being taken with their etymological meanings of movement activation (*emovere*) of the senses (*aisthesis*). Sense is not purely passive in this respect. It is an activity of creation that both receives and creates the sensible.

Aesthetic emotion is a complex emotion that cannot be assimilated to basic emotions such as joy or sadness which may be felt while listening to a piece of music. It is linked with aesthetic experience, but any aesthetic experience is not necessarily associated with aesthetic emotion. It is the result of activation and of a resonance of the various layers of psychic functioning (originary, primary and secondary) from the sensory impact. A multidirectional dynamic and symbolising trajectory of shaping, picturing, staging and wording is activated.

This dynamic is to be found at the relational level, where aesthetic emotion seems to open a pathway between the intimate, the singular and one or more others. This brings us to the notion of empathy, a notion that is becoming a source of interest again these days in the fields of neuroscience, psychoanalysis and sociology. Allow me to emphasise the fact that, from the beginning, the *Einfühlung* (inside feeling) is used to designate the aesthetic relation between a subject and an object, a piece of art and the surrounding world, to designate the way in which she/he is affected by a shape from sensoriality (Vischer, 1873).

Several psychoanalysts have put forward the idea of the possibility of transformation of aesthetic emotion. For Segal (1979), the aesthetic emotion experienced by the recipient of the piece of art corresponds to the unconscious reliving of the artist's deep depressive experiences. Segal suggests that there is a mechanism of identification with the latter at the moment when she/he faces his/her own depression and expresses it in his/her creative process. Through identification with the artist, the subject revisits his/her own precocious depressive anxieties that had been overcome by some sort of "successful grief re-establishing their own objects and internal world".[2] The recipient of the piece of art "therefore feels re-established and enriched".[3] Meltzer and Williams (2000/1988) argue that aesthetic emotion fundamentally organises the psyche from the aesthetic shock constituted by birth and the encounter with one's mother's face. According to them, the shock felt on listening to the piece of music is similar to the impact of that primary aesthetic experience. "In order to live an aesthetic experience, we let ourselves be enthused by the formal and external qualities of the piece of art and then we have to face our doubts and suspicions regarding its internal qualities."[4] According to Lecourt (1995), "the beautiful object" is defined thanks to its subjective encounter during therapy where it seems to have two main characteristics: "*it evokes the mark of the lost object*" and is therefore akin to an imaginary encounter with the mother's body, and it "produces the right excitement (like the right note)".[5] The encounter between the traces of the first feelings in relation to the objects – which are characterised by their sensorimotor qualities, their shapes and their containing qualities – and the "truthfulness of the excitement which allows to taste the experience without being overwhelmed by it" gives birth to the emotion provided by the "beautiful object".[6] Bollas (1989) defines a transformational object "identified by children from what they feel as what modifies the experience of the self".[7] The mother continually transforms the interior and exterior environment of her baby. She supports it in "a continuity of being" and – through the maternal tone which is hers – gives him/her "an aesthetics of being", a "private culture" which constitutes the backdrop of interactions. The memory of the transformational object, of the "*experience of the aesthetic moment*" as a metamorphosing process is "re-enacted" in the encounter with the aesthetic object. Art potentially shapes our quest for transformations.

The clinical case of Sarah[8]

I General information on this case (presentation and biographical data, diagnosis and treatment, modality of the introduction of music therapy)

Sarah is a 34-year-old woman, with no psychiatric antecedents, mother of three boys.[9] The team which welcomed her a few days earlier in the post-psychiatric emergency service were preoccupied by her major depressive collapse with suicidal thoughts and sometimes incoherent words – but not a clearly identified delirious speech. Her husband had just left the family home. That separation was a particularly painful, unexpected and disorganising event. Sarah was feeling *devastated, empty* and *lifeless*. Her *life made no more sense*. It seemed to her that her *husband had left with part of her identity*. Her state would have required a longer hospitalisation, but she and her family turned down this suggestion. Ambulatory care was therefore organised at the medico-psychological centre where I work as a psychiatrist. This care combined a nursing interview every week and a psychiatric consultation with psychotherapeutic aims every two weeks. I was in charge of the latter. The doctor in charge renewed the anti-depressant and anti-psychotic thermoregulatory treatment that had been prescribed at the hospital.

The first stage of this ambulatory follow-up care allowed her to go on with her everyday life thanks to the help of a home-help. She stopped her treatment on her own initiative at the same time as she started her professional life again. During interviews, she only parsimoniously revealed a few elements of her history: her parents' divorce when she was 16, her father's alcoholism afterwards, two younger brothers whom she hardly ever saw for they lived far away, her encounter when she was a teenager with a *brilliant young man* who became her husband. It was as if she was not supposed to remember or yearn for anything. Her psychic vitality was subdued.

Her speech remained a variation on the theme of absence, the impossibility for her to live without her husband. It seemed that that "being deficiency" was irreducible and unattainable. It communicated to me a feeling of powerlessness. The exposition to silence and suicidal ideas was painful for her as well as for me. The complexity of the processes at stake remained inaudible, hidden under a surfacing fake-self. It was then, in that seeming dead-end in the face-to-face psychotherapeutic process where words only cannot be used as a medium for the representative processes, that I thought about sharing musical listening with her.

I thereby hoped to create a sensible space of encounter and contact, a secure modality of being-together in order to try to make audible what had no listening place, what had no possibility for psychic representations, and in order to insufflate a living shape, a moving shape in a fixed and frozen situation. I hypothesised that the qualities of plasticity and mobilisation of sensory-motivity and of the affects of the sound and musical medium, as well as the "relational plasticity" (my empathy) and the sharing of affects, would potentially bring about transformations so that the destructivity that was taking place, the freezing of the processes of representation, might be blocked.

2 Evaluation procedures (for indication and follow-up)

Before engaging in my music therapy proposal, I carried out a psycho-musical assessment in order to better perceive Sarah's positioning as regards music.

This assessment, which has been developed by Verdeau-Paillès (2004), is made up of three sections:

- an interview oriented towards the sound and musical history of the subject, his/her tastes, his/her relation to sound and music in everyday life, his/her musical knowledge . . .;
- a receptive test consisting of the listening to 10 musical excerpts that are adapted to the patient according to the data gathered during the interview and that cover a wide range of emotions and musical styles;

- an active test during which the subject is invited to spontaneously explore a varied instrumentarium.

Sarah's psycho-musical assessment revealed her sensibility to the sound dimension of her environment. She enjoyed listening to music while playing (*it stimulates the gesture*) but not while preparing her class activities (*music speaks to me very loudly*). She owned *a good hi-fi system with nice sound*. She found that music *gave her courage*. She particularly liked classical music and her favourite composer was Mozart. She also listened to songs (Charles Aznavour, Léo Ferré) and to original film soundtracks. She did not like hard rock or metal music. Between the ages of 8 and 10, she played the organ a little with a friend of her parents. She still owned that instrument; it *remains in its cover*. From her childhood's sound environment, she mentioned the silence and her isolation in her bedroom during the day: "*My mother could not stand noise*." What about at night? At night she mentioned the footsteps of her father who sometimes came into her room. That sound memory aroused vivid anxiety and silent tears. *How can I talk about that with words?* She did not say any more and I respected her silence.

Listening to the 10 extracts showed her capacity to focus and a good receptivity to music: she gave rich and personal answers, had evocative and figurative modes of listening and according to the grid of analysis, showed a prevalence of motor answers.

While playing with the instruments, she enjoyed exploring all of them, except for the triangle, *because of the points*, she said. She sought sensual sounds and showed a preference for the xylophone that she chose to improvise and with which she used rhythm as much as melody. She became absorbed and seemed to forget about me.

That assessment confirmed the fact that sound and music are the objects of an actual investment and of a psychic mobilisation, but also that more than being just a prerequisite, it marks a passing, a transition. It had at once opened up a field of possible exploration of her history and psychic life, a field which seemed inaccessible until then after several months of encounters. It also showed a richness of expression that contrasted with the previous follow-up. She managed to "use" and "manipulate" her moving shapes suggested by the music. Her imaginary life that seemed fixed now seemed to be able to spread out and suggested that thanks to that detour she would be able to tame her interior life. By taking it again afterwards, it seemed to have brought the germs of elements that developed later on, as is often the case with early interviews.

From that assessment onwards, each session gave rise to the collection of musical data and writing on the unfolding of exchanges. The notes took into account the clinical state of the day, the verbal and nonverbal associativity (gestures, mimics and postures), and the dynamics of transfer (transfers on the sensorimotor attractor that is the sound and musical medium, on the materiality of the frame, but also intersubjective transfers).

In parallel, the pieces of music that had been listened to were filed by session, in the order in which they had been listened to, in order for me to be able to keep and easily reuse the sound pieces that I had suggested. This made it easier to link the notes taken during the sessions and take them over later on in order to get an overview of several sessions. It also helped me to rework a particularly important and significant session in the therapeutic process.

3 Introduction to the technique used

As my institute is not equipped for music therapy, I use my usual consulting room, my laptop, a hard drive that contains a large music library and that I regularly update with the results of my musical research, and two good-quality speakers.

At the beginning of each 45-minute weekly session (always at the same time and on the same day), Sarah shared with me her preoccupations, her mood, her everyday life and her thoughts on the previous session.

Then, we alternated moments of music listening with moments of verbal expression. I sat beside her during the listening so that our listening was directed towards the same source in a sort of co-presence. My pivoting chair allowed me to then sit face to face with her, so as to listen to her speaking to me about her own listening. I invited her to word her feelings, her emotions, her images, her memories, her associations of ideas, her pleasure or displeasure, etc., on listening to the music. It was also possible not to say anything if nothing came to mind. The frame thereby suggested created a space in which Sarah could oscillate between a psychic state similar to a game or a dream, with me only beside her, and an interaction face to face with me. Such a system invites the subject to move from a sensorial experience and the representation of a thing to narration. It has a double mirror function: that of the music and that of the therapist. It aims to facilitate musical investment, emotional investment but also representational investment.

My interventions particularly sought to revitalise the associative flux and to attract Sarah's attention to an image, a word. I tried to let myself be carried away by her visions, her associative constructions, and to dive into a shared emotional experience, to let myself "feel with her".

In the interval between two sessions, I pre-selected several music pieces. We only listened to two or three pieces per session that seemed more relevant at that specific moment, prompted by our interrelation and of the day's speech. I addressed a message or a musical gesture that established a presence in the sharing of emotions and that testified to my research to come and support her; it aimed to say something in a nonverbal register about what I perceived and understood of Sarah's emotional experience, of her pain. The choice gives free rein to a form of underground weaving, of musical accompaniment, of echoing, of pre- and unconscious contact. It is the expression of my counter-transference.

At any moment, Sarah was free to bring with her a piece of music that she wished to share with me during a session. She only did that twice.

Most of the pieces chosen were taken from classical and contemporary music. Then came original soundtracks from films and world music. In front of Sarah, I chose to associate pieces of music with her psycho-musical assessment. Some of them are reassuring and containing, either because they create a soothing and reliable musical environment, or a feeling of balance and self-contemplation, or because they bring about gaiety or humour. Other pieces were chosen in order to allow Sarah to explore affects such as anxiety, anger, strangeness, fear, etc. This alternation was aimed at not reinforcing the defence mechanisms of repression of affects and not hampering a process of elaboration that can only be born from contrast, difference and strangeness. In contact with Sarah, I felt the need for musical listening not to be felt only as "healthy food" to calm her down, heal her like a therapeutic mothering, but also as a welcoming space to receive painful affects, *clouds of sensations* in order to project into shape something that had not happened.

4 Treatment proper

The one-year study window allowed me to gather data relative to the 30 sessions of which I extract in this chapter the specificities of my relation with Sarah, the themes at stake and the transitional sessions. These data are fragmentary but they seem to me to give a sufficient insight into the salient features of the whole clinical process.

The therapeutic relation with Sarah had a few singular features.

- Sarah cancelled some appointments in order to control the interval in the relationship. She was sometimes led to mention *things that she did not want to think about any more*, she felt *a threat* within her that she was *afraid to awake*, but she also felt profoundly that she *must do something for her and her children later*. She seemed to need to use, to "take", to "leave" the care plan, without being punished; she needed to check that I was here, that I could answer her and see her quickly in spite of a few missed appointments. She did not want to *feel dependent*, but she needed to perceive infallible availability. Through these processes of taking/leaving, through that investment/disinvestment pattern, she seemed to be trying to make me feel what she had gone through during her childhood.
- Moreover, Sarah had a particularly intense and "penetrating" look, as though to see behind the eyes. That particular way of staring at me made me somehow uncomfortable. I wondered whether she was trying to recognise me, to recognise something behind "my surface". Did she doubt my being the actual me? Was she wondering what I was trying to plot? A place where I would divulge my emotions and my perceptions? Was she looking for the mirror of my look?

- On several occasions, I was invaded by the fear that music might repeat a violation of Sarah's intimate space. Wasn't my wish to make her listen to such and such a part causing a re-enactment of her fear of the other's desire against which she was defenceless? That fear signalled the weight and investment of my thoughts that had been created by her revelation, by that real event that kept me from perceiving Sarah differently. Letting myself be limited – within psychic care – by the weight of that real event might cause a repetition of the way in which she felt her father's abuse as a tearing apart, a rupture of her access to dreams and her capacity to play.

The therapeutic process was marked by three main themes developed in the course of our sessions.

- A little girl's anxiety while being alone in the dark watching out for the worrying noises of the night. That theme came back recurrently with multiple variations since the psycho-musical assessment.
- A quest for harmony with no wrong notes. Her quest for and ideal *harmonious family* that would be a place of *total accomplishment*, like a *marvel factory* where *oblivious children would be playing*, like a *welcoming and benevolent nature*, which was largely exposed during the first six sessions, gradually toned down. During session 20, when a piece of music could have recalled that theme, she said that the *music did not correspond to her any longer.*
- A fake-self organisation that, as it revealed itself, allowed for a quest for identity. In order to respond to her parents' expectations, Sarah was *good as gold as a little girl.* Her excessive devotion to her husband, with whom she *acted as the perfect wife*, made the relationship inauthentic, boring and monotonous. Sarah felt as though she were *in the superficial*, as though *there was nothing solid underneath*, as though she *nipped in the bud* any creative capacity in order to *conform* to the image of the ideal spouse. She started to feel like putting into shape creative ideas; in particular, she felt like writing.

Elaborative crossings concentrated on three transitional sessions appeared against the ground made up of these themes. These sessions seemed to be animated by an associative and transferential flux that opened up a particular time and space (paradoxically out of time, but inscribed in the time lapse of the session), thereby giving a feeling of density to the experience. They were characterised by a feeling of astonishment and of shared amazement. It was as if the seizure of a multisensory shape, the transformation of chaos through creation and the way one found to represent oneself and create meaning were conjugated in the therapeutic relation in order to be linked with a feeling of beauty and to create aesthetic emotion. That aesthetic emotion gives the feeling of experiencing a revelation, a possible meaning or a support in order to go a little bit further.

These elements are hard to describe, systematise and categorise. In order not to deprive them of their singularity, not to freeze them and deprive them of their mobility, not to isolate them and make them lose their multiple resonance, I propose to describe them as closely as possible to the clinical experience of session S30 so as to attempt to draw out the representative fluxes at stake and called up by the musical listening in the interrelation.

Before that, let me evoke more briefly S15 and S17:

- *The music I liked the best is the one I liked the least*, said Sarah during S15. Sarah was surprised and affected by this paradox that she heard herself uttering very naturally on that day. The pieces of music she *liked the best* were the one which opened up some interrogations, the ones in which she heard a cry, the cry from something unattainable, which was suffered to appear. They were the ones that called for something, the ones which repeated in order to transform. The ones she preferred were those, which gave her the possibility to tame her anxiety, her fear, her anger in order to transform them, to inscribe the painful events in her life into her story. They were the ones which were linked *in torment.*
- S17: Sarah remembered the death of her little brother, who was born shortly after her and who suffered from cystic fibrosis and was heavily handicapped. No one ever mentioned him at home. She remembered the *profound sorrow* of her mother, who *kept her from seeing him.* Her mother was *too absorbed and too sad* and could not maintain a warm and living contact with her. Sarah would stay *alone, facing excessive requirements and responsibility* for her age. She was responsible for restoring her mother, for *dragging her out of her darkness*, and in order to do that she had to be *well-behaved* and to tell her ceaselessly *how much she loved her.* These repeated words shared no link with her subjective feelings; they detached her language from her profound experience (which she described as *incredible violence*). She experienced the ambivalence of her feelings towards her mother. With that memory, she opened up a space that had remained in the shadows until then.

5 A detailed session: "Sounds and Perfumes Are Turning in the Evening's Air"; discussion around that session

At the beginning of the session, Sarah told me that *she* was feeling well ... *but ... that she felt a grey and ugly backdrop.... There was still something, like danger, somewhere...*

That *grey backdrop* made me think of a dream that I had had one night after a supervision session. In that dream, I saw Paul,[10] whose family name evokes the "parent". There was a memory lapse in that dream that I would like to link with a theoretical point regarding "the Forces of Destiny" (C. Bollas), quoted in an article by Golse (2010) that I had read shortly before and the title of which – "Se souvenir dans le corps, se souvenir dans la tête"[11] – I had found very telling. My thought was empty and I was facing some grey thickness, as I was sitting on a desk, between the sofa and the piano in the supervision room. After this momentary distraction, my attention shifted back to Sarah's speech as she was talking about her art professor and his proposition to participate in a choir *during lunch break*. She remembered her professor's taste for painting and visiting a Francis Bacon exhibition. She explained to me how much she had not liked those paintings, *the colour red, the flesh, the distorted features, the viscera*. I was struck by her evoking this painter at the very moment when *Francis Bacon: The Logic of Sensation* by Gilles Deleuze was sitting on my desk at home. I thought about the notion of Diagramme that is evoked in that book and I mentally represented myself what it designates, that is, the painter's gesture as he tries to erase, to sweep away what the image shows, the figurative data, in order to recreate a zone of indeterminacy, to reintroduce chaos, shapelessness by disfiguring the image, by emptying it of meaning in order to give a chance, a possibility for a new shape to emerge. I questioned myself on the fact that a period of grief, a break-up might constitute some sort of "psychic Diagramme" to Sarah. Then, my ear took me out of my thoughts about Diagramme, when I heard her mention a CD that she had looked for but which she could not find. It was a CD with which that professor had acquainted her: *Voices of the World*. She had wanted to bring it with her that day so as to share with me one of the songs that she *used to listen to in a loop at the time*, but she forgot it. During our last session she had brought an extract from the soundtrack of the cartoon *Kirikou*, which had precisely made me think of a CD called *A Capella, Voice of the World*; I had selected it from my music library the previous day in order to be able to listen to it with her.

We listened to one of the songs on the album: "Angira", sung by three Madagascan sisters from Tirahea (meaning wealth). Sarah heard in *the chorus of women, a voice that was having trouble making itself heard. She liked that voice, an African voice that brought solace and warmth. African mothers have a direct skin-to-skin contact with their children*. She wondered whether that voice that was having trouble making itself heard might be *her voice*. She thought about Kirikou and the witch again and said *that she would also like to write a tale, an inverted tale in which the villain wizard would be handsome*.

The feeling of strangeness and mystery in this *inverted tale* project oriented me towards another suggestion of music: the third movement of *Toward the Sea II: Cape Cod* by Japanese composer Toru Takemitsu. Sarah said that this music was *somehow frightening … (silence), the pinch of the guitar*[12] *is threatening. The flute … (silence). I don't like the gasp for air. It takes me back … (silence). The harp evokes the forest, the water, it's beautiful. It hides or softens things before something worse comes*.

She then mentioned her favourite painter, Van Gogh. She quoted and described *the paintings that particularly moved her*, among which *the last one,*

"Wheatfield with Crows", in which *life and death coexist.* She explained to me that *what she liked about it were the turning colour touches.* She also thought about *The Starry Night.* I pictured those paintings in my head with her. She sometimes gets absorbed into *this type of paintings, turning colour touches* at home and she *could spend hours doing that.* Wondering what can fascinate her in that manner about that *turning movement*, she mimicked the gesture of painting like that on the desk. She remained silent. I looked at her and also got absorbed in her gesture. I merged into her gesture, into the rhythm of her fingers painting virtually on the desk. I thought about an episode during which, as I was practising a left-hand part in broken arpeggios from a sonata by Mozart, trying to find "sonority and the right curve", my daughter had asked me why I kept practising the same thing since I "knew the piece". She felt as if I was *drowning in my notes.* I then thought about *La noyée*[13] (an excerpt from the soundtrack of *Amélie*), the first piece Sarah had brought to *"describe"* herself. I thought I could feel what she meant when she talked about getting absorbed in a gesture or a sound. Shortly before, I had taken my collection of preludes by Debussy out again and had found my daughter's handwriting in it. She had written her name at the bottom of every single page of the prelude "Sounds and Perfumes Are Turning in the Evening Air" so that I might not forget about her as I was absorbed in this piece that marked my going back to playing after a rather long pause. Time seemed to be suspended; she was absorbed in her gesture and I was looking at her doing it while the prelude and its sonorities were on my mind.

As if painting virtually on the table were not enough any more, Sarah turned towards the wall and resumed the same gesture on the vertical part of the wall, getting absorbed again. Suddenly, she stopped. She went and fetched the tissue box as she did so many times (so much so that I was careful to check that it was in the right place before I went to get her in the waiting room so that she could reach it "with her eyes closed"). She told me that she had just understood something and that *she needed to talk now otherwise she wouldn't dare to.* That gesture was *one of masturbation, that of her father on her back while she was staring at the wall against which was her bed.* She cried and then told me *that she'd overcome a new obstacle on the path to her nebula.* Something *was becoming clearer.*

The emergence of the formal signifier (Anzieu, 1987) "it is turning" which is present in the cyclic figures of the harp in Toru Takemitsu's piece marked a decisive moment in that session. From a sound channel, "it is turning" shifted to an auditory channel and to a visual channel in the paintings by Van Gogh. The gesture on the desk mimicking the paintbrush painting turning colour touches on the canvas called up motivity. Some questions emerged: what does this gesture mean? What is this type of movement telling me? Inscribed in repetition, the gesture that turned horizontally on the desk absorbed us both and modified our perception of time. An immaterial and ungraspable process seemed to take a perceptive and material shape. Through that materialised shape which became figurable and noticeable, the psyche could begin to take hold of it. It was the change of orientation of the gesture from horizontality to verticality on the wall that awoke the mnestic cenesthetic traces of the traumatic memory and the possibility of vocalising it and sharing it with me. The traumatic experience felt solitarily calls for someone else's recognition.

Sarah created a shape from sensory-motivity before being able to create meaning. A form of stowage of body sensations and mind thoughts was created. After the silence of intimate experience, the emotion of renewed feelings found a voice of expression through language. Sarah touched and understood in her body as well as in her mind. The "aisthetic" experience, the emotional experience that accompanied her, paved the way to internalisation and the appropriation of that experience. Sharing affects is an essential part of this work, since the experience had not found many possibilities for experimentation until then. It facilitated my own regression in identifying with Sarah. This can be called counter-transferential movement, normal projective identification and empathy.

Aesthetic emotion comes to reveal the fecundity of the encounter between the material at work in the music and psyches concerned. It occurs at the moment when a shape – a discovered shape, incorporated, transformed, reinvented, shared – is constituted and comes out of the unshaped. It reveals itself in the moment of shock when it takes shape in the form of an advent, an appearance that engages a vital movement from an opaque and dreadful zone. That movement is opposed to the horror of a once lethal time that is frozen and testifies to the "upsetting feeling of existence". That moment "gathers all that had been heard from the one to the other until then. The felt emotion "suddenly sparkling" entails a crossing (Franck, 2007).[14] It acts as a "smuggler": it reshuffles, it transforms and it opens up and brings something to light. Sarah *can see more clearly*. It is as if the aesthetic emotion created by the piece of art generated a favourable momentum to the work of symbolisation and subjective appropriation of the experience and as if the work of symbolisation and appropriation – that creation of the psyche – in turn generated an aesthetic emotion.

It is also an emotion that links subjects in the presence of the piece of art (a piece that is itself shaped by other subjects, composers, interpreters) and subjects in the presence of one another – through multidirectional transfers. Aesthetic emotion draws a bridge between oneself and the others and testifies to the "desperate attempt and sometimes success to meet someone else" (Franck, 2007).[15]

6 Discussion and comments on the activity of symbolisation in this clinical case

That therapeutic process goes through several interdependent stages: a possibility for historicisation (narrating allows the constitution of the past as past), the presence of a symbolic musical form within a therapeutic relation (a whole that serves as a container and a contained), the acquisition of a capacity for reflection.

During a first stage of the follow-up, Sarah needed to establish a feeling of security. Music creates a protecting and containing envelope, a support structure. It is "*mother music*" and has a "*feeding*" function, its filling, consoling, soothing function as a carrying object that holds (Lecourt, 2005). Music also gave me the capacity to dream at a moment when I was stuck in front of the monotonous and repetitive aspect of her distress, in front of the painful feeling of hollowness, of emptiness, in front of the suicidal risk.

Listening to pieces of music opened up an *intermediary area* in which Sarah could find a playful dimension by playing with the enigmatic messages in the music. The space for exchange created by the care plan weaves links, all the while maintaining a bearable distance.

The double aspect of countenance and potentiality for transformation through music and the intersubjective relation allowed Sarah to give flexibility to her defence mechanisms, to cut some slack in order to facilitate the implementation of her own representations. She was able to become once again the subject of traumatic situations from which she had had to withdraw herself in order to be able to survive psychically, in order to drown in astonishment and nothingness. The care plan seems to have played the part of an "*aesthetic container*" (Guillaumin, 1997).[16] That "container" term designates the transformative potentialities of the contained.

Over time, Sarah managed to represent herself, her own psychic functioning and her own representative activity. From "*that's what the music is saying!*" (which implied that it was not her), she came to *prefer the music she did not like*, the music that recognised, heard and reflected something unknown within her, something that scared her but for which she developed an interest, partly through identification with my own interest.

Progressively, Sarah grasped herself in the link to the object-music and the object-other-subject therapist. Then, through an internal reflexive function inherited from that link which experimented with these objects, she grasped herself in a relationship with herself. Her making of an internal reflexivity, of "I see myself, I hear myself, I feel myself", the constitution of an "internal psychic mirror" testified to the internalisation of the mirror function of music and to our interrelation, a reflexive mirror that introduced both a link of similarity and a gap.

Of course, Sarah's psychotherapeutic care went on for much longer after that period of observation. Progressively, she did not need the music in order to be able to express her psychic life. Today, she writes short stories and has joined an art class at the school of art. Their first work theme was movement! That access to creativity is the major step forward that this therapy permitted her to take.

Conclusion

The work of symbolisation spreads out against a complex and utterly mobile framework. It is multidirectional between two polarities: sensuality and signification from a double bodily and relational anchoring. This clinical experience from sound and musical mediation leads to the perception of aesthetic emotion as a witness and a generator of the fluidity of the representative processes at stake from sensations, images and words. Starting from the original sensory-affective-motor end, where emotion is not yet differentiated from sensory perception, from the "inside feeling", the *Einfühlung*, a multisensorial, multi-significant, multi-transferential, multidirectional motion phase – crossing all the layers of the psyche – draws in a complex and creative network of inter-weavings, disconnections/recombinations, interpenetration and circulation of elements that belong to the patient(s), the nursing staff, the artists summoned in their artistic creation, the sound material used during the session, and beyond that … to culture and to the human community. It gives an intense feeling of presence to oneself, to the other, to the world, and a feeling of suspension of the linear continuity of time. It gives the feeling of a "living movement within the self", of a "movement that opens up a space", of a "movement that overflows the dimension of the 'Ego' but is not outside of language", of a movement linked to the impression of "feeling oneself being alive" (Boissière, 2014).[17]

Other research regarding aesthetic emotion is also being carried out in our laboratory with picture mediation (art therapy). That research trend shows the desire to fully integrate the aesthetic dimension to our art therapy practices.

Notes

1 Chapter translated by Léa Boichard, Agrégée and PhD student in English language and literature, Jean Moulin University-Lyon 3, Jean Monnet University-Saint-Etienne.
2 Translated by the author.
3 Translated by the author.
4 Translated by the author.
5 Translated by the author.
6 Translated by the author.
7 Translated by the author.
8 I draw on Kenneth Bruscia's (1991) model for case presentation which contains 42 cases of music therapy.
9 Words in italics are Sarah's own expressions.
10 Another patient of mine from the same period and whom I also talked about during supervision.
11 "Remembering in the body, remembering in the head"; translated by the author.
12 At first, Sarah heard a guitar instead of the harp.
13 *The one who drowned*; translated by the author.
14 Translated by the author.
15 Translated by the author.

16 Translated by the author.
17 Translated by the author.

References

Aigen, K. (2007). In defense of beauty: A role for the aesthetic in music therapy theory, part I – The development of aesthetic theory in music therapy. *Nordic Journal of Music Therapy, 16*(2), 112–128.

Aigen, K. (2008). In defense of beauty: A role for the aesthetic in music therapy theory, part II – Challenges to aesthetic theory in music therapy: Summary and response. *Nordic Journal of Music Therapy, 17*(1), 3–18.

Anzieu, D. (1985). *Le Moi-peau.* Paris: Dunod.

Anzieu, D. (1987). *Les enveloppes psychiques.* Paris: Dunod.

Boissière, A. (2014). *Musique et mouvement.* Paris: Manucius.

Bollas, C. (1989). L'Objet transformationnel. *Revue Française de Psychanalyse, 4,* 1181–1196.

Bruscia, K. E. (1991). *Case studies in music therapy.* Phoenixville, PA: Barcelona Publishers.

Franck, A. (2007). *Beautés et transfert.* Paris: Hermann psychanalyse.

Gaston, T. (1964). The aesthetic experience and biological man. *Journal of Music Therapy, 1*(1), 1–7.

Golse, B. (2010). Se souvenir dans la tête, ou se souvenir dans le corps. In J. Aïn (Ed.), *Réminiscences* (pp. 31–52). Toulouse: Eres.

Guillaumin, J. (1997). Esthétique et identité. *Adolescence, 15*(1), 19–31.

Lecourt, E. (1987). L'enveloppe musicale. In D. Anzieu (Ed.). *Les enveloppes psychiques* (pp. 199–222). Paris: Dunod.

Lecourt, E. (1995). Le beau et la question de la sublimation. *La Revue de Musicothérapie, 15*(2), 43–54.

Lecourt, E. (2005). *Découvrir la musicothérapie.* Paris: Eyrolles.

Maiello, S. (2010). À l'aube de la vie psychique: Réflexions autour de l'objet sonore et de la dimension spatio-temporelle de la vie prénatale. In J. Aïn (Ed.), *Réminiscences* (pp. 103–116). Toulouse: Erès.

Malloch, S. N. & Trevarthen, C. (Eds.). (2009). *Communicative musicality: Exploring the basis of human companionship.* Oxford: Oxford University Press.

Meltzer, D. & Williams, M. H. (2000). *L'appréhension de la beauté.* Paris: Edition du Hublot. (Original work published 1988 as *The apprehension of beauty: The role of aesthetic conflict in development, violence and art,* The Clunie Press.)

Mueller, J. (1964). The aesthetic experience and psychological man. *Journal of Music Therapy, 1*(1), 8–15.

Nordoff, P. & Robins, C. (1977). *Creative music therapy: Individualized treatment for the handicapped child.* New York: John Day Company.

Roussillon, R. (2000). *Besoin de créer.* Intervention à l'institut d'art contemporain. Retrieved from http://reneroussillon.wordpress.com/création/institut-dart-contempo.

Salas, J. (1990). Aesthetic experience in music therapy. *Music Therapy, 9*(1), pp. 1–15.

Segal, H. (1979). Psychanalyse et esthétique. *Revue Française de Psychanalyse, 5–6,* 875–900, en appui sur les travaux de M. Klein sur *la position dépressive.*

Stern, D. (1998). Les bébés et la musique: Réflexion sur les aspects temporels de l'expérience quotidienne d'un nourrisson. *Revue de Psychanalyse de l'enfant, 23*, 88–111.
Tsiris, G. (2008). Aesthetic experience and transformation in music therapy. *Music Therapy, 8*(3). Retrieved from https://voices.no/index.php/voices/article/view/416.
Verdeau-Paillès, J. (2004). *Le bilan psycho musical de la personnalité.* Courlay: J. M. Fuzeau.
Vischer, R. (1873). *Über das optische Formgefühl. Ein Beitrag zur Aesthetik.* Leipzig: Hermann Credner.
Winnicott, D. W. (1975). *Jeu et réalité: L'espace potentiel.* Paris: Gallimard. (Original work published 1971 as *Playing and reality*. Harmondsworth: Penguin)

Further reading

Brun, A. & Roussillon, R. (2014). *Formes primaires de symbolisation*. Paris: Dunod.
Lecourt, E. (1992). L'objet-beauté en art-thérapie. *Le Journal des psychologues, 103*, 23–25.
Lecourt, E. (1996). L'étude de cas en psychopathologie et en musicothérapie. *La Revue de Musicothérapie, 16*(5), 1–5, 31–33.
Lecourt, E. (1998). The role of aesthetics in countertransference: A comparison of active versus receptive music therapy (pp. 137–159). In K. E. Bruscia (Ed.), *The dynamics of music psychotherapy*. Gilsum, NH: Barcelona Publishers.
Roussillon, R. (1999). *Les enjeux de la symbolisation à l'adolescence.* In International Society for Adolescent Psychiatry, GREUPP "Adolescence", pp. 7–23.
Roussillon, R. (2007). Le langage et l'objet. *Revue française de psychanalyse, 71*(5), 1441–1447.
Roussillon, R. (2012). On souffre du non-approprié de l'histoire: On guérit en l'intégrant. *Le Carnet PSY, 167*(9), 36–41.
Roussillon, R. (2012). *Manuel de pratique clinique.* Issy-les-Moulineaux: Elsevier Masson.
Winnicott, D. W. (1975). "La crainte de l'effondrement", in Figures du vide. *Nouvelle revue de psychanalyse, 15*, 35–43.

Chapter 3

Dramatherapy work in the treatment of schizophrenic psychoses

Johannes Junker

Introduction

The purpose of this chapter is to give an overview of evidence-based literature on the topic of dramatherapy and to also make suggestions for the further development of a dramatherapy method in this area. Dramatherapy will be defined in detail so that it can be discerned from other related subjects and also to clarify what has been published in the defined subject area so far and what those publications' goals and results have been. Focus will be on possible effects in the treatment of schizophrenia and on singling out specific dramatherapy methods.

Using an empirical case study, the chapter will conclude by describing an evaluated dramatherapy method that allows for quantitative research that might comply with current medical quality standards.

Literature review

In 2006 Lambros Yotis published "A review of dramatherapy research in schizophrenia: methodologies and outcomes" and in 2007 Rachel Ruddy and Kim Dent-Brown published "Drama therapy for schizophrenia or schizophrenia-like illness". Both these articles show clearly that only a very small amount of quantitative evaluation of dramatherapy methods with schizophrenic patients has been done so far. Yotis states that "quantitative research in dramatherapy, in particular randomized controlled trials, has disadvantages and limitations, as does any research in the psychotherapeutic field" (2006, p. 191). He describes several dramatherapy trials with quantitative methods which unfortunately use neither a sufficient number of participants nor exactly defined dramatherapy methods or randomized controlled trials. A full account of Yotis's interesting research is included in Chapter 10 of this volume. What is also lacking is a critical debate on quantitative versus qualitative research methods (i.e. Leichsenring & Rüger, 2004). What is of interest for future trials is his collection of case studies that, according to his research, show evidence of "the positive effect of brief periods of dramatherapy on the lack of motivation, socialization deficits and poor affective relationships of patients with schizophrenia, all of which are aspects of the 'negative syndrome' (Andreasen, 1982) of this disorder": Emunah (1983); Johnson (1984); Langley and Langley (1983); Whitelock (1987); Grainger (1990); Landy (1994); Mitchell (1996); Snow (1996); Van der Wijk (1996); Yotis, Kravariti, Theodoridou and Megaloeconomou (2003). These were mostly carried out in in-patient or day-care clinics or in psychiatric rehabilitation clinics, and concentrate on different issues in their research. Grainger (1990), for example, focuses on the cognitive processing of reality by letting patients play with real-life scenarios. Snow (1996), however, focuses on the patients' phantasy world by letting them transform their psychotic experiences into images and allowing them to integrate these phantasies into their inner self. Landy (1994) uses distancing techniques such as masks and phantasy roles to help them learn to control their excessive emotions. Mitchell (1996) describes the value of the collective creativity which takes place if the emphasis is on the ritual nature of the dramatherapy setting.

Yotis cites two more research methods which do not initially aim to gauge quantitative effectiveness, but which contain important aspects from the scientific research tradition. He states that "the new paradigm research (Payne, 1993) proposes a responsive, interactive way of approaching truth, which values the subjective experience, self-determination, and interdependency of all participants" (2006, p. 196). This participatory research method tries to record the positions of all participants in the setting in order to find out from their different viewpoints if progress has been made as intended (e.g. Junker, Oostrik & Scharf, 2008). This ensures that the dramatherapist, who participates, also takes on the role of the observing scientist, which complies with the natural situation in this particular setting. This is the approach increasingly used by the social sciences; it is not yet used in evidence-based medical research, however.

Another approach Yotis describes is the research branch based in theatre. Landy (1996) comments on this as follows: "when the therapeutic process is one based in an artistic, dramatic experience, then we need to look more closely at dramatic ways of knowing that reveal mysteries and yield new knowledge" (p. 40). This theatre-based branch has two arms. The first one "intends to create public performances focusing on a play and the people in it and on the actor–spectator communication" (Yotis, 2006, p. 196). Yotis refers to Andersen-Warren (1996), Emunah (1994), McKay (1996) and Johnson (1994), who is currently very popular in the Netherlands. The latter puts special emphasis on communication in and with the group and on the feeling of belonging to a group, on recognizing common signs showing that one belongs to a group and that one has a common goal. Using this dramatherapy approach it is possible to work individually with a schizophrenic patient in a group setting. There are a lot of dramatherapy pioneers who have worked in this way, for example, Bielanska, Cechnicki and Budzyna-Dawidowski (1991) from Poland. The second arm of this research branch applies "the use of a dramatic text to create a healing environment within the group without opening the group work to the public, the element of the play being a springboard of inspiration for the group members" (Yotis, 2006, p. 197). Yotis (1997), for example, worked with a modern interpretation of Aristophanes' "Birds", and McNiff (1998) and Grainger (1999) used an interpretation of Aristophanes' "Frogs" with schizophrenic patients. Using this dramatherapy process with the same type of patient group in a day-care clinic, Andersen-Warren (1996) chose the style of a melodrama because of its strict and simple structure.

Yotis's article illustrates that research on dramatherapy with schizophrenic patients can include quantitative, qualitative and theatre-based methods. They are all used to evaluate positive and negative symptoms, cognitive functions, mental representations, levels of social contact, of conversation and of verbal expressions. Sometimes existing standardized psychological tests are used, whereas other researchers have developed their own testing methods. None of the tests quoted by Yotis comply with the requirements of evidence-based medical research on levels 1 and 2, nor do those quoted by Oster, Melches and Hamberger (2014) and Hamberger et al. (2016).

In 2007, Rachel Ruddy and Kim Dent-Brown published "Drama therapy for schizophrenia or schizophrenia-like illness". In their literature review on the topic of dramatherapy and schizophrenia, they list 183 articles; out of these, however, only five use relevant randomized controlled groups in connection with a double-blind method. They delineate dramatherapy by using an internationally recognized definition, i.e. that of the British Association of Dramatherapists (BADTH):

> Dramatherapy has as its main focus the intentional use of healing aspects of drama and theatre as the therapeutic process. It is a method of working and playing that uses action methods to facilitate creativity, imagination, learning, insight and growth.
>
> (BADTH, n.d.a)

This is an important delineation, as there is not yet an internationally valid definition of dramatherapy; this also becomes evident in the same article where two of the five chosen methods are from psychodrama and three dramatherapy methods, which were carried out in China (Qu, Li & Xiao, 2000; Zhou & Tang, 2002). It is important to differentiate psychodrama and dramatherapy, which is not always done in the literature. In a narrow sense, these would also have to be excluded, unless they used the same psychodrama techniques that are also used in dramatherapy, which would mean there is an accidental overlap that is equally valid. These possible overlaps must be described, otherwise in research it would be classed as a methodological uncertainty. The above-mentioned two articles do not give sufficient information on this subject, however. The authors also include in their selection two trials (Gutride,

Goldstein & Hunter, 1973; Whetstone, 1986) that contain role play, but those were not carried out by dramatherapists. According to them the methods are, however, described sufficiently, so that they can be counted as part of the dramatherapy range of methods (Ruddy & Dent-Brown, 2007, p. 6). The selected patient group is very broadly categorized as suffering from schizophrenia or "schizophrenia-like illness" (Ruddy & Dent-Brown, 2007, p. 3). From today's perspective this must be defined in a more differentiated and detailed manner.

Furthermore, they list precisely how and where they searched using various terminology and what methods they used to measure effectiveness. They describe the basic parameters in all five trials and most of all discuss the different groups of patients with their illnesses and the methods used including an evaluation of the goals of the trial. The five trials are evaluated in a table according to methods, participants, interventions, results and final evaluation. None of the selected tests comply with the standards of evidence-based research. The two authors then summarize their findings as follows: "Randomized Studies are possible in this field. The use of drama therapy for schizophrenia and schizophrenia-like illnesses should continue to be put under evaluation as its benefits, or harms, are unclear" (Ruddy & Dent-Brown, 2007, p. 2).

This illustrates that currently there are no exactly defined methods in dramatherapy; neither is there a precise diagnosis or fine-tuning for the participants in a standardized setting, nor are there exact medical research methods or meta-analysis.

Insights into related sciences

It is not really helpful to look to related sciences for guidance, as all the therapy sciences are trying to find solutions for exactly the same problems. A little detour into the realm of psychodrama will illustrate this.

Psychodrama

Psychodrama therapists already have professional credibility and thus only indirectly face the same problems as a group trying to establish a new profession. Training in psychodrama takes place at postgraduate level and therefore is not a basic professional training course. Therapists who use psychodrama already have a therapeutic qualification that allows them to practise as recognized therapists. Thus, in Germany, for example, this method is generally used in addition to a recognized psychotherapy treatment. In spite of this, it is only natural that psychodrama therapists would like to see their results measured and validated and therefore encompass scientific benchmarking processes that are increasingly used as standard methods in all health care professions. As mentioned above, there are also no valid findings in psychodrama research in relation to schizophrenia. This is not really surprising as this form of therapy has not been extensively applied to that particular illness. The reasons for this might also be their different starting points. In a special edition (Sonderheft No. 3) from 2011 of "Empirische Forschung und Wissenschaft" (Stadler & Wieser, 2011), a psychodrama and sociometry magazine, an article titled "Qualitative Psychodramaforschung" (Hintermeier, 2011, §§89–107) states the following:

> As psychodrama therapy training is turning more and more into an academic discipline, a person unfamiliar with methodology sometimes has to do practical research for their Master thesis. Even though they have been around for a long time, qualitative research methods are less well known to a person who is new to research than quantitative ones.

And yet, according to Hintermeier, these dramatherapists would be ideally suited for psychodrama therapy process research and would fit in with the spontaneous and creative approach in psychodrama including more open approaches. This illustrates that psychodrama also deals with the necessity of an academic and scientific discourse and is looking for its ground rules. What is striking is that, according to the author quoted above, quantitative research methods are better suited to this subject matter. She does not mention, however, that the results so far are not even considered in evidence-based medical research at the moment.

Guidelines in psychiatry

However, the results from research developments until today are still encouraging, even though in the last German guidelines on schizophrenia in 2006 (Gaebel, 2006) artistic therapies were introduced under the collective term "creative therapies" as a complementary therapy without any notable research. This assessment does not yet include research from 2009 (Gold) and 2013 (Ulrich, Houtmans & Gold), which was mentioned above, and gives us reason to believe that a revision of the guidelines on schizophrenia from 2006, which will be concluded in 2016, will lead to a more favourable assessment of artistic therapies. These practice guidelines are aimed at increasing the quality of psychiatric treatments. Medical reports and diagnoses are processed and summarized through meta-analyses and systematic reviews and are thus set apart from subjective individual experiences as described in many reports. German guidelines follow international standards from the US and UK. They stipulate the so-called evidence-based medical standard which can be systematically summed up as follows:

I.a meta-analysis of at least three randomized controlled trials (RCTs);
I.b at least one RCT or meta-analysis of fewer than three RCTs;

II.a at least one controlled non-randomized trial with a high degree of method design;
II.b at least one quasi-experimental trial with a high degree of method design;
III at least one non-experimental descriptive trial (comparative clinical trial, correlation trial, case studies);
IV reports/recommendations of expert committees, clinical experience of recognized authorities.

The recommendations were divided up into three levels of recommendation. The three levels of recommendation were determined by the strength of the available supporting evidence:

A I.a and I.b;
B Evidence level II.a, II.b, III or evidence from level I which does not, however, relate to the specific question under review and is therefore extrapolated or deduced;
C Evidence level IV or derivations from II.a, II.b or III. GCP: Good Clinical Practice – a treatment standard which is broadly agreed on and where no experimental scientific research is possible or desired (Falkei et al., 2006, p. 7).

Creative therapies, as artistic therapies are called in these guidelines, are given the grade "GCP". Therefore artistic therapies in Germany are very keen to obtain good evidence-based studies in their specialist field. At present all four artistic therapies (art, music, drama and dance therapy) are gathered under this collective name and therefore are able to support one another in their scientific aspirations. However, these formerly separate developments in each field are now starting to collaborate and plan and perform research together.

There is, of course, a lot of resistance to these standards that have been imposed by the science-oriented Western medicine. This type of measuring instrument cannot be used to prove the effectiveness of many methods which, because of their multifacetedness, are of a different value altogether, work on a different timescale or enhance healing processes that begin to stimulate certain mental inner forces in order to help achieve long-term success (Fydrich & Schneider, 2007). Also, the forgery of evidence-based trials in drug trials and placebo research are at present shattering the credibility of this approach (Rief, Hofmann & Nestoriuc, 2008, pp. 1626–1628).

Despite this fundamental criticism, it is nevertheless necessary to deal with and get acquainted with the current structures, to react to what is demanded by health insurance providers, medical and other related empirically based fields and to find ways of verifying one's actions.

As there are not yet sufficient evidence-based studies in dramatherapy available at the levels outlined above, it is necessary to work on the next steps to achieve this. One of the building blocks could be a high-quality trial which would be used to describe and systematically analyse dramatherapy indications, diagnosis and method within a narrowly defined patient group. This is the only way comparability might become possible.

Draft of a dramatherapy trial with schizophrenic patients

As described above, the dramatherapy method used must be defined in detail by the authors and the scope of the conditions and the setting where dramatherapy is to take place for the duration of the trial must be outlined clearly. The scientific methods used and their evaluation and assessment must also be described precisely.

In the following I will outline the dramatherapy method, as in my view this is where the most confusion exists. All other scientific parameters stem from the relevant evidence-based medical survey tradition and should of course be used accordingly.

The BADTH definition is used as a basis for the description of the method that follows:

> Dramatherapy is a form of psychological therapy in which all of the performance arts are utilised within the therapeutic relationship. Dramatherapists are both artists and clinicians and draw on their trainings in theatre/drama and therapy to create methods to engage clients in effecting psychological, emotional and social changes. The therapy gives equal validity to body and mind within the dramatic context; stories, myths, playtexts, puppetry, masks and improvisation are examples of the range of artistic interventions a dramatherapist may employ. These will enable the client to explore difficult and painful life experiences through an indirect approach.
>
> (BADTH, n.d.b)

Concrete dramatherapy methods can be derived from this definition and it can also be used to distinguish dramatherapy from other types of therapy. A further essential step is to select which of the dramatherapy interventions we should focus on. Should the dramatherapy unit in question be described as a whole or should we concentrate on those parts where we expect to effect the greatest possible change? Is the "warming up" part which serves as an introduction to playing or the choice of the play's topic already part of the expected change, or is it only the actual core area, for example, the improvisation itself? In all cases it must be pointed out what is included in the survey, why and in what way. This is of great importance because it is the only way in which the actual characteristics of therapeutic intervention can be abstracted and how we can find out if they had an effect or not. Limiting the scope to what is essential allows us to detect what is so special about dramatherapy intervention. The following example will illustrate this point.

During dramatherapy with six schizophrenic male patients who were all diagnosed with F20 "schizophrenia" or F20.3 "undifferentiated schizophrenia" according to the ICD 10 (Deutsches Institut für Medizinische Dokumentation und Information, 2015), the following method was used in their therapy for one year: Each therapy unit lasts 60 minutes and consists of three parts where each part has a different focus. Part one always consists of getting to know the room and becoming aware of oneself in the room and encountering the other participants there. All the exercises used in this part are taken from actors' training courses (cf. Junker, 1998, pp. 142–146). Part two consists of making up a story, staging it by defining the different roles, picking a role and designing the set and subsequently acting out the story. Part three consists of the discussion and evaluation afterwards. Part one is, of course, of very high relevance to this patient group as it can have an impact on negative symptoms. Many different variations can be worked out here on the themes of sharing a common reality, experiencing a room that is being used together with others, encountering oneself and then others within the boundaries of a safe space. This always serves as a starting point which enables participants to put on a play together. In part two all the exercises of part one are combined in new variations; they are used in different ways and expanded on. Part three brings the patients back to the narrative, i.e. talking about one's experience, what has become visible to oneself and others, what is important or not important and how can it be interpreted in one's present life situation. This also includes how certain things are reiterated, what one has the courage to tell others and what one wishes to tell others. From this it becomes clear that part two is the centrepiece of the dramatherapy method; this is where the specific features of dramatherapy intervention stand out most clearly. A dramatherapy trial can thus focus on this part.

Junker's (1998) survey can be used as a basis for a possible structure:

1. Finding a topic. This can be inspired by various materials, for example, the genre of the stage-set (e.g. a throne room, a climbing wall) or the costumes (e.g. a monk's habit, a hunter's hat).
2. Collecting ideas. Ideas are gathered on the chosen topic. This is guided by specific questions as to a possible location, possible roles and a possible plot.
3. Choosing an idea. Each participant is now asked about his decision for a particular idea that has by now been slightly elaborated on and the idea that receives the most agreement is picked.
4. The story. The plot and the parts and places therein are being discussed and decided on. The plot is fine-tuned by deciding on the key objective of the story, i.e. if conflicts should be part of the story, how the story should end (a tragic, happy or even open ending).
5. Choice of stylistic devices. This can be used to increase or decrease, for example, temper, the drama of the plot. The group can use this as a way

to express their relationship with the common story and what they want to emphasize when they perform it.

6 Choice of roles. The roles that need to be filled are shared out. This is all about their curiosity about a particular role as well as about discovering new ways of behaving, thinking and feeling in this role. We look at all the roles in the story as this has an influence on the relationship between them, for example, between protagonist and antagonist.
7 Playing area and decoration including costumes. Defining the playing area in a dramatherapy room is a necessary aid to orientation and the safety of the playing area is a fundamental prerequisite for "play-acting". This is where the story gets attached to a space and even pinned down by objects. In this way all participants, i.e. actors, director and spectators, then know why an object is in a certain place in the room and for what purpose.
8 Role interview. This is where the roles in the story are picked. Patients pick their role according to their individual goal in dramatherapy. The role interview is always carried out by the therapist and serves to detect the suspense between the patient's freedom of choice to choose a particular role and the goal of the therapy. This creates a balance between what patients think they are able to do in a particular role and what they cannot actually do yet and which they may now dare to do through play-acting in a safe environment. To help them act more confidently, they are offered props, i.e. text, a prompter or an assistant who helps them in the play when they give a sign, or time-outs when the scene is stopped and the next sequence can be discussed.
9 Discussing the first scene. The beginning of the first scene is determined in detail. Who stands where, who initiates an action, who responds, what are the rules of the play, can the director interfere and, if yes, how? A clearly defined structured beginning is set.
10 Discussion of the entire play sequence. The director gives a summary of the whole story with regard to the different roles and the set beginning.
11 The play. The play is taking place within the set parameters. The participants can decide after the first scene which role they want to take. This is meant in the broad sense of the theatre, i.e. they may choose to be actor, director or spectator or they may enhance their chosen role. The therapist's observation plays a big part here, he/she needs to see and appreciate all patients in their chosen positions and in relation to their therapy goal.
12 Appraisal. Here we talk about the different qualities of being a spectator, of picking a role and changing it. Initially experiences are shared and then discussed in the context of the story in question. What happened the way it was supposed to happen when the sequence of the scenes was planned beforehand, how did the actors perform their roles and how relevant are the therapist's observations to the patient's therapy goal? This is also

where the stage is set for the next steps in the therapy (cf. Junker, 1998, pp. 142–163).

In the survey quoted, three treatment phases unfolded where the sequences described above can be grouped into different subject areas. During the first phase patients wanted to play with stories from their imagination, in the second one with generalized everyday situations and in the third phase with stories that deal with autobiographical material. These different focuses can be integrated into the prescribed sequence without any problems.

This little foray into the description of a survey might serve to illustrate just how important the precise structuring and description of content within the structure is if you want to find out what researchers actually mean when they talk about dramatherapy. Only then does a survey become comprehensible and can be repeated and evaluated. And in this way the core areas of the relevant therapeutic methods can be compared with one another.

To put it in a nutshell, the question crops up more and more whether dramatherapy activities should become more science-oriented. The starting points in various European countries and in the US are very different and this is reflected in their research traditions. Neither the UK nor the Netherlands, Belgium, Italy or Latvia, where dramatherapy has its strongest academic roots, demand as much evidence-based medical science as Germany. Switzerland has chosen its own path; dramatherapy there does not have to withstand academic verification at all. Therefore the biggest demand for verification is in Germany where its scientific tradition is the weakest. It is becoming increasingly necessary that the artistic therapies see themselves as one academic unit and start initiating mutually coordinated research projects, as is happening in art therapy where a joint library stock is being built up by three German universities, i.e. Hochschule für Kunsttherapie Nürtingen, Alanus Hochschule Alfter and Hochschule für Künste im Sozialen Ottersberg (Elbing, Schulze, Zillmann & Ostermann, 2008; Elbing, Schulze, Zillmann, Raak & Ostermann, 2009; Elbing & Schulze, 2011; Schulze, 2014). These three universities of applied sciences have been cooperating in a research association since 2008 whose goal is to coordinate their research plans and to initiate and undertake common research projects. Cooperation also exists between Universität Witten-Herdecke and Universität Ulm where joint doctoral colloquiums about dramatherapy can be carried out.

This leads to the development of different research centres and in time helps to establish an academic community. This is also supported by the Bundesarbeitsgemeinschaft Künstlerischer Therapien, an umbrella organization of 11 German professional associations from the areas of art, music, dance and drama therapy whose common goal is to advance the establishment of these professions in the German health system (Hamberger & Hamdorf, 2011).

References

Andersen-Warren, M. (1996). *Therapeutic theatre*. Philadelphia, PA: Jessica Kingsley Publishers.

Andreasen, C. N. (1982). Negative versus positive schizophrenia. *Psychiatry, 39*, 789–794.

BADTH (British Association of Dramatherapists). (n.d.a). *About dramatherapy*. Retrieved from http://badth.org.uk.

BADTH (British Association of Dramatherapists). (n.d.b). *Dramatherapy*. Retrieved from http://badth.org.uk/dtherapy.

Bielanska, A., Cechnicki, A. & Budzyna-Dawidowski, P. (1991). Drama therapy as a means of rehabilitation for schizophrenic patients: Our impressions. *American journal of psychotherapy, 45*(4), 566–575.

Deutsches Institut für Medizinische Dokumentation und Information. (2015). *Internationale statistische Klassifikation der Krankheiten und verwandter Gesundheitsprobleme*, 10. Revision, German Modification. Retrieved from www.dimdi.de/static/de/klassi/icd-10-who/kodesuche/onlinefassungen/htmlamtl2005/index.htm?gf20.htm+.

Elbing, U. & Schulze, C. (2011). www.arthedata.de: Eine wissenschaftliche Datenbank für Kunsttherapie. In P. Petersen, H. Gruber & R. Tüpker (Eds.), *Forschungsmethoden Künstlerischer Therapien* (pp. 167–178). Wiesbaden: Reichert.

Elbing, U., Schulze, C., Zillmann, H. & Ostermann, T. (2008). Arthedata: Aufbau und technische Realisierung einer wissenschaftlichen Datenbank für Kunsttherapie. *Zeitschrift für Musik-, Tanz- und Kunsttherapie, 19*(3), 121–125.

Elbing, U., Schulze, C., Zillmann, H., Raak, C. K. & Ostermann, T. (2009). Arthedata: An online data base of scientific references on art therapy. *European Journal of Integrative Medicine*. doi:10.1016/j.eujim.2009.01.001.

Emunah, R. (1983). Drama therapy with adult psychiatric patients. *The Arts in Psychotherapy, 10*, 77–84.

Emunah, R. (1994). *Acting for real: Drama therapy process, technique, and performance*. New York: Brunner Mazel Publishers.

Falkei, P., Gaebel, W., Weinmann, S. & Wobrock, T. (2006). DGPPN (Hrsg.) S3 – *Praxisleitlinien in Psychiatrie und Psychotherapie Band 1: Behandlungsleitlinie Schizophrenie*. Retrieved from: www.dgppn.de/fileadmin/user_upload/_medien/download/pdf/kurzversion-leitlinien/s3-praxisleitlinien-bd1-schizophrenie-methodenreport.pdf.

Fydrich, T. & Schneider, S. (2007). Evidenzbasierte Psychotherapie. *Psychotherapeut, 52*(1), 55–68. http://doi.org/10.1007/s00278-006-0522-x.

Gaebel, W. (Ed.). (2006). *Behandlungsleitlinie Schizophrenie: Praxisleitlinien in Psychiatrie und Psychotherapie* (Bd. 1). Darmstadt: Steinkopff.

Gold, C. (2009). Systematische Übersichtsarbeit und Meta-Analyse. *Musiktherapeutische Umschau, 30*(1), 74–77.

Grainger, R. (1990). *Drama and healing: The roots of drama therapy*. London: Jessica Kingsley Publishers.

Grainger, R. (1999). *Researching the arts therapies: A dramatherapist's perspective*. London: Jessica Kingsley Publishers.

Gutride, M., Goldstein, A. & Hunter, G. (1973). The use of modeling and role playing to increase social interaction among asocial psychiatric patients. *Journal of Consulting and Clinical Psychology, 40*, 408–415.

Hamberger, C. & Hamdorf, T. (2011). Fragmentierter Entwurf eines Bauplans: Zur aktuellen Etablierungsdynamik der künstlerischen Therapien. *Zeitschrift für künstlerische Therapien, Kunst & Therapie, 2*, 72–83.

Hamberger, C., Melches, J. & Oster, J. (2016). Berufsgruppenanalyse Künstlerischer Therapeutinnen und Therapeuten (BgA-KT). *Ergebnisse und Resümee. Musiktherapeutische Umschau, 37*(1), 41–59.

Hintermeier, S. (2011). Qualitative Psychodramaforschung. *Zeitschrift für Psychodrama und Soziometrie, 1*, 89– 107.

Johnson, D. R. (1984). Representation of the internal world in catatonic schizophrenia. *Psychiatry, 47*(4), 299–314.

Johnson, D. R. (1994). Shame dynamics among creative arts therapists. *The Arts in Psychotherapy, 21*(3), 173–178.

Junker, J. (1998). *Dramatherapie en Schizofrenie: Johannes Junker en Ge Cimmermans* (G. Cimmermans, Ed.). Nijmegen: Triprint.

Junker, J., Oostrik, H. & Scharf, A. (2008). Heilt Spielen! Eine Fallstudie. In D. Müller-Weith, L. Neumann & B. Stoltenhoff-Erdmann (Eds.). *Spielend leben lernen* (pp. 67–111). Berlin.

Landy, R. J. (1994). *Drama therapy: Concepts, theories and practices* (2nd ed.). Springfield, IL: Charles C. Thomas.

Landy, R. J. (1996). Drama therapy and distancing: Reflections on theory and clinical application. *The Arts in Psychotherapy, 23*(5), 367–373.

Langley, D. & Langley, G. (1983). *Dramatherapy and psychiatry*. London: Croom Helm.

Leichsenring, F. & Rüger, U. (2004). Psychotherapeutische Behandlungsverfahren auf dem Prüfstand der Evidence based medicine. *Zeitschrift für Psychosomatische Medizin, 2*, 203–217.

McKay, B. (1996). Conceptual and methodological issues of research in drama therapy. In D. Read Johnson & R. Emunah (Eds.), *Current approaches in drama therapy* (pp. 314–328). London: Charles C. Thomas Publishers.

McNiff, S. (1998). *Art based research*. London: Jessica Kingsley Publishers.

Mitchell, S. (1996). *Dramatherapy: Clinical studies*. London: Jessica Kingsley Publishers.

Oster, J., Melches, J. & Hamberger, C. (2014). Berufsgruppenanalyse Künstlerischer Therapeutinnen und Therapeuten (BgA-KT): Ergebnisse und Resümee 1. *Musiktherapeutischen Umschau, 4*, 314–326.

Payne, H. (1993). *Handbook of Inquiry in the Arts Therapies: One River, Many Currents*. London: Jessica Kingsley Publishers.

Qu, Y., Li, Y. & Xiao, G. (2000). The efficacy of dramatherapy in chronic schizophrenia. *China Journal of Psychiatry, 33*, 237–239.

Rief, W., Hofmann, S. G. & Nestoriuc, Y. (2008). The power of expectation: Understanding the placebo and nocebo phenomenon. *Social and Personality Psychology Compass, 2*(4), 1626–1628.

Ruddy, R. & Dent-Brown, K. (2007). Drama therapy for schizophrenia or schizophrenia-like illnesses. *Cochrane Reviews, 1*. Retrieved from www.thecochranelibrary.com.

Schulze, C. (2014). Forschungsverbund Kunsttherapie: Arbeitsprogramm und erste Ergebnisse. *Zeitschrift für Musik, Tanz- und Kunsttherapie, Sonderheft Forschung, 25*, 186–190.

Snow, S. (1996). Focusing on mythic imagery in brief dramatherapy with psychotic individuals. In A. Gersie (Ed.), *Dramatic approaches to brief therapy*. London: Jessica Kingsley Publishers.

Stadler, C. & Wieser, M. (Eds.). (2011). *Psychodrama: Empirische Forschung und Wissenschaft*. Wiesbaden: VS Verlag.
Ulrich, G., Houtmans, T. & Gold, C. (2007). The additional therapeutic effect of group music therapy for schizophrenic patients: A randomized study. *Acta Psychiatrica Scandinavica, 116*(5), 362–370.
Whetstone, W. (1986). Social dramatics: Social skills development for the chronically mentally ill. *Journal of Advanced Nursing, 11*, 67–74.
Whitelock, J. (1987). Dramatherapy in a psychiatric daycentre. In S. Jennings (Ed.), *Dramatherapy: Theory and practice for teachers and clinicians* (pp. 569–577). London: Routledge.
Wijk, J. B., van der. (1996). Van Rummikub tot Rollenspel: de verschillende gezichten die het vak dramatherapie kan hebben in de behandeling van kinderen en jongeren met een psychiatrische stoornis. *Tijdschrift voor Creatieve Therapie, 3*, 16–21.
Yotis, L. (2006). A review of dramatherapy research in schizophrenia: Methodologies and outcomes. *Psychotherapy Research, 16*(2), 190–200.
Yotis, L., Kravariti, C., Theodoridou, D. & Megaloeconomou, T. (1997). The Leros Hospital Drama Group: A stage for deinstitutionalisation. *Collection of abstracts and lectures of the 12th International Conference for the Psychotherapy of Schizophrenia*. London: ISPS.
Yotis, L., Kravariti, C., Theodoridou, D. & Megaloeconomou, T. (2003). The role of dramatherapy in the psychiatric reform: The paradigm of Leros. *Teradia Psychiatrikis, 81*, 48–58.
Zhou, Y. & Tang, W. (2002). A controlled study of psychodrama to improve self-esteem in patients with schizophrenia. *Chinese Mental Health Journal, 16*, 669–671.

Chapter 4

Therapeutic effects of brief group interactive art therapy with war veterans

Alexander Kopytin and Alexey Lebedev

Introduction

One of the crucial tasks with which art therapists are now confronted is the study of the therapeutic efficacy of art therapy interventions applied with different client groups and conditions. Though there are many empirical examples of the therapeutic effects of art therapy, most of them are presented in the form of qualitative case studies. Very little published art therapy research which satisfies "specific rules of evidence" (Goldner & Bilsker, 1995) are currently available in Russia (Ionov, 2004; Kopytin, 2011) and elsewhere (Rusted, Sheppard, & Waller, 2006).

Though advances in medical art therapy have become more evident throughout the last two decades (Malchiodi, 1999a, 1999b), it is still often underestimated and even ignored among medical professionals as reliable treatment modality, because

> there is a conspicuous absence of research oriented to outcome studies in support of art therapy in medical and nursing journals. Art therapy is briefly listed in medical and psychiatric nursing textbooks as a mind–body adjunctive therapy. Most adjunctive or complimentary therapies are described as lacking in positive outcome studies.... In other words, research is not evidence based.
>
> (Hagen, 2007, p. 145)

One of the biggest clinical populations that need relevant therapeutic interventions consists of various stress-related disorders, post-traumatic stress disorders (PTSD) in particular. As the recent survey of AATA members has shown (Elkins & Deaver, 2013), various stress-related disorders belong to the main area of American art therapists' specialization. A large majority of respondents reported specializing in the areas of mood/anxiety disorders (41.8%) and PTSD (29.3%) (respondents could select up to three specializations among 36 areas of specialization indicated in the survey).

War veterans establish a significant clinical group with which art therapy can be used together with other medical and paramedical interventions to reduce stress-related symptoms and to improve the social adaptation of ex-servicemen. In the Russian Federation many combat veterans of military campaigns in different regions of the country and abroad suffer from mental disorders as a result of their service. Although the value of art therapy with war veterans who have suffered psychological trauma has been studied (Foa, Kean, & Friedman, 2000; Golub, 1984; Haeseler, 1998; Lobban, 2014), little research that is grounded in specific *rules of evidence* has been conducted to support the multifaceted effects of art therapy as their treatment. Further clarification of art therapists' specific contribution to ex-servicemen's mental well-being and social adaptation is needed, taking into account the clinical nature of stress-related disorders, the culture of war veterans, and their personal characteristics.

Combat veterans have been identified with having high levels of emotional tension and instability, low impulse control, difficulties in interpersonal relations, distorted reactions to others, ambivalent and inadequate self-perception, and difficulties in securing existential meaning (Apchel & Tsygan, 1999; Kolov, Ostapenko, & Krivtsov, 2005). They may have a retrospective orientation toward life, or may organize their lives around those values and norms that were acceptable in combat situations while feeling themselves to be lonely and unsafe in civilian life (Apchel & Tsygan, 1999; Kolov et al., 2005).

Foa et al. (2000) found that different interventions were helpful, depending upon the goals and conditions of treatment. Interventions may be aimed at: (a) uncovering and working through traumatic material while avoiding reactions; (b) reducing restlessness through relaxation and withdrawal of attention; (c) improving communication skills and reducing agoraphobic reactions through group interaction; and (d) improving self-esteem by stimulating creativity. These authors suggested that as a treatment modality for war veterans and other traumatized persons, art therapy may help reduce symptoms and promote other positive effects, such as improved impulse control and interpersonal skills, and alleviation of dissociation, anxiety, night fears, and distortions in perception. Artistic activity also may have a positive effect on the client's social functioning, which in turn can lead to better self-esteem, sense of hope, socially adaptive behavior, and decreased feelings of shame. Foa et al. (2000) suggested that these positive effects may be the result of a combination of general psychological processes (e.g., relaxation, cognitive working-through) with nonverbal and creative processes.

Haeseler (1998) and Lobban (2014) comment on the importance of the group context in their work with war veterans, as it provides a sense of human interdependence and community, "with the advantage of having a cohesive peer group ready to listen and learn from each other" (Lobban, 2014, p. 5). Lobban presents relevant excerpts of recordings using the participants' own words to illustrate that group art therapy with veterans who have PTSD enables them to communicate on an emotional level, which is usually avoided by employing both conscious and unconscious defenses. All this

> supports the theory that in art therapy unconscious, unprocessed material is expressed through image-making, then decoded using cognitive appraisal mechanisms, which involves reduced avoidance and increased tolerance of emotions and leads to improved insight. When done in a group setting this reduces isolation by promoting a sense of reconnection.
>
> (Lobban, 2014, p. 6)

However, no attempts have been made to assess the impact of art therapy interventions on quality of life among war veterans, though this criterion becomes more widespread in various outcome studies. Quality of life is considered as an integral characteristic related to a person's physical, mental, social, and spiritual functioning and is based on his or her subjective perception. Quality of life can be one of the indicators of one's psychosocial adaptation in general. Improvement of patients' quality of life as a result of their treatment is considered to be one of the significant measures of therapeutic efficacy and goals of treatment.

The goal of the present study was to assess the therapeutic effects of brief group interactive art therapy with patients being treated in a specialized psychotherapy unit for war veterans. The hypothesis of the study was as follows:

1 Group interactive art therapy is an effective intervention, which can be used with war veterans to reduce symptoms and improve personality functioning and quality of life.
2 These effects will be more apparent in the experimental group than in the control group.

Method

Location

The study took place in a specialized psychotherapy department within a regional clinical hospital for war veterans. The hospital is administered by the Ministry of Public Health and offers complex treatment for war veterans. The psychotherapy department was established in 1997 to provide quality medical and psychosocial support to war veterans residing in the Volgograd region of the Russian Federation who were involved in military campaigns in the Northern Caucasus, Afghanistan, and other geopolitical "hot spots." All of the patients experienced emotional disorders that, due to their severity, could not be treated outside the hospital setting.

The staff of the psychotherapy department includes psychiatrists, psychotherapists, clinical psychologists, and nurses. The treatment emphasis combines medical and psychosocial interventions, and includes occupational therapy, counseling, individual and group verbal therapy, and group interactive art therapy. The general goal is not only to reduce the clients' symptoms but to enable personality reconstruction and social integration as well.

Participants

Male and female patients of different ages made up the experimental (Group 1) and control (Group 2) groups (Table 4.1). The inclusion criteria were that participants had been diagnosed with having non-psychotic mental disorders and had been involved in military campaigns either in the Russian Federation or abroad. Participants were excluded from the study if they experienced severe mental disorders and were older than 55 years.

A total of 112 patients were enrolled in the study. The department chief randomly assigned participants to the experimental group ($n=62$) or control group ($n=50$). From the complete list of patients being treated in the department, every second patient was referred to group art therapy and every first patient was referred to occupational therapy, the standard treatment that served as the control condition. Patients in both groups continued to receive psychopharmacological treatment and physiotherapy. The participant ages in the groups varied from 25 to 53 years; participant mean age (*M*) in Group 1 was 38 years and the mean age (*M*) in Group 2 was 35 years. Most patients in

Table 4.1 Participant demographics and diagnoses

Demographic	*Group 1* (n = 62)	*Group 2* (n = 50)
Male	57 (92%)	45 (90%)
Female	5 (8%)	5 (10%)
Age 20–29 years	15 (29%)	13 (26%)
Age 30–39 years	29 (47%)	23 (47%)
Age 40–49 years	10 (16%)	9 (18%)
Age 50+ years	8 (13%)	5 (10%)
Diagnoses (ICD-10)†		
Neurotic, stress-related, and somatoform disorders[a]	17 (24%)	14 (28%)
Affective disorders (depression)[b]	10 (16%)	7 (14%)
Organic mental disorders[c]	35 (60%)	29 (58%)

Notes
† *International Statistical Classification of Diseases and Related Health Problems* (ICD-10), World Health Organization (1992).
a ICD-10 codes F43.22, F45.3, F48.0, and F43.23.
b ICD-10 codes F32.0, F32.10, F32.11, and F33.01.
c ICD-10 codes F06.6 F06.4, F06.3, F06.2, and F07.0.

both groups were diagnosed as having stress-related and somatoform disorders, affective disorders, and organic disorders (Table 4.1). The main presenting problem was a decreased or unstable mood that was often associated with anxiety, irritation, difficulties in relationships, low impulse control, absence of interest in life, tiredness, apathy, poor sleep, and feelings of pain and discomfort in the body.

A majority of the participants were involved in local military campaigns, whereas 75 had fought in Afghanistan or the Northern Caucasus. The average length of stay in the hospital was one month.

Measures

The instruments were chosen to assess symptomatic improvement in the participants' conditions and changes in their self-perception, cognitive functioning, and quality of life. To assess symptomatic improvement, the following tools were used: Symptomatic Checklists, SCL-90 (Derogatis, 1983); Questionnaire of Depressive Conditions (QDC; Bespalko, 2004), and the Integrative Anxiety Test (Bizyuk, Wasserman, & Iovlev, 2005). The QDC is a quantitative tool that measures the absence or presence of depressive symptoms, according to its first scale, and distinguishing endogenous and neurotic depression, according to its second scale. The Integrative Anxiety Test provides a general index and measure for personality and situational anxiety, as well as specific scales for both these types of anxiety, such as Emotional Discomfort, Asthenic Component, Phobic Component, Perception of Perspectives, and Social Phobic Reactions. To assess changes in personality functioning, self-perception, cognitive skills, and quality of life, instruments included the self-report General Condition–Activity–Mood Test (Doskin, Lavrenteva, Miroshnikov, & Sharay, 1973); Silver Drawing Test (SDT) and Draw-a-Story (DAS; Silver, 2002, 2010); and the World Health Organization Quality of Life Questionnaire (Burkovskij, Kotsubinskij, Levchenko, & Lomachenkov, 1998; Kuyken, Orley, Hudelson, & Sartorius, 1994; World Health Organization Group, 1998).

The Questionnaire includes 100 questions that help to assess the six main spheres of quality of life, such as physical and psychological functioning, level of independence, social relationships, environment, and spiritual life.

All the measures were taken pre- and post-treatment: at the beginning of treatment in the hospital and again after one month and not long before participants' discharge (usually during the 12th and 13th sessions). To compare statistical differences between pre- and post-test results in two groups, the researchers used *t*-test, Mann-Whitney, and chi-square measures. The *t*-test enabled a statistical comparison of pre-test and post-test results in the groups, whereas the Mann-Whitney measure compared Group 1 and Group 2 data.

Art therapy intervention

Participants in Group 1 took part in group interactive art therapy three times per week in after-lunch sessions that lasted two-and-a-half hours. Group sessions usually consisted of 5–8 patients. The course of art therapy lasted one month and included 12–14 sessions that were facilitated by the second author, a psychiatrist and trained art psychotherapist. Each session was structured with warm-up activities, a main art-based activity with discussion, and closure. Basic art materials were available, such as crayons and pastels, colored pencils, gouache and acrylic paints, and white paper of different sizes.

Group art therapy involved various art-based activities that corresponded with the appropriate stages of treatment and group dynamics aimed at different therapeutic targets. For example, participants created individual and group squiggle drawings that encouraged warming up, creative stimulation, and the safe release of emotions and stimulation, and also presented their current emotional state through drawing. Drawing tasks and themes were introduced to allow clients to develop interpersonal skills and mindfulness; to express and understand their own self-perception; to perceive their attitude to others and position in a group, their disease and resources; and to gain perspective on their past and present life situations. Directives included "realistic and metaphoric self-portraits," "my life line," "positive and negative feelings," "my resources in the past and present," "challenging life situations and how I overcome them," "personal coat of arms," "my life achievements and goals," and "presents I give myself and others." Issues that arose from group dynamics were also worked through using art-based activities and discussion.

Results

The pre-treatment measures found no significant overall difference ($p > .05$) in patients' scores between those who received art therapy and those who did not receive art therapy at the start of treatment. However, significant differences ($p < .05$ to .001) were found after one month between the groups in mean scores on several measures.

As for SCL-90 Symptom Checklists, there was a statistically significant difference in the post-test ($M = .47$, $m = .07$) to post-test ($M = .67$, $m = .10$) scores in the Depression Scale, $t = -1.62$, $p < .05$, and in the post-test ($M = 0.45$, $m = 0.07$) to post-test ($M = 0.73$, $m = 0.13$) scores in the Hostility Scale, $t = -1.91$, $p < .05$, between groups. Statistical significance was in favor of the experimental (art therapy) condition, while the difference between groups in other scales was insignificant at the end of treatment (Table 4.2).

Comparison of post-test scores in the experimental and control groups for the QDC indicated a lower level on the Depression/Nondepression Scale in the experimental group as compared to the control group, and no significant difference in Endogenous/Neurotic Depression Scale between groups. There

Table 4.2 Pre- and post-test results in experimental and control groups

Measurements and scales	*Experimental group* M ± m *(n = 62)*		*Control group* M ± m *(n = 50)*	
	Pre	*Post*	*Pre*	*Post*
SCL-90				
Somatization	1.11 ± .09	.56 ± .07	1.10 ± .09	.62 ± .08
Obsessive–compulsivity	1.21 ± .19	.63 ± .08	1.18 ± .10	.79 ± .10
Interpersonal sensitivity	1.04 ± .10	.55 ± .07	1.02 ± .10	.70 ± .11
Depression	1.05 ± .10	.47 ± .07	1.00 ± .09	.67 ± .10*
Anxiety	1.06 ± .10	.44 ± .07	1.07 ± .12	.61 ± .10
Hostility	1.09 ± .11	.45 ± .07	1.17 ± .13	.73 ± .13*
Phobic anxiety	.56 ± .09	.28 ± .07	.56 ± .08	.34 ± .08
Paranoid ideation	.83 ± .10	.51 ± .07	.94 ± .12	.61 ± .11
Psychotism	.60 ± .08	.26 ± .06	.56 ± .08	.40 ± .08
Additional scales	1.20 ± .11	.58 ± .10	1.23 ± .11	.66 ± .09
Global severity index	.99 ± .08	.48 ± .06	.99 ± .08	.62 ± .09
Personality severity index	49.74 ± 2.86	31.26 ± 3.13	53.91 ± 3.32	38.41 ± 4.44
Positive symptom distress index	1.71 ± .07	1.29 ± .04	1.60 ± .06	1.32 ± .05
Questionnaire of Depressive Conditions				
Depression–No Depression Scale	79.76 ± 3.07	66.18 ± 2.59	81.32 ± 3.51	73.69 ± 3.05*
Endogenous–Neurotic Depression Scale	40.73 ± 1.50	47.12 ± 1.46	42.52 ± 1.96	45.22 ± 2.03
Integrative Anxiety Test				
Personality anxiety				
General index	7.57 ± .23	4.44 ± .38	7.48 ± .24	6.56 ± .36**
Emotional discomfort	7.74 ± .19	4.88 ± .32	7.56 ± .27	6.38 ± .37*
Asthenic component	7.29 ± .25	4.96 ± .35	7.67 ± .34	6.59 ± .36*
Phobic component	5.95 ± .29	3.54 ± .37	5.30 ± .44	5.31 ± .37***
Perception of perspectives	7.40 ± .27	5.00 ± .36	7.41 ± .24	6.34 ± .36*
Social phobic reactions	5.00 ± .40	4.00 ± .42	4.96 ± .47	4.31 ± .44*

Situational anxiety				
General index	6.64 ± .31	3.58 ± .35	6.33 ± .44	5.28 ± .46*
Emotional discomfort	5.88 ± .35	3.50 ± .30	5.67 ± .48	4.91 ± .44*
Asthenic component	6.76 ± .34	4.10 ± .34	6.93 ± .40	5.34 ± .43*
Phobic component	5.05 ± .39	3.04 ± .34	5.30 ± .42	4.34 ± .46*
Perception of perspectives	7.19 ± .32	4.82 ± .38	6.48 ± .41	5.88 ± .41
Social phobic reactions	5.29 ± .40	4.16 ± .36	5.52 ± .43	5.16 ± .41
General Condition–Activity–Mood Test				
General condition	3.75 ± .15	5.39 ± .11	3.77 ± .20	5.01 ± .14*
Activity	3.82 ± .13	5.22 ± .12	3.94 ± .19	4.54 ± .17***
Mood	4.13 ± .15	5.48 ± .12	4.14 ± .21	4.77 ± .18***
Silver Drawing Test				
Emotional content scale	2.89 ± .22	3.42 ± .13	2.60 ± .76	3.05 ± .19*
Self-image scale	3.26 ± .17	3.56 ± .09	3.20 ± .65	3.23 ± .16*
Ability to select	3.67 ± .08	4.49 ± .07	4.00 ± .13	4.05 ± .14***
Ability to combine	4.22 ± .10	4.69 ± .08	4.50 ± .14	4.45 ± .13***
Ability to represent	3.69 ± .12	4.62 ± .07	4.09 ± .16	4.14 ± .16***
Total in cognitive scales	11.69 ± .23	13.82 ± .16	12.55 ± .33	12.68 ± .31***

Notes
* $p < .05$;
** $p < .005$;
*** $p < .001$.

was a statistically significant difference in the experimental group's post-test scores ($M=66.18$, $m=2.69$) as compared to the control group's post-test scores ($M=73.69$, $m=3.05$) in the Depression/Nondepression Scale, $t=-2.11$, $p<.05$, and no significant difference in Endogenous/Neurotic Depression Scale between groups, $t=.59$, $p>.05$ (Table 4.2).

Comparison of mean pre-test and post-test scores in the experimental group for the Integrative Anxiety Test indicated a significant decrease in General Indices and most Scales of Personality and Conditional Anxiety ($p<.05$), whereas a decrease in scores was less evident in the control group. There was a statistically significant difference in the post-test ($M=4.44$, $m=0.38$) to post-test ($M=6.56$, $m=0.36$) scores in the General Index of Personality Anxiety Scale, $t=-3.16$, $p<.005$, and in the post-test ($M=3.58$, $m=0.35$) to post-test ($M=5.28$, $m=0.46$) scores in the General Index of Situational Anxiety Scale, $t=-2.39$, $p<.05$, between groups in favor of experimental group at the end of treatment (Table 4.2).

For the General Condition–Activity–Mood Test scores there was a statistically significant difference in the post-test ($M=5.39$, $m=0.11$) to post-test ($M=5.01$, $m=0.14$) scores in the General Condition Scale, $t=2.55$, $p<.05$, in the post-test ($M=5.22$, $m=0.12$) to post-test ($M=4.54$, $m=0.17$) scores in the Activity Scale, $t=4.08$, $p<.001$, and in the post-test ($M=5.48$, $m=0.12$) to post-test ($M=4.77$, $m=0.18$) scores in the Mood Scale, $t=3.47$, $p<.001$, between groups in favor of the experimental one (Table 4.2).

Comparison of mean post-test to post-test scores in the experimental and control groups for the Draw-A-Story and the Silver Drawing Test indicated a more significant increase on the Emotional Content and Self-Image scales and on three cognitive scales in the experimental group as compared to the control one. There was a statistically significant difference in the post-test ($M=3.42$, $m=0.13$) to post-test ($M=3.05$, $m=0.19$) scores in the Emotional Content Scale, $t=1.91$, $p<.05$, in the post-test ($M=3.56$, $m=0.09$) to post-test ($M=3.23$, $m=0.16$) scores in the Self-Image Scale, $t=2.08$, $p<.05$, and in the post-test ($M=13.82$, $m=0.16$) to post-test ($M=12.68$, $m=0.31$), $t=4.46$, $p<.001$, total scores in cognitive scales, between groups in favor of the experimental one (Table 4.2). The increased scores in cognitive scales are indicative of such improvements as the ability to select and combine ideas, and represent a story. These and other abilities are basic for effective cognitive functioning and creativity (Bruner, Olver, & Greenfield, 1966; Piaget & Inhelder, 1967; Zeki, 2000).

As for the Questionnaire of Quality of Life, the improvement in quality of life was significantly more evident in the experimental group than in the control group. While significant increase in the control group was only in the Sleep and Rest subsphere (F3), the experimental group demonstrated significant increase of results in the majority of subspheres (F1, F2, F3, F4, F5, F8, F9, F10, F19, and F21) and spheres: in the physical sphere (I), in the level of independence (III), in the perception of environment (IV), and in the spiritual sphere (VI), as well as in the Total Score Reflecting Health and Quality of Life and the General Index of quality of life and health (G).

Comparison of post-test scores in the experimental and control groups for the World Health Organization Quality of Life Questionnaire indicated that participants in the art therapy group had a significantly higher General Quality of Life and Health Index (M=14.3, m=0.51) as compared to participants in the control group (M=11.86, m=1.07), t=3.24, p<.05. Also, mean post-test scores were significantly higher (M=88.98, m=1.93) in the experimental group as compared to the control group (M=78.95, m=4.48), t=4.12, p<.05, as well as in the subspheres of Life Activity/Energy/Fatigue (F2; I Physical Sphere) (M=14.43, m=0.46 and M=12.14, m=0.92, accordingly), t=2.04, p<.05; Cognition/Memory/Concentration (F5; II Psychological Sphere) (M=14.77, m=0.39 and M=12.5, m=0.95, accordingly), t=2.94, p<.05; Mobility (F9; III Level of Independence) (M=17.1, m=0.59 and M=14.12, m=1.11, accordingly), t=3.21, p<.05; Physical Safety and Protection (F16) (M=15.5, m=0.54 and M=12.43, m=0.73, accordingly), t=3.39, p<.05; Medical and Social Aid (F19; V Environment) (M=14.5, m=0.50 and M=12.36, m=0.73, accordingly), t=2.75, p<.05; and Spirituality/Religion/Personal Values (F24; VI Spiritual Sphere) (M=16.03, m=0.48 and M=13.0, m=0.90, accordingly), t=4.12, p<.05.

As a result of comparison of post-test scores in the experimental and control groups, most significant differences were revealed in such spheres as spiritual, physical, and level of independence, while the least significant difference was found in the sphere of social relationships among all main six spheres. As for the most considerable difference with regard to post-test scores in the spiritual sphere, it can be indicative of the considerable improvement in patients' satisfaction with spiritual aspects of their existence that include their system of beliefs and values giving meaning and perspective in their life. It is also indicative of the increase in patients' creative stance in the world (Burkovskij et al., 1998).

Conclusion

The results of the study confirm that group interactive art therapy used in the form of a brief intervention provides various positive effects on symptomatic status, cognitive abilities, creativity, and quality of life of patients treated at the psychotherapy department of the hospital for war veterans. Though certain positive effects were also observed in the control group, these effects were less evident than in the experimental group.

A significant increase in Emotional Content and Self-Image scores as well as cognitive scores in the Silver Drawing Test observed in the experimental group after one month of art therapy appears to be one of its specific effects, which was absent in the control group. These findings support publications indicating an important role of image formation and artistic activity in cognition and creative solutions of various cognitive tasks and their ability to improve self-esteem (Calvin, 1986; Gardner, 1982; Horowitz, 1983; Solso, 1994).

One of the important findings of the study includes complex improvement in patients' quality of life, especially with regard to such main spheres as the spiritual and physical spheres and level of independence.

One of the limitations of the study was that patients with more severe stress-related conditions, such as PTSD, were absent in both Group 1 and Group 2 because only a few of them were hospitalized in the department over the course of study. This category of patients in particular should be studied further regarding art therapy efficacy. Possible bias in how the drawings in this study were scored, given that there was no test–retest analysis and no inter-rater measure, also should be taken into account.

References

Apchel, V. Y., & Tsygan, V. N. (1999). *Stress and coping with stress*. St. Petersburg: Peter.

Bespalko, I. G. (2004). *The scale for quick psychological measurement of unstructured depressive disorders: The manual for doctors and psychologists*. St. Petersburg: Psychoneurological Research Institute.

Bizyuk, A. P., Wasserman, L. I., & Iovlev, B. V. (2005). *The use of Integrative Anxiety Test (ITT): The manual*. St. Petersburg: Psychoneurological Research Institute.

Bruner, J. S., Olver, R. R., & Greenfield, P. M. (1966). *Studies in cognitive growth*. New York: Wiley.

Burkovskij, G. V., Kotsubinskij, A. P., Levchenko, E. V., & Lomachenkov, A. S. (1998). *The use of the Questionnaire of Quality of Life (World Health Organization) in psychiatric practice: The manual for doctors and psychologists*. St. Petersburg: Psychoneurological Research Institute.

Calvin, W. H. (1986). *How brains think: Evolving intelligence, then and now*. New York: Basic Books.

Derogatis, L. R. (1983). *The Symptomatic Checklists (SCL-90-R) administration, scoring and procedures manual – II*. Towson, MD: Clinical Psychometric Research.

Doskin, V. A., Lavrenteva, N. A., Miroshnikov, M. P., & Sharay, V. B. (1973). Test for differential self-measuring of the functional state. *Voprosy Psihologii, 6*, 141–145.

Elkins, D., & Deaver, S. (2013). American Art Therapy Association, Inc.: 2011 membership survey report. *Art Therapy: Journal of the American Art Therapy Association, 30*(1), 36–45.

Foa, E. B., Kean, T. M., & Friedman, M. J. (Eds.). (2000). *Effective therapy of PTSD: Practice guidelines*. New York: Guilford Press.

Gardner, H. (1982). *Art, mind, and brain*. New York: Basic Books.

Goldner, E. M., & Bilsker, D. (1995). Evidence-based psychiatry. *Canadian Journal of Psychiatry, 40*(2), 97–101.

Golub, D. (1984). Symbolic expression in post-traumatic stress disorder: Vietnam combat veterans in art therapy. *The Arts in Psychotherapy, 12*, 285–296.

Haeseler, M. P. (1998). Crossing the border: Cultural implications of entering a new art therapy workplace. In A. R. Hiscox & A. C. Calisch (Eds.), *Tapestry of cultural issues in art therapy* (pp. 327–346). London: Jessica Kingsley.

Hagen, L. (2007). Art therapy and medicine. In D. Spring (Ed.), *Art in treatment: Transatlantic dialogue* (pp. 143–158). Springfield, IL: Charles C. Thomas.
Horowitz, M. J. (1983). *Image formation and psychotherapy*. New York: Jason Aronson.
Ionov, O. (2004). *Art therapy in complex rehabilitation of psychiatric patients*. Master's thesis, State Scientific Center of Forensic Psychiatry in the Name of V. P. Serbsky, Moscow.
Kolov, S. A., Ostapenko, A. V., & Krivtsov, A. G. (2005). Psychological study of post-traumatic stress disorder. *Vestnik Psychoterapii, 13*, 23–35.
Kopytin, A. (2011). *Art therapy of mental disorders*. St. Petersburg: Rech.
Kuyken, W., Orley, J., Hudelson, P., & Sartorius, N. (1994). Quality of life assessment across cultures. *International Journal of Mental Health, 23*(2), 5–27.
Lobban, J. (2014). The invisible wounds: Veterans' art therapy. *International Journal of Art Therapy: Inscape, 19*(1), 3–18.
Malchiodi, C. (Ed.). (1999a). *Medical art therapy with adults*. London: Jessica Kingsley Publishers.
Malchiodi, C. (Ed.). (1999b). *Medical art therapy with children*. London: Jessica Kingsley Publishers.
Piaget, J., & Inhelder, B. (1967). *The child's conception of space*. New York: Norton.
Rusted, J., Sheppard, L., & Waller, D. (2006). A multi-centre randomized control group trial on the use of art therapy for older people with dementia. *Group Analysis, 39*, 517.
Silver, R. (2002). *Three art assessments: The Silver Drawing Test of cognition and emotion; Draw a Story: Screening for depression; and stimulus drawings and techniques*. New York: Brunner-Routledge.
Silver, R. (2007). *The Silver Drawing Test and Draw a Story: Assessing degression, aggression, and cognitive skills* (2nd ed.). New York: Routledge.
Silver, R. (2010). *Identifying risks for aggression and depression through metaphors: The mouse, the bride and the use of humor*. Dewitt, NY: Purple Finch Press.
Solso, R. L. (1994). *Cognition and the visual arts*. Cambridge, MA: MIT Press.
World Health Organization. (1992). *The ICD-10 classification of mental and behavioural disorders: Clinical descriptions and diagnostic guidelines*. Geneva: Author.
World Health Organization Group. (1998). The World Health Organization quality of life assessment (WHOQOL): Development and general psychometric properties. *Social Science and Medicine, 46*(12), 1569–1589. doi: 10.1016/S0277-9536(98)00009-4.
Zeki, S. (2000). *Inner vision: An exploration of art and the brain*. Oxford: Oxford University Press.

Chapter 5

A neglected area in schizophrenia treatment and research: the efficacy of art therapy

Results of a pilot randomized controlled trial and qualitative study

Christiane Montag and Karin Dannecker

Fostering creativity and self-expression in people suffering from severe mental disorders like schizophrenia not only looks back on a long tradition (Dannecker, 2006b; Killick & Schaverien, 1997; Navratil, 1965; Prinzhorn, 1922), but might even become a more central therapeutic means in recovery-oriented, modern psychiatry (Deutsche Gesellschaft für Psychiatrie und Psychotherapie, Psychosomatik und Nervenheilkunde (DGPPN); NICE, 2014). Over the past decades, individual or group art therapy has been a common adjunctive treatment option in hospital settings (Patterson, Debate, Anju, Waller & Crawford, 2011), where it is valued as a nonverbal, resource-oriented "form of therapy in which the making of visual images ... contributes towards externalisation of thoughts and feelings which may otherwise remain unexpressed" (Waller & Gilroy, 1992, p. 5). Like in the other creative ("arts") therapies, an aesthetic form is used to "contain" and give meaning to a patient's experience, to allow for psychological development and to open alternative ways of self-experience and relating with others (NICE, 2014, p. 217).

A wide range of theoretical considerations argue in favor of a routine application of art therapy – especially in patients with psychotic disorders, who often show reduced verbal capabilities, formal thought disorder and difficulties in symbolic representation like mentalizing emotions, and here, art therapy might often be more suitable than other forms of exploratory psychotherapy (Ruddy & Milnes, 2005). Patient with schizophrenia might experience a weakened basic sense of self, a reduced sense of agency and dysfunctional self–other differentiation, on the one hand, and problems making sense of their own and other people's mental states, on the other (Brüne, 2005; Sass & Parnas, 2003). In consequence, the ability to regulate interpersonal closeness and distance might be compromised, and the experience of emotions can become overwhelming. Clinical experience suggests that art therapy might specifically account for these problems by using a tripartite relationship between the patient, the therapist and the artifact, allowing a finer regulation of interpersonal contact and emotional intensity (Killick & Schaverien, 1997;

Patterson, Crawford, Ainsworth & Waller, 2011). Many scholars underline the importance of art therapy in fostering the expression of one's inner life – whether its contents be unusual, "abnormal" or "unspeakable" – in a validating and non-judgmental creative space (Patterson, Crawford et al., 2011) and its potential to promote cognitive understanding of the disease and coping skills (Hanevik, Hestad, Lien, Teglbjaerg & Danbolt, 2013). Importantly, the creative process may also strengthen the vulnerable sense of self, of agency and ownership in psychoses, foster benign self-awareness (Green, Wehling & Talsky, 1987; Springham, Findlay, Woods & Harris, 2012; Teglbjaerg, 2011) and establish the notion of self-efficacy in the process of recovery (Harrow, Hansford & Astrachan-Fletcher, 2009). Art therapy in psychotic people can help to restore orientation and structure within internal and external experiences, and the artistic "externalization" of inner states or experiences can become subject to cautious distancing and reality-testing (Dannecker, 2006a). Moreover, art therapy might help to recover mentalizing function in psychosis by stimulating the formation of mental representations of thoughts and feelings, to develop a "language" for the mental processes of oneself and others and to understand mental states by the ascription of meaning (Springham et al., 2012). Some art therapeutic techniques also invite one to jointly reflect about images and artifacts and to share one's experience in the group, which might provoke decentration and perspective-taking (Dannecker, 2006a). The establishment of joint attention may, not only in developmental terms, but also during recovery from mental illness, form the basis of the ability to represent und to reflect about mental states (Isserow, 2008). The recent focus on mentalization and reflective functioning in art therapy (Franks & Whitaker, 2007; Havsteen-Franklin & Altamirano, 2015; Michaelides, 2012) might parallel the general tendency of psychodynamically or psychoanalytically oriented art therapists to modify their technique when treating patients with psychotic or borderline psychostructural organizations. Arts therapies therefore rather emphasize the patients' capacities for reflection and self-awareness, as well as "supportive and interactive experiences, with less emphasis on the use of 'uncovering' psycho-analytic approaches" (NICE, 2014, p. 216). However, despite the long history of art-making and art therapy in the treatment of schizophrenia and the wealth of therapists' narrative accounts of treating psychotic people, neither theoretical foundations nor illness-specific methodological modifications for this disorder have been outlined in a comprehensive, generally accepted form and none of the individual approaches has been systematically empirically tested (Brooker et al., 2007; Dannecker, 2006a; Greenwood, 2012; Gühne et al., 2012; Killick & Schaverien, 1997; Waller, 1993; Wood, 2013).

From a theoretical point of view, the advantages of art psychotherapy might seem obvious, and clinical experiences as well as reported anecdotal evidence strongly suggest its broad use in the treatment of psychoses. However, the upsurge in interest in recent decades in the scientific foundations and in proof of the efficacy of different psychotherapeutic techniques will not stop short of art psychotherapy. As for any other remedy, desired properties and potential adverse effects, their specificity and differential indication, as well as external validity and cost-effectiveness of psychotherapeutic techniques and interventions, are to be substantiated in high-quality scientific research. As a matter of fact, demands for an evidence-based practice not only aim at providing the right treatment, with a minimum of risk, for the right disorder as reflected through recommendations by scientifically grounded clinical guidelines, but also are advanced by reimbursement systems to ensure efficient practice (Lambert, 2013). A strong recommendation by national treatment and practice guidelines for a therapy requires higher levels of scientific evidence, like suggestive findings from meta-analyses and larger randomized controlled trials (RCT), while non-randomized or naturalistic research and case studies result in less compelling evidence (DGPPN).

Considering these desiderata, and in contrast to the wealth of clinical experience, naturalistic reports and subjective accounts of the healing properties of art-making, the use of art therapy in the treatment of psychoses has received only limited empirical support. However, as a part of the broader spectrum of "arts therapies", i.e. together with music, dance movement, drama and body psychotherapy, art therapy was subjected to an overarching meta-analysis that suggested that all the creative therapies were effective when compared with any other control condition – especially in reducing negative psychotic symptoms. "Arts therapies" were therefore recommended by the British NICE guidelines as an adjunctive treatment for schizophrenia in 2009 (NICE, 2009). In Germany, the creative therapies were endorsed by the guidelines on psychosocial therapies in severe mental disorders with a recommendation grade B, the slight downgrading being due to the inhomogeneity of studies (Deutsche Gesellschaft für Psychiatrie und Psychotherapie, Psychosomatik und Nervenheilkunde (DGPPN)).

However, regarding art psychotherapy alone, only two RCTs were included in the meta-analysis and had already been identified in Ruddy and Milnes' earlier systematic review (Ruddy & Milnes, 2005). The literature search of these authors yielded 61 studies of art psychotherapy in psychoses, among which were only two RCTs (total $n = 137$). Both studies compared the effects of art psychotherapy in addition to treatment as usual (TAU) with TAU alone in outpatients (Ruddy & Milnes, 2005). The RCT conducted by Green et al. (1987) included 47 patients with schizophrenic and major affective psychoses or personality disorders who received 10 sessions of art therapy or TAU. Patients who had completed the art therapy course showed a more positive attitude toward themselves and a better ability to get along with others. Richardson, Jones, Evans, Stevens and Rowe (2007) randomized 90 patients with a diagnosis of chronic schizophrenia to either 12 sessions of group art therapy or to standard care. Results at post-treatment and the 6-month follow-up indicated positive effects of art therapy on negative symptoms, but did not have any effect on other measures like psychosocial functioning or quality of life. Another study was conducted in hospitalized patients in Beijing and showed positive effects of group art therapy compared to TAU on psychotic symptoms (PANSS[1]), self-concept and social functioning (Meng et al., 2005).

However, knowledge gained from small trials may be limited due to bias and insufficient statistical power, and study designs that compare the intervention of interest with TAU usually provide information about the efficacy of *any* additional treatment or of a mere "higher dose" of psychotherapy compared to offering no adjunct, but do not allow statements about its specificity. Researchers therefore strive to compare interventions with "active" control conditions to control for the effects of common factors like therapeutic bond and support, facilitation of hope and use of resources, exploration and integration of problems.

Adopting a far more rigorous design, the largest published, three-arm RCT of group art psychotherapy – the "Multicenter Study of Art Therapy in Schizophrenia: Systematic Evaluation" (MATISSE) – was conducted in 417 stabilized outpatients with schizophrenia randomized to group art therapy or an activity group plus TAU, or TAU alone (Crawford et al., 2012a, 2012b). All randomized patients were assessed at 12 and 24 months using the "intention to treat" principle, but group differences could not be determined with respect either to the primary outcomes, i.e. global functioning and symptom load at 24 months, nor to the secondary outcome measures, i.e. global functionig and symptoms at 12 months, but also social function, general well-being, quality of life, drug adherence, client satisfaction and group attendance. Therapists in this pragmatic trial were required to employ treatment principles flexibly "to fit with the needs of participants" (Crawford et al., 2012b, p. 2).

However, the MATISSE trial had limitations, which were mainly due to substantial problems of attendance, and should therefore not be too readily generalized: according to the authors, "Almost 40% of participants randomised to group art therapy did not attend any sessions. Among those who did, few attended regularly" (Crawford et al., 2012b, p. 4). Only 31% of patients who were randomized to the art therapy intervention had attended 10 or more sessions; the median level of attendance was 11 sessions in the art therapy group over a one-year period. Although attendance was not related to study outcomes, very low group sizes might still have affected group dynamics, interaction between participants and peer support. Short-term outcome data were not recorded, so that benefits during or shortly after the intervention phase might have gone unnoticed. Secondary analyses were also limited by the small amount of sessions administered and did not yield significant differences in effectiveness of art therapy in subgroups formed with respect to the severity of negative symptoms or pre-existing preferences for this kind of therapy. The authors conclude that the "Identification of patients with schizophrenia who may benefit most from group art therapy remains elusive" (Leurent et al., 2014, p. 1703). However, qualitative analyses could confirm that patients who had engaged with art therapy indeed reported personal benefits like having developed higher self-esteem, social confidence and sense of agency (Patterson, Borschmann & Waller, 2013).

Subsequently, results of the MATISSE study sparked a lively discussion about the future of art psychotherapy and the caveats of related research. The questions raised covered the problem of the specificity and consistency of treatment, its clear description including necessary adaptations and observation of the complex needs of people with schizophrenia, therapists' appropriate experience, as well as participants' adherence and preferences (Attard & Larkin, 2016; Patterson, Waller, Killaspy & Crawford, 2015; Wood, 2013). Other issues were related to study design and implementation, like the choice and timing of relevant outcome parameters including participants' opinions, the necessity of piloting, subgroup analyses and process research, or statistical issues (Holttum & Huet, 2014). In summary, the initial disappointment about the negative results of the MATISSE study yielded to a fruitful scientific debate and further development within the professional field (Crawford, Barnicot, Patterson & Gold, 2016). By now, a growing number of systematic reviews have explored the existing evidence for art therapy across different disorders (Maujean, Pepping & Kendall, 2014; Slayton, D'Archer & Kaplan, 2010; Van Lith, 2016; Van Lith, Schofield & Fenner, 2013) or specifically with respect to the treatment of psychoses (Attard & Larkin, 2016) and – the available data still being limited – demonstrated persistent interest in and motivation for the empirical validation of art therapy in psychotic disorders.

Evidence from a pilot randomized-controlled trial

Concurrent with the final stages of the MATISSE trial but prior to its publication, another study of art therapy was prepared as a collaboration between the Art Therapy Department, Weissensee School of Art (Kunsthochschule Berlin-Weißensee) and the Department of Psychiatry and Psychotherapy of the Charité University of Medicine (Charité Universitätsmedizin) in Berlin.[2] The research project was planned as a pilot study with the main objectives to: (1) evaluate the feasibility of an efficacy trial of art therapy, delivered in an inpatient setting, for patients with schizophrenia during acute psychotic episodes, and (2) collect preliminary data on the effects of art therapy on psychotic and depressive symptoms as well as global functioning. The rationale for this study was, on the one hand, to prepare a larger trial and, on the other, to focus on the effects that art therapy would exert not only on the negative, but also on the positive symptom dimension during acute psychotic episodes that required hospitalization. A third aspect evolved from theoretical considerations that two main effective factors might be particularly relevant for change during recovery from acute psychosis, which were selected as potential, at least partially specific targets of art therapeutic interventions: the ability to mentalize and the recovery of the sense of self as creative agent

(Frith, 2004; Montag, 2015; Sass, 2014). These should be accounted for in the exploratory part of the study by looking at the surrogate measures cognitive empathy, mentalizing capacity and self-efficacy, respectively, in the course of treatment. Finally, videotaping of the session was carried out for subsequent process analysis.

The pilot study was conceptualized as a single-blind, parallel-group RCT and compared inpatients receiving a six-week course of 90 minutes of art therapy twice weekly in addition to standard care with standard hospital care alone. Due to the brevity of an average hospital stay in Germany, the intervention and follow-up periods of six and 12 weeks, respectively, were kept relatively short. Patients had a diagnosis of schizophrenia according to DSM-IV and were between 18 and 64 years old. Exclusion criteria were all DSM-IV axis-I disorders other than schizophrenia, antisocial personality disorder, relevant use of alcohol or illegal drugs, severe somatic disease, insufficient German-language competence, inability to give informed consent, acute suicidal intention, aggression and hospitalization according to the Berlin Mental Health Act. Patients were also excluded when treatment in a group setting was complicated by (1) marked psychomotor agitation or impulsivity, (2) hostility and aggression, (3) severe paranoid ideation related to the setting or to group members. Patients who were professionally involved in the making or the reception of art, or had attended art therapy as an outpatient before admission, were not included. In addition, patients' active and passive interest in art was documented on a four-point Likert scale (not at all – occasionally – regularly – passionate), but no significant group differences were found.

Primary outcomes were psychotic and depressive symptoms, measured by the Scales for the Assessment of Positive and Negative Symptoms (Andreasen, 1983, 1984) and the Calgary Depression Scale for Schizophrenia (Müller et al., 1999), as well as global psychosocial functioning (Saß, Wittchen, Zaudig & Houben, 2003). Secondary outcome measures were inter alia parameters of mentalizing function and self-efficacy/locus of control. Mentalizing was operationalized as cognitive empathy, (1) measured with the Reading the Mind in the Eyes test (Baron-Cohen, Wheelwright, Hill, Raste & Plumb, 2001) that requires the inference of complex emotional mental states from photographs depicting the eye regions of 36 persons, and (2) using the Levels of Emotional Awareness Scale (LEAS) (Lane, Quinlan, Schwartz, Walker & Zeitlin, 1990; Subic-Wrana, Thomas, Huber & Köhle, 2001), which assesses the ability to imagine, to recognize and to express one's own and others' emotions when presented with written emotion-laden scenarios. The development of the LEAS was based on Piaget's model of emotional-cognitive development, which comprises five hierarchically ascending levels (Lane & Schwartz, 1987). The increasing complexity and elaboration of the awareness of the story-evoked emotional mental states, imagined from both first- and third-person perspective, is reflected by higher scores of the LEAS-self and LEAS-other scales, respectively. Self-efficacy and locus of control were estimated using the Questionnaire for Competence and Control (Krampen, 1991), which consists of four primary subscales (self-concept of own ability, internality, social externality and fatalistic externality) and two secondary scales that were used for analysis (self-efficacy and overall externality). Moreover, potential confounding variables like verbal intelligence and verbal memory were measured. Analyses were conducted as both per-protocol (completer) analysis and intention-to-treat analysis.

After baseline exams, 58 patients were randomized to either art therapy or standard care. Patients who were allocated to art therapy were then offered a trial therapy session in which they were introduced to the setting and the fact that all sessions were videotaped. Group size fluctuated between three and six patients. A single art therapist with long-standing experience in the treatment of patients with psychoses conducted all sessions. She was helped by a co-facilitator who videotaped the intervention. The setting was a small art studio in the clinic, containing a variety of art materials such as poster paint, pencils, color pencils, markers, crayons, pastels, different size paper and brushes, drawing boards, clay, tools, an easel, storage facilities and art books.

The psychodynamically founded therapeutic approach focuses on the assumption that the art therapy process involves psychic experiences, emotional and cognitive processes, the relationships between patient, therapist and the art work, and the process of creation. The paradigms of theory, practice and research are based on the visual arts, psychoanalysis and relational-oriented psychotherapy (Dannecker, 2006b, 2017). The therapeutic aims in the treatment of psychosis can be outlined as helping the patient develop a sense of self and of agency through creation of symbolic forms (Killick & Schaverien, 1997, p. 17). The art therapy setting constitutes a containing function for the patient's unintegrated state of mind (Killick & Schaverien, 1997, p. 38). Experiences of fragmentation as a defense against overwhelming anxieties can be counteracted through the creation of an object – helping to transform unbearable states of mind into a tangible external form. The mere discharge of destructive uncontrollable impulses and fantasies is contrasted by the creative process, which intrinsically involves decision making, phases of doing, distancing, looking and reflecting together with the therapist and in a group setting with other people. The capacity to develop mentalizing processes, to understand oneself and the other originates in this situation. The increase of self-esteem through the production of a relatively long-lasting art object contributes to the positive effects which can be felt as authorship. Patients experience being capable of creating something that stimulates communication and often surprising new views about themselves, which differ from the predominantly pathological self-concept.

Thus, in our project the approach was non-directive and supportive – patients could choose to create whatever they wanted and use any available material they liked. They were encouraged to find their own image at their own pace. Interventions by the art therapist were aimed at supporting the creative process and helping to understand the image. The last 30 minutes of a session were reserved for a shared viewing and reflecting on the images. The focus was on capturing phenomenologically what one sees, how the process of creation and the choice of material had occurred. Each patient was encouraged to present his/her image and to talk about it. Other patients were invited to comment and share their observations and ideas. If a patient did not want to share his/her image, this wish was respected. Interpretations were avoided, but the therapist stimulated the process of reflection. Also, the patient's autonomous decision making about the handling of his/her artwork was crucial. Regular video-based supervisions confirmed the treatment fidelity of the therapist.

Patients assigned to the control group received standard hospital treatment without an offer of art therapy, expression-focused ergotherapy or passive reception of visual arts. Standard treatment covered a broad spectrum of verbal psychotherapies for patients with psychoses like cognitive behavioural therapy and modified psychodynamic interventions in individual and group settings, as well as occupational therapy, music therapy, cognitive and social skills training, excursions, relaxation and sports. As individualized treatment plans were arranged routinely with all patients, the "total dose" of nonpharmacological therapies was not necessarily smaller in the control group. Patients who were discharged or transferred to a day clinic within the intervention period were actively encouraged to attend the remaining art therapy sessions. All patients received a designed reminder card of session and examination dates and were intensively motivated by personal contact and phone calls to participate.

Results will be discussed briefly in the following, and can be grouped into aspects of feasibility, preliminary data on efficacy regarding symptoms and functioning, and exploratory findings regarding mentalizing and self-efficacy (see Montag, Haase, Seidel, Herrmann & Dannecker, 2014, for a detailed report).

Experience of the trial generally suggests feasibility of this and similar RCTs under routine hospital conditions. A total of 122 hospitalized patients were screened, about half of whom met the inclusion criteria. Out of 29 patients randomized to art therapy, 12 left the art therapy group early, after an average of about two sessions. Of those, five patients did not complete the introductory session. Only in three patients was dropout caused by study- or intervention-related factors: fear of videotaping or inability to tolerate the group setting. Nine out of 29 patients left the control group early, among these were three patients who withdrew their consent because of dissatisfaction with the randomization result. In all but three patients, reasons for dropout were not study-related, but mainly caused by unplanned discharge or inability to attend after planned discharge from hospital. The data of 59% of patients randomized to art therapy and 69% receiving standard care were analyzed at post-treatment, and 55% versus 66% at the 12-week follow-up. Compared to trials conducted with chronic outpatients (Green et al., 1987; Richardson et al., 2007), dropout rates in hospitalized patients tended to be higher, and the also high attrition rates of the MATISSE study are hardly comparable because of its greater length (Crawford et al., 2012b). In summary, the adherence of patients can be considered to be satisfactory if the exacerbated state of the participants and the ubiquitous wish to leave the hospital as early as possible is kept in mind. Moreover, attendance at art therapy sessions was good, as soon as participants were engaged in the group and as long as they stayed in the hospital. Only three patients attended fewer than 12 (around eight or nine) art therapy sessions because of alternative occupations after discharge. Two individuals were lost to the 12-week follow-up. As suggested by Crawford et al. (2012b), recruitment and attendance of patients might be less challenging in RCTs with patients receiving inpatient treatment. This was confirmed in the present study, although an initial inability to consent, high symptom load and related cognitive dysfunction or lack of interest in art therapy in some cases prevented inclusion. Art therapy as a focus of the study was well accepted, and some patients articulated their wish to help nonpharmacological research. Future inclusion of an attractive, active control condition might even facilitate recruiting, as patients were looking forward to the new form of treatment. However, intolerance of art therapy, unplanned discharges and withdrawal of consent presented a problem, so that a substantial share of participants did not receive the allocated intervention and were not willing to shoulder the burden of a return to continue the study on an outpatient basis. The inclusion of a run-in period before randomization to test acceptance and tolerability of all study arms or the exclusion of subjects who do not engage with the intervention after randomization might reduce the number of formal dropouts and render intention-to-treat analyses less conservative, but can introduce new bias (Fergusson, Aaron, Guyatt & Hebert, 2002; Little et al., 2012). On the other hand, psychotherapy research always has to consider personal preferences, and the question "what works for whom" is the subject of a broad field of current and future research (Barber et al., 2013, pp. 461ff.). In our study, art therapy completers were more often female and had significantly higher verbal intelligence than patients leaving the control group early and art therapy dropouts, but did not differ from the other groups in symptom severity at baseline or in education. Hence, art therapy might have particularly attracted a subgroup of patients with a better a priori prognosis. This problem indicated probable selection bias in the per-protocol sample and was accounted for statistically, but could also reflect a general trend regarding hospital service use.

Primary outcome measures were determined in both the per-protocol and intention-to-treat samples. Even if results from such a small RCT have to be considered with great caution, they suggest a greater mean reduction of positive symptoms in patients assigned to art therapy compared to standard care at post-treatment and at 12-week follow-up in the per-protocol, and also at post-treatment in the intention-to-treat sample. In addition, negative symptoms were significantly lower in the art therapy group at follow-up, although not maintained in the intention-to-treat analysis. Also, global psychosocial functioning seemed to be higher in patients who had been randomized to art therapy at post-treatment and follow-up, but there were no significant group differences as for depression ratings.

These preliminary results point in a direction similar to that of findings of the other smaller and shorter RCTs comparing art therapy to standard care – like that of Richardson et al., who reported reductions in negative symptoms and better social functioning in patients randomized to art therapy after 12 sessions and at the six-month follow-up, and of Meng et al., who found an increase in overall mental health and social functioning associated with twice-weekly group art therapy over 15 weeks (Meng et al., 2005; Richardson et al., 2007). Results also substantiate evidence from other creative therapies (Gold, Heldal, Dahle & Wigram, 2005; NICE, 2014) that foster the notion that the arts therapies might be particularly effective in reducing core negative symptoms in psychosis. In our study, negative symptoms scores in patients who had completed the art therapy course further improved during the follow-up period, while they deteriorated again in the control group. This finding may lead to speculate that the initiation of art therapy or other creative processes during an acute psychotic episode could prevent an increase of negative symptoms after remission. Although this was linked to neither depressive symptoms nor self-ratings of self-efficacy, art therapy might protect people from experiencing discouragement, hopelessness, lack of motivation or anhedonia and may activate resources of self-expression, self-help and social contact during recovery.

Moreover, art therapy's effect on positive symptoms in acutely psychotic patients in our study seemed somewhat unexpected but promising. As previous studies were conducted in stabilized outpatients, an individual "floor effect" might have concealed these properties. Patients who underwent art therapy mainly reported stress reduction brought about by concentrated work during sessions, which may bear some parallels with concepts of mindfulness, on the one hand, and to the sharing of routine activities in therapeutic communities like the Soteria, on the other (Ciompi et al., 1992). Notably, many acutely ill psychotic patients show formal thought disorders, and psychosis itself can be conceived of as a disorder of symbolization, representation or mentalization. There is only insufficient evidence on the phase-specific assignment of individual therapies or complex treatment schedules, but it could be speculated that verbal and cognitive psychotherapies do not always account for the specific needs of patients during acute psychotic states, while art therapy might specifically help the restoration of basic representational deficits. Moreover, it should be stressed that no adverse events related to art therapy were noticed and there was no indication that psychodynamic therapies may kindle emotional intensities in psychotic patients leading to undesired effects (Mueser & Berenbaum, 1990; Patterson et al., 2011b). In contrast, the results of this study rather suggest that the art therapy setting and the artwork may "contain rather than stimulate anxiety", even in acutely psychotic patients (Brooker et al., 2007; Killick & Schaverien, 1997; Patterson et al., 2011b).

In close relationship to the expression of psychotic symptoms, difficulties in the ability to mentalize, i.e. to recognize, to infer and to reflect about one's own and others' mental states, have consistently been reported in schizophrenia (Brüne, 2005). Although the improvement of mentalizing functions as an "active ingredient" may lie at the core of any psychotherapy (Fonagy, Gergely, Jurist & Target, 2002), its particular importance in the treatment of psychoses has been theorized (Brent, 2009; Lempa, von Haebler & Montag, 2016). Here, art therapy may bear additional benefits, as it was suggested that it mediates between concrete and symbolic ways of thinking (Greenwood, 2012). Psychotic patients may externalize their inner states in a concrete physical way – the artwork then allows them to reflect upon, to clarify and to re-internalize the meaning of internal states, and to develop a mentalizing stance; the intentional use of symbolic representations, of a "mentalistic" language and perspective-taking are encouraged (Dannecker, 2006a, 2017; Franks & Whitaker, 2007; Springham et al., 2012). An exploratory objective of the present study aimed at determining changes in mentalizing abilities during the course of art therapy compared to the control condition. Patients randomized to art therapy showed at post-treatment a significantly higher complexity and elaboration in their reflections on others' mental states, measured with the Levels of Emotional Awareness Scale (Subic-Wrana et al., 2001). Mentalization regarding own mental state at six weeks was nominally higher in patients who had received art therapy than standard care, but the group difference missed statistical significance. Results, though tentative, might suggest that – as well as in psychotic patients – art therapy might be associated with a recovery of the ability to reason about own and others' emotional mental states. In contrast, no changes were detected for cognitive empathy measured in the Reading the Mind in the Eyes test. This might be explained by the fact that art therapy fosters emotional awareness by introspection and imagination, rather than the ability to recognize emotions from facial expressions. Another exploratory question was whether art therapy would also promote a creative sense of agency in the course of the recovery of psychotic patients, which was – coarsely – defined as self-efficacy or reduced externality. However, though externality scores nominally decreased in our art therapy group until follow-up, but did not do so in controls, no significant influence of art therapy on externality or self-efficacy was determined in our study.

The multiple limitations of this small RCT are reported in detail in (Montag et al., 2014), the most striking of which refer to the lack of an "active" control condition, low case numbers and insufficient statistical power. Despite this, the quantitative results of this study encourage the conducting of further research in the field of art therapy, and the tentative findings regarding the positive effects of art therapy in patients suffering from psychoses may find independent substantiation.

The qualitative evidence

Art therapy research is not restricted to quantitative methods. The questions of how and why the art media, the special setting and the intervention of the therapist have an effect on the participants of a research project are central in the qualitative approach. As the above results from the RCT pilot study show positive benefits for the participants, we wanted to probe how and why these results occurred. This means that, regarding the qualitative evaluation, we needed to ask about the fundamental factors effective in art therapy. Therefore the specific characteristics of art therapy have to be taken into consideration; some of them are listed below:

- Both art and therapy move between the inner and the outer, between the spoken and the unspoken world.
- The setting of an art room provides a physical space where one can safely try out materials and get involved in exploring fantasies, which are then put into visible form. This arouses thinking processes like structuring and mentalizing capacities.
- The sensory qualities of the art materials stimulate somatic memories and open the ways to symbolic representations and help to lift memory blocks.
- Art is the evidence of an activity. Thus the products are unique physical and relatively lasting artifacts, which are visible, can be touched and are at the disposal for reviewing.
- Art therapy circumvents consciousness and makes unconscious psychological relationships visible.
- It also works with people who are normally incapable of participating in psychodynamically oriented therapy aimed at consciously gaining insight (e.g., people who are mentally or emotionally disabled or impaired through trauma or developmental deficits) (Dannecker, 2013; Gilroy, 2011).

The potential of art therapy can be summarized from a mentalizing viewpoint: handling art materials is a natural way in which feelings and thoughts and relationships can be evaluated on a basically nonverbal, sensorimotor, perceptual and visible symbolic level. Patients are encouraged to mentalize implicitly by creating with representations of physical reality, but actually undergoing and feeling emotions, ultimately leading to the capacity to create an explicit mental perception of this reality. When clients use nonverbal means such as art, they have an opportunity to grow mentally even though their cognitive competence may not be fully developed (Verfalle, 2016, p. xvi).

Many art therapists argue that relying on the matrix of art itself makes the application of visual research strategies evident since they are intrinsically much more consistent with the field than social or empirical research approaches. Visual research can be manifold. It centers on the image and the artistic medium aiming to produce and represent knowledge, which is based on the assumption that they provide a wealth of information about the meaning of the work as well as the artist or creator behind the work. Collecting data, the researchers themselves may analyze the visual components according to knowledge from art history, aesthetics, art development and art psychology. They may react to their research subject artistically and make their own responses.

Art-based inquiry as a data-gathering method involves the researcher or the research participants' intense engagement in creative activities (materials, processes and people actively creating) that structurally guide the question. Visual research methods extend the understanding of what happens in art therapy and how the results may be evaluated. The need to critically examine existing phenomena such as the subjective bias must be considered. But the gains from visual research for art therapists can be broad: it illuminates or constructs knowledge while it privileges the practice and perspective of the artist (Kapitan, 2010, pp. 167–180).

However, the main issue persists for art therapy research: changes and developments, which are conceived through the art processes and products, must be translated into linear descriptive language and the inherent shortenings must be overcome (Gilroy, 2011).

In our pilot project we applied quantitative and qualitative methods of evaluation, which tried to gather information about the patient in a structured framework. Therefore, we systematically collected all the images which the patients had created, taking photographs of them after each session. The visual approach in art therapy includes gathering information for the purpose of diagnostic assessments.

Henceforth, the analysis of visual data, the artwork, can be carried out under several aspects:

- systematic analysis of the use of the material, style, traces, forms, colors, choice of material, composition, opposites, rhythm, use of space;
- analysis of the content;
- documentation of the changes in content, working style, choice of material;
- origination process of the artwork, the reaction to it, interaction with others and the therapist;
- comparison of the patient's and the therapist's subjective experiences (Dannecker, 2013).

Another special visual research method is video documentation. We videotaped each session. This material bears an invaluable additional potential to analyze the processes in our art therapy project. Interactions and modi of relatedness with the patients in the group and with the therapist, interruptions, affects and general behavior, visible reactions, the process of the creation of images from the very first line or brush-stroke to the finished image – all can be registered with many more details and documented with greater objectivity than with any other method.

Parameters of the therapeutic process and the therapist's interventions as well as the above-mentioned characteristics of the creative process and the resulting artwork can then be paralleled to the pre-defined outcome measures of the study, and possible associations between process and outcome can be determined.

Presently all information and data are being evaluated in a separate project in a doctoral study. This qualitative visually based evaluation is, naturally, a complex and time-consuming process. Since this qualitative evaluation is in process it cannot be fully presented in this chapter. However, to give an idea of the approach, we depict examples of three patients' images – in each case the first and the last image produced during the art therapy treatment. Two vignettes show additional images created in the middle of the complete process.

Patient A was a male patient who showed high scores in the improvement of emotional awareness and mentalization capacity. In his first image (Figure 5.1) we see a pencil drawing of a leaf, and his last image (Figure 5.2) is an

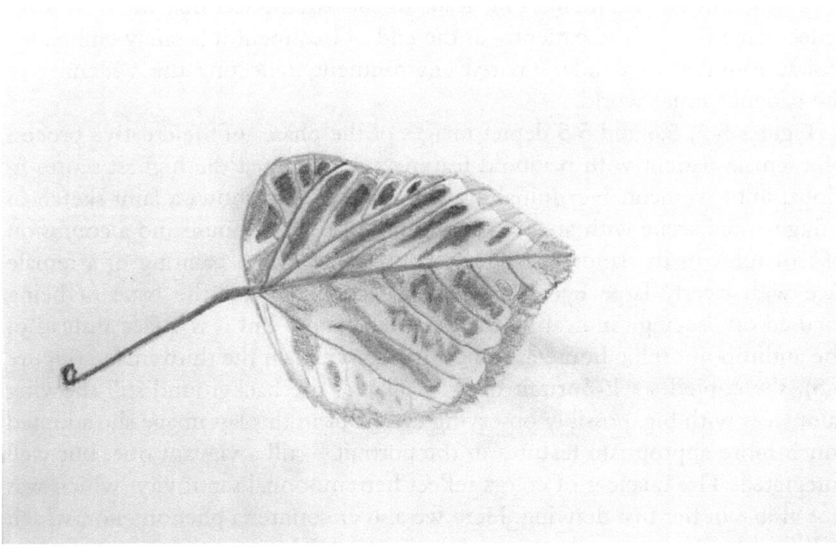

Figure 5.1

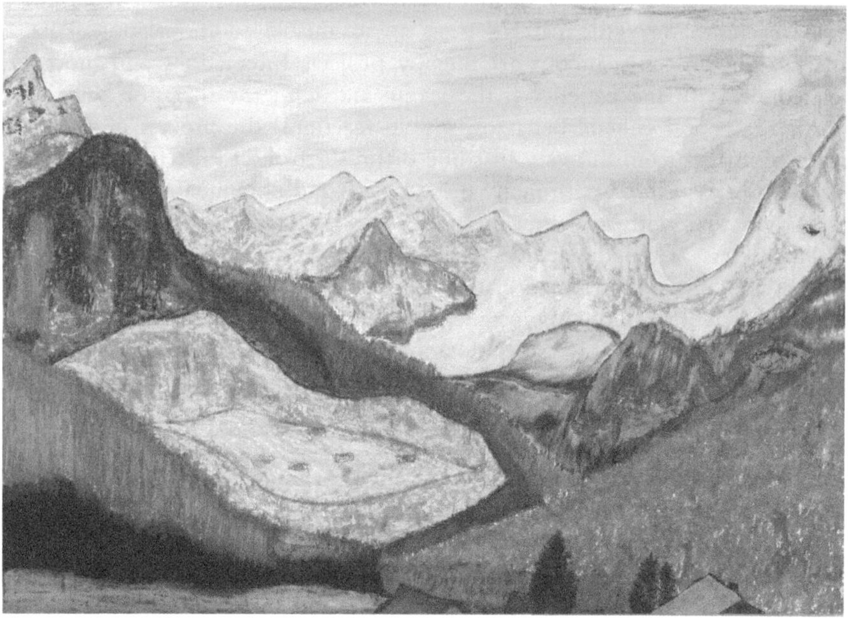

Figure 5.2

elaborated landscape with a great variety of colors and perspective. The basic oval form of the leaf is repeated in the landscape. Now it is embedded in a large spacious environment. This leads to the assumption that the oval form reflects an aspect of the patient – at the end of treatment it is safely embedded and surrounded in a differentiated environment, reflecting the widening of the patient's inner world.

Figures 5.3, 5.4 and 5.5 depict images of the phases of the creative process of a female patient with paranoid features who attained the highest scores in global improvement. Her initial drawing (Figure 5.3) shows a faint sketch of a fragmented scene with an anthropomorphic-seeming house and a confusion of structures in the landscape. Her second image was a painting of a female face with overly large eyes (Figure 5.4). It still mirrors the issue of being focused on "seeing" indicating the paranoid state – but it is a face instead of the anthropomorphic house as in her first drawing. In the third image (Figure 5.5), she copied a self-portrait of Frida Kahlo, the background still showing faint faces with big, possibly observing eyes. But in this last image she adopted much more appropriate features in the portrait – still a vigilant one, but well integrated. The nuances of colors reflect her emotional sensitivity, which was not visible in her first drawing. Here we also encounter a phenomenon which will be taken into consideration in the research: the issue of copying from a motif, as it was done here as well as in the previous patient's last image

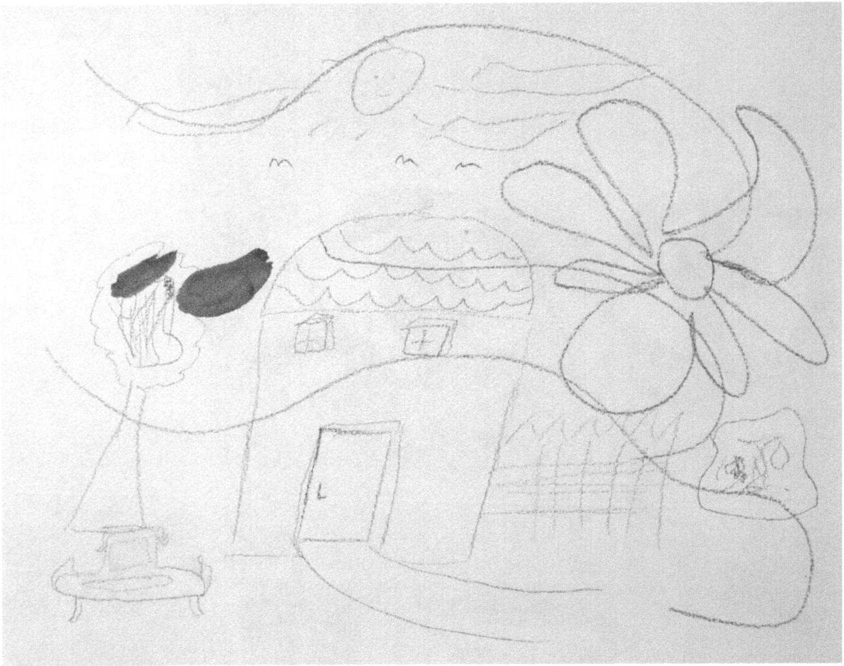

Figure 5.3

(Figure 5.2). The theme of the "borrowed image" is also dealt with by Elizabeth Stone in Chapter 8 of this book.

The last vignette is about a young adult woman who first drew a three-quarter profile (Figure 5.6). It was very much a self-portrait, although not intentionally. Like the other two patients, her use of pencil and faint lines seemed to reflect her cautious approach to art material, needing some control and avoiding emotional expression. Her convergence to colors shows a daring step, as depicted in Figure 5.7: strongly primary-colored bubbles seem to hang heavily over her. The perspective of the face is complex: it looks above to the colors, curiously and anxiously all at once. Being in close exchange with the art therapist during the session, searching for moments of joint attention to the newly arising image, she created a colorful self-portrait leaning against the edge of the paper, reflecting a bold and expressive manner and style (Figure 5.8). This woman also had the highest improvements in global functioning according to the RCT.

The qualitative evaluation of the art therapy process, including the images, videotapes and other visually gained data, will be compared to the RCT outcome parameters such as psychotic symptoms, mentalizing capacities, antipsychotic doses, etc.

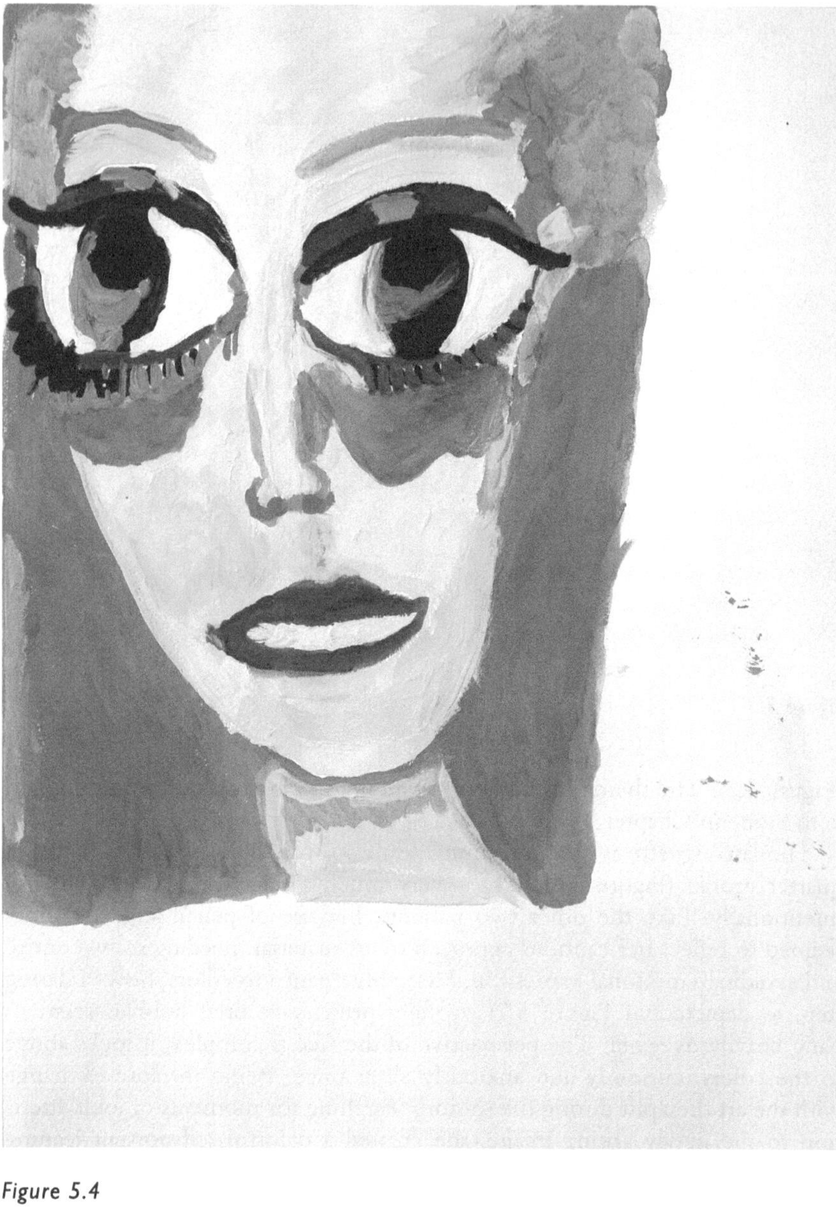

Figure 5.4

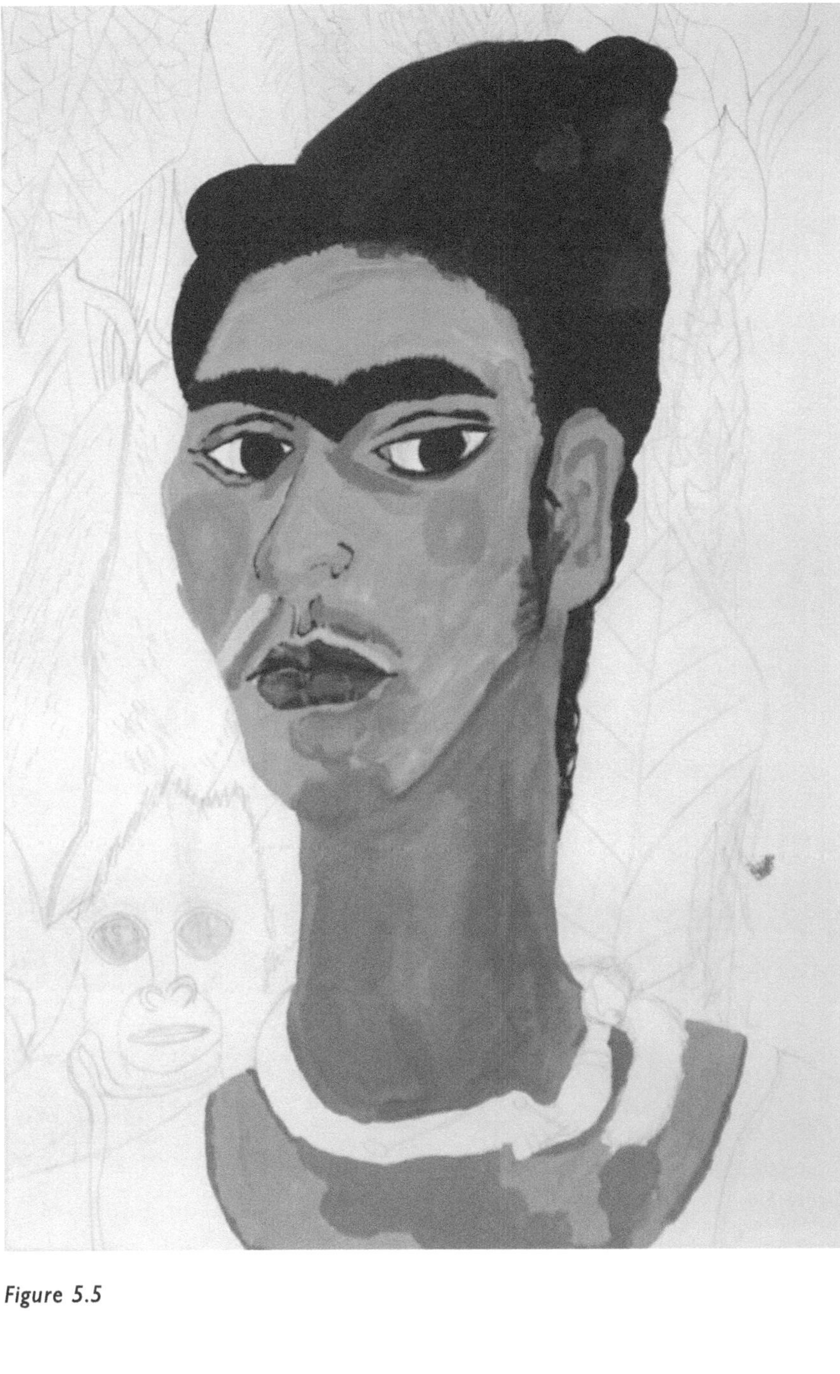

Figure 5.5

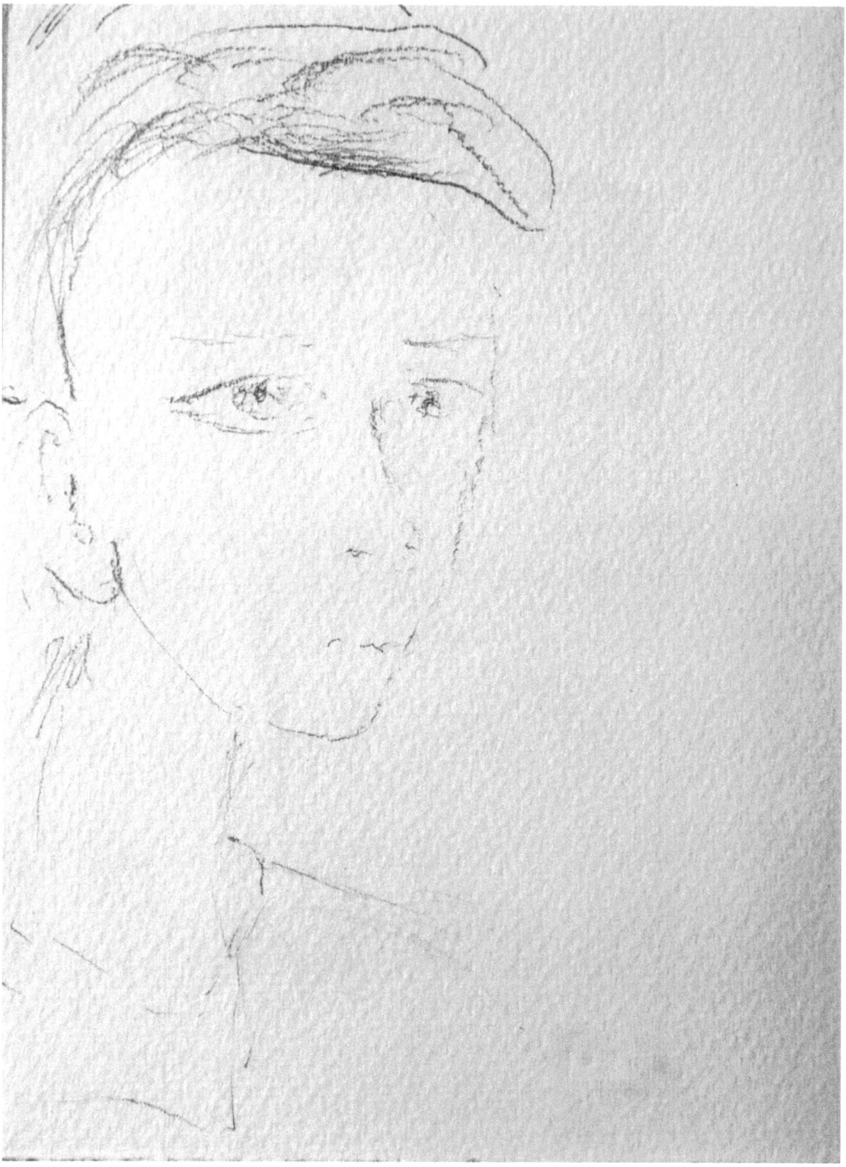

Figure 5.6

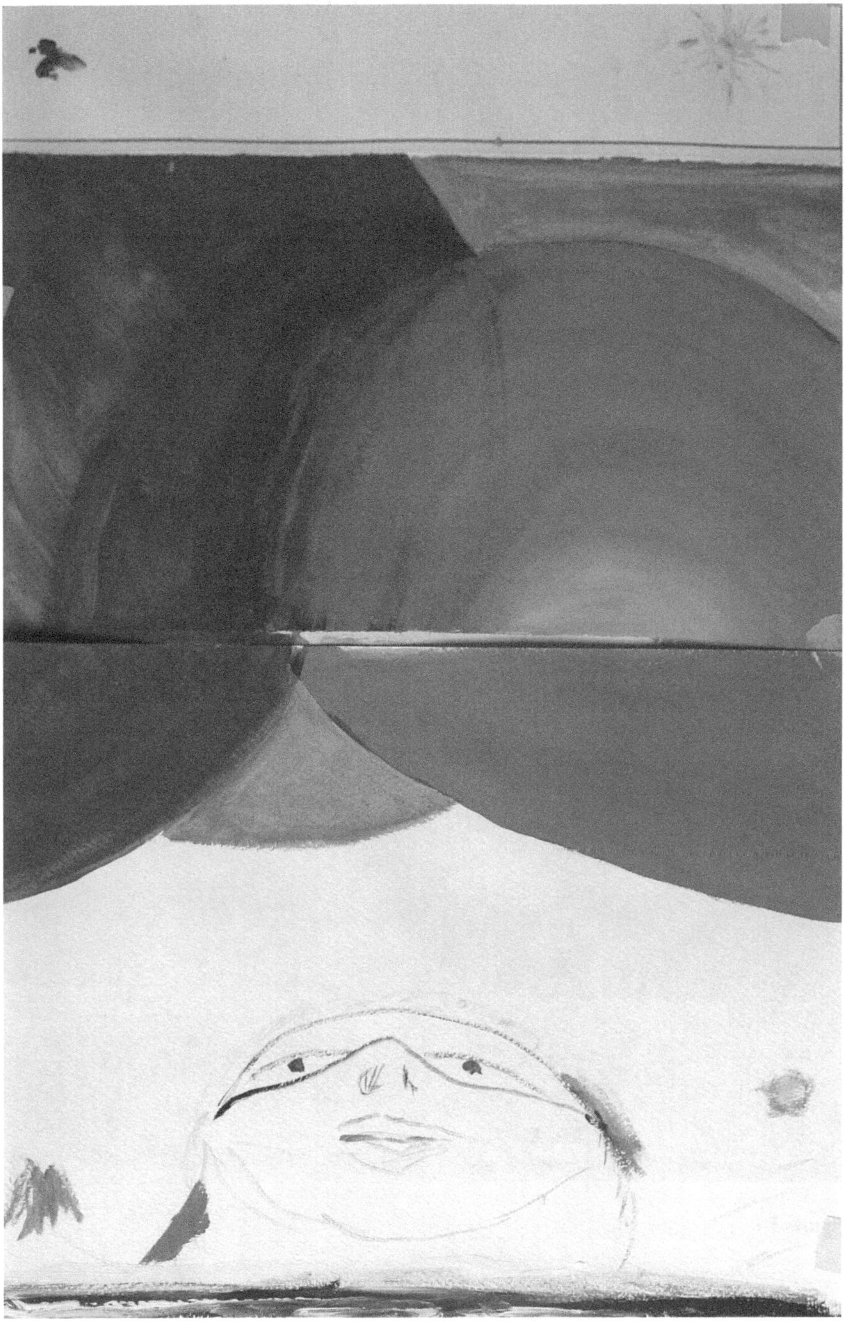

Figure 5.7

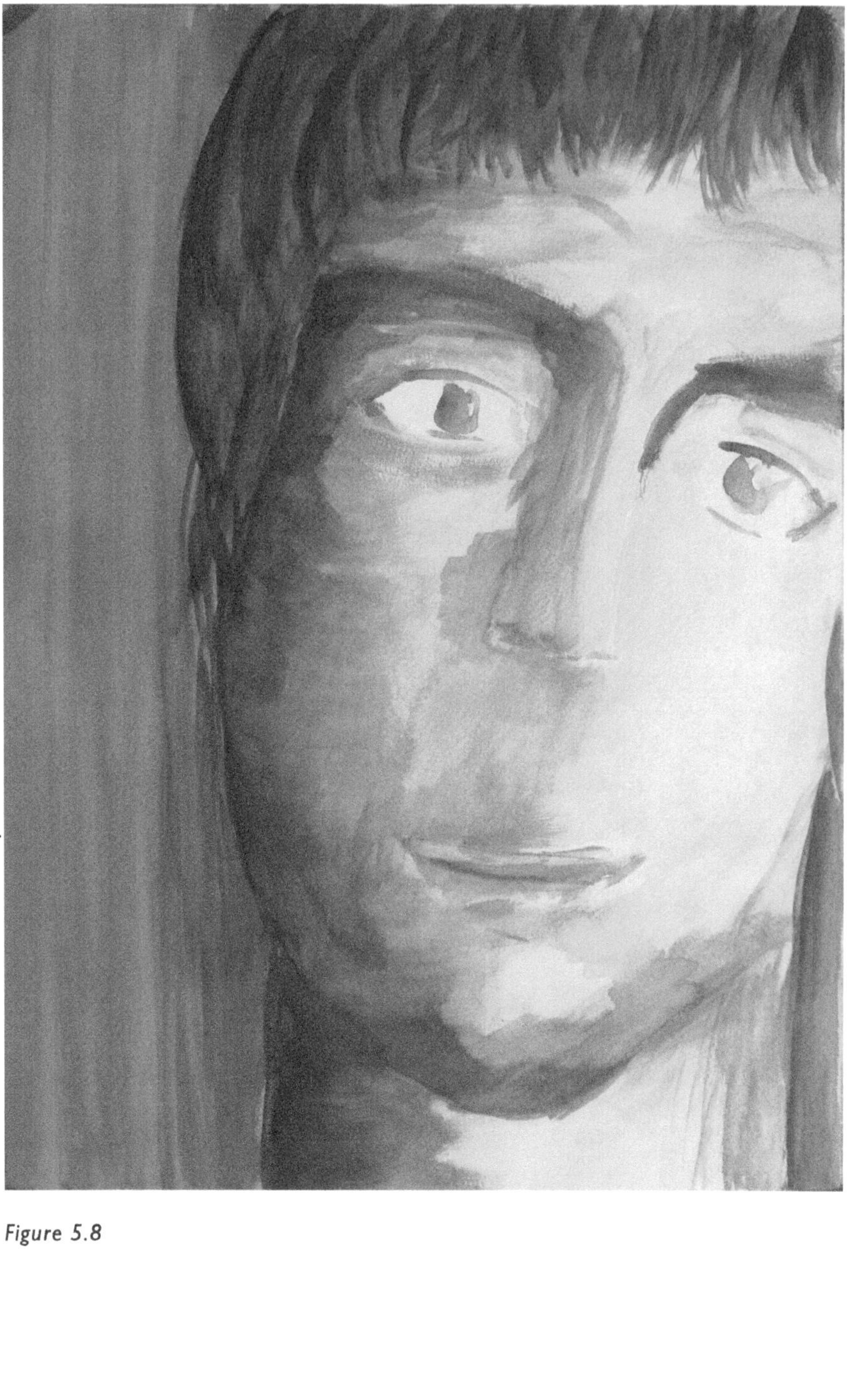

Figure 5.8

The ongoing research combining quantitative and qualitative parameters is, to our knowledge, among the first carried out in art therapy. We hope that this project might encourage other arts therapists as well as researchers from different professions to include both empirical, "medically oriented" designs and art-based, visual methods in their scientific work. We believe that interdisciplinary collaboration provides an effective path to integrate the qualitative and quantitative approaches to research in the arts therapies.

Notes

1 PANSS: The positive and negative syndrome scale for schizophrenia (Kay, Fiszbein & Opler, 1987).
2 Design and results of the pilot study have been reported in greater detail elsewhere (Montag et al., 2014) and contributed to the doctoral dissertation of Laura Haase (2016). The trial was registered at www.ClinicalTrials.gov (identifier: NCT01622166).

References

Andreasen, N. C. (1983). *Scale for the assessment of negative symptoms (SANS)*. Iowa City, IA: University of Iowa.

Andreasen, N. C. (1984). *Scale for the assessment of positive symptoms (SAPS)*. Iowa City, IA: University of Iowa.

Attard, A. & Larkin, M. (2016). Art therapy for people with psychosis: A narrative review of the literature. *Lancet Psychiatry*.

Barber, J. P., Muran, C., McCarthy, K. & Keefe, J. R. (2013). Research on dynamic therapies. In M. J. Lambert (Ed.), *Bergin and Garfield's handbook of psychotherapy and behavior change* (pp. 443–494). Hoboken, NJ: Wiley.

Baron-Cohen, S., Wheelwright, S., Hill, J., Raste, Y. & Plumb, I. (2001). The "Reading the Mind in the Eyes" test revised version: A study with normal adults, and adults with Asperger syndrome or high-functioning autism. *J Child Psychol Psychiatry, 42*, 241–251.

Brent, B. (2009). Mentalization-based psychodynamic psychotherapy for psychosis. *Journal of Clinical Psychology: In Session, 65*, 803–814.

Brooker, J., Cullum, M., Gilroy, A., McCombe, B., Mahony, J., Ringrose, K., et al. (2007). *The use of art work in art psychotherapy with people who are prone to psychotic states: An evidence-based clinical practice guideline*. London: Goldsmiths, University of London.

Brüne, M. (2005). "Theory of mind" in schizophrenia: A review of the literature. *Schizophr Bull., 31*, 21–42.

Ciompi, L., Dauwalder, H. P., Maier, C., Aebi, E., Trutsch, K., Kupper, Z. & Rutishauser, C. (1992). The pilot project "Soteria Berne": Clinical experiences and results. *Br J Psychiatry Suppl.*, 145–153.

Crawford, M. J., Barnicot, K., Patterson, S. & Gold, C. (2016). Negative results in phase III trials of complex interventions: Cause for concern or just good science? *Br J Psychiatry, 209*, 6–8.

Crawford, M. J., Killaspy, H., Barnes, T. R., Barrett, B., Byford, S., Clayton, K., et al. (2012a). Group art therapy as an adjunctive treatment for people with schizophrenia: A randomised controlled trial (MATISSE). *Health Technol Assess., 16*, iii–76.

Crawford, M. J., Killaspy, H., Barnes, T. R., Barrett, B., Byford, S., Clayton, K., et al. (2012b). Group art therapy as an adjunctive treatment for people with schizophrenia: Multicentre pragmatic randomised trial. *BMJ, 344*, e846.

Dannecker, K. (2006a). Fragmenterung im schizophrenen Erleben: Ein Beitrag aus der Kunsttherapie. *Praxis Klinischer Verhaltensmedizin und Rehabilitation, 73*, 204–212.

Dannecker, K. (2006b). *Psyche und Ästhetik: Die Transformationen der Kunsttherapie* (1st ed.). Medizinisch Wissenschaftliche Verlagsgesellschaft: Berlin.

Dannecker, K. (2013). ArteFakte: Forschung in der Kunsttherapie. In W. Rössler & B. Matter (Eds.), *Kunst- und Ausdruckstherapien: Ein Hanbuch für die psychiatrische und psychosoziale Praxis* (pp. 35–51). Stuttgart: Kohlhammer.

Dannecker, K. (2017). Der ästhetische Moment. Intersubjektivität und Veränderungsprozesse in der Kunsttherapie. In F. von Spreti, P. Martius & F. Steger (Ed.), *Kunst-Therapie: Künstlerisches Handeln – Wirkung – Handwerk.* Stuttgart: Schattauer.

Deutsche Gesellschaft für Psychiatrie und Psychotherapie, Psychosomatik und Nervenheilkunde (DGPPN). (2012). *Behandlungsleitlinie "Psychosoziale Therapien bei Menschen mit schweren psychischen Erkrankungen"*. Berlin, Heidelberg: Springer.

Fergusson, D., Aaron, S. D., Guyatt, G. & Hebert, P. (2002). Post-randomisation exclusions: The intention to treat principle and excluding patients from analysis. *BMJ, 325*, 652–654.

Fonagy, P., Gergely, G., Jurist, E. & Target, M. (2002). *Affektregulierung, Mentalisierung und die Entwicklung des Selbst.* Stuttgart: Klett-Cotta.

Franks, M. & Whitaker, R. (2007). The image, mentalisation and group art psychotherapy. *International Journal of Art Therapy: Formerly Inscape, 12*, 3–16.

Frith, C. D. (2004). Schizophrenia and theory of mind. *Psychological Medicine, 34*, 385–389.

Gilroy, A. (2011). *Art therapy, research and evidence based practice.* London: Sage.

Gold, C., Heldal, T. O., Dahle, T. & Wigram, T. (2005). Music therapy for schizophrenia or schizophrenia-like illnesses. *Cochrane Database Syst Rev.*, CD004025.

Green, B. L., Wehling, C. & Talsky, G. J. (1987). Group art therapy as an adjunct to treatment for chronic outpatients. *Hosp Community Psychiatry, 38*, 988–991.

Greenwood, H. (2012). What aspects of an art therapy group aid recovery for people diagnosed with psychosis? *ATOL: Art Therapy Online, 1*(4).

Gühne, U., Weimann, S., Arnold, K., Ay, E.-S., Becker, T. & Riedel-Heller, S. (2012). Künstlerische Therapien bei schweren psychischen Störungen. Sind sie wirksam? *Nervenarzt, 83*, 855–860.

Haase, L. (2016). *Eine randomisiert-kontrollierte Pilotstudie zur psychodynamischer Kunsttherapie in akuten psychotischen Episoden: Machbarkeit, Einfluss auf die Symptomatik und die Mentalisierungsfähigkeit.* Doctoral dissertation, Psychiatrische Universitätsklinik der Charité im St. Hedwig-Krankenhaus, Medizinische Fakultät, Charité – Universitätsmedizin Berlin.

Hanevik, H., Hestad, K. A., Lien, L., Teglbjaerg, H. S. & Danbolt, L. J. (2013). Expressive art therapy for psychosis: A multiple case study. *The Arts in Psychotherapy, 40*, 312–321.

Harrow, M., Hansford, B. G. & Astrachan-Fletcher, E. B. (2009). Locus of control: Relation to schizophrenia, to recovery, and to depression and psychosis – A 15-year longitudinal study. *Psychiatry Res., 168*, 186–192.

Havsteen-Franklin, D. & Altamirano, J. C. (2015). Containing the uncontainable: Responsive art making in art therapy as a method to facilitate mentalization. *International Journal of Art Therapy, 20*, 54–65.

Holttum, S. & Huet, V. (2014). The MATISSE trial: A critique – Does art therapy really have nothing to offer people with a diagnosis of schizophrenia? *Sage OPEN*, 1–11.

Isserow, J. (2008). Looking together: Joint attention in art therapy. *International Journal of Art Therapy, 13*, 34–42.

Kapitan, L. (2010). *Inroduction to art therapy research*. New York: Routledge.

Kay, S. R., Fiszbein, A. & Opler, L. A. (1987). The positive and negative syndrome scale (PANSS) for schizophrenia. *Schizophr Bull., 13*, 261–276.

Killick, K. & Schaverien, J. (1997). *Art, psychotherapy and psychosis*. London: Routledge.

Krampen, G. (1991). *Fragebogen zu Kompetenz- und Kontrollüberzeugungen (FKK)*. Göttingen: Verlag für Psychologie Dr. C. J. Hogrefe.

Lambert, M. J. (2013). Introduction and historical overview. In M. J. Lambert (Ed.), *Bergin and Garfield's handbook of psychotherapy and behavior change* (pp. 3–20). Hoboken, NJ: Wiley.

Lane, R. D., Quinlan, D. M., Schwartz, G. E., Walker, P. A. & Zeitlin, S. B. (1990). The Levels of Emotional Awareness Scale: A cognitive-developmental measure of emotion. *Journ. Pers Assess., 55*, 124–134.

Lane, R. D. & Schwartz, G. E. (1987). Levels of emotional awareness: A cognitive-developmental theory and its application to psychopathology. *Am J Psychiatry, 144*, 133–143.

Lempa, G., von Haebler, D. & Montag, C. (2016). *Psychodynamische Psychotherapie der Schizophrenien: Ein Manual*. Gießen: Psychosozial-Verlag.

Leurent, B., Killaspy, H., Osborn, D. P., Crawford, M. J., Hoadley, A., Waller, D. & King, M. (2014). Moderating factors for the effectiveness of group art therapy for schizophrenia: Secondary analysis of data from the MATISSE randomised controlled trial. *Soc Psychiatry Psychiatr Epidemiol., 49*, 1703–1710.

Little, R. J., Cohen, M. L., Dickersin, K., Emerson, S. S., Farrar, J. T., Neaton, J. D., et al. (2012). The design and conduct of clinical trials to limit missing data. *Statistics in Medicine, 31*, 3433–3443.

Maujean, A., Pepping, C. A. & Kendall, E. (2014). A systematic review of randomized controlled studies of art therapy. *Art Therapy: Journal of the American Art Therapy Association, 31*, 37–44.

Meng, P., Zheng, R., Cai, Z., Cao, D., Ma, L., Liu, J., et al. (2005). Group intervention for schizophrenia inpatient with art as medium. *Acta Psychologica Sinica, 37*, 403–412.

Michaelides, D. (2012). An understanding of negative reflective functioning, the image and the art psychotherapeutic group. *International Journal of Art Therapy, 17*, 45–53.

Montag, C. (2015). Zum Konzept der Mentalisierung in Theorie und Behandlungstechnik der Psychosen. *Forum der Psychoanalyse, 31*, 375–393.

Montag, C., Haase, L., Seidel, D., Herrmann, U. & Dannecker, K. (2014). A pilot RCT of psychodynamic group art therapy for patients in acute psychotic episodes: Impact on symptoms and mentalising capacity. *PLoS One, 13*, October.

Mueser, K. T. & Berenbaum, H. (1990). Psychodynamic treatment of schizophrenia: Is there a future? *Psychol Med., 20*, 253–262.

Müller, M. J., Marx-Dannigkeit, P., Schlosser, R., Wetzel, H., Addington, D. & Benkert, O. (1999). The Calgary Depression Rating Scale for Schizophrenia:

Development and interrater reliability of a German version (CDSS-G). *J Psychiatr Res.*, *33*, 433–443.

Navratil, L. (1965). *Schizophrenie und Kunst*. Munich: Deutscher Taschenbuchverlag.

NICE (National Institute for Clinical Excellence). (2009). Schizophrenia: Core interventions in the treatment and management of schizophrenia in adults in primary and secondary care. *NICE Clinical Guideline 82*. London: NICE.

NICE (National Institute for Health and Care Excellence). (2014). Psychosis and schizophrenia in adults: The NICE guideline on treatment and management. *NICE Clinical Guideline 178*. London: NICE. Retrieved from www.nice.org.uk/guidance/cg178/evidence/fullguideline-490503565.

Patterson, S., Borschmann, R. & Waller, D. (2013). Considering referral to art therapy: Responses to referral and experiences of participants in a randomised controlled trial. *International Journal of Art Therapy*, *18*, 2–9.

Patterson, S., Crawford, M. J., Ainsworth, E. & Waller, D. (2011). Art therapy for people diagnosed with schizophrenia: Therapists' views about what changes, how and for whom. *International Journal of Art Therapy*, *16*, 70–80.

Patterson, S., Debate, J., Anju, S., Waller, D. & Crawford, M. J. (2011). Provision and practice of art therapy for people with schizophrenia: Results of a national survey. *J Ment Health*, *20*, 328–335.

Patterson, S., Waller, D., Killaspy, H. & Crawford, M. J. (2015). Riding the wake: Detailing the art therapy delivered in the MATISSE study. *International Journal of Art Therapy*, *20*, 28–38.

Prinzhorn, H. (1922). *Die Bildnerei der Geisteskranken*. Berlin: Springer.

Richardson, P., Jones, K., Evans, C., Stevens, P. & Rowe, A. (2007). Exploratory RCT of art therapy as an adjunctive treatment in schizophrenia. *Journal of Mental Health*, *16*, 483–491.

Ruddy, R. & Milnes, D. (2005). Art therapy for schizophrenia or schizophrenia-like illnesses. *Cochrane Database Syst Rev.*, CD003728.

Saß, H., Wittchen, H. U., Zaudig, M. & Houben, I. (2003). *Diagnostisches und Statistisches: Manual Psychischer Störungen – Textrevision- DSM-IV-TR*. Göttingen: Hogrefe.

Sass, L. A. (2014). Self-disturbance and schizophrenia: Structure, specificity, pathogenesis (current issues, new directions). *Schizophr Res.*, *152*, 5–11.

Sass, L. A. & Parnas, J. (2003). Schizophrenia, consciousness, and the self. *Schizophr Bull.*, *29*, 427–444.

Slayton, S. C., D'Archer, J. & Kaplan, F. (2010). Outcome studies on the efficacy of art therapy: A review of findings. *Art Therapy: Journal of the American Art Therapy Association*, *27*, 108–118.

Springham, N., Findlay, D., Woods, A. & Harris, J. (2012). How can art therapy contribute to mentalization in borderline personality disorder? *International Journal of Art Therapy*, *17*, 115–129.

Subic-Wrana, C., Thomas, W., Huber, M. & Köhle, K. (2001). Levels of Emotional Awareness Scale (LEAS): Die deutsche Version eines neuen Alexithymietests. *Psychotherapeut.*, *46*, 176–181.

Teglbjaerg, H. S. (2011). Art therapy may reduce psychopathology in schizophrenia by strengthening the patients' sense of self: A qualitative extended case report. *Psychopathology*, *44*, 314–318.

Van Lith, T. (2016). Art therapy in mental health: A systematic review of approaches and practices. *The Arts in Psychotherapy*, *47*, 9–22.

Van Lith, T., Schofield, M. J. & Fenner, P. (2013). Identifying the evidence-base for art-based practices and their potential benefit for mental health recovery: A critical review. *Disabil Rehabil., 35*, 1309–1323.

Verfalle, M. (2016). *Mentalization in arts therapies*. London: Karnac Books.

Waller, D. (1993). *Group interactive art therapy: Its use in training and treatment*. London: Routledge.

Waller, D. & Gilroy, A. (Eds.). (1992). *Art therapy: A handbook*. Buckingham: Open University Press.

Wood, C. (2013). In the wake of the Matisse RCT: What about art therapy and psychosis? *International Journal of Art Therapy, 18*, 88–97.

Chapter 6

Changes in well-being of schizophrenic patients after movement therapy

Results of a multicenter RCT study

Valerie Pohlmann, Sabine C. Koch, and Thomas Fuchs

Introduction

Achievements and unmet needs in the treatment of schizophrenia

Comprising a number of psychopathology domains, schizophrenia appears as a heterogeneous clinical syndrome (Buchanan & Carpenter, 1994). Patients with schizophrenia experience positive psychotic symptoms including delusions, hallucinations, and disorganization of thought and behavior, as well as negative symptoms, which are conceptualized as a deficit or loss of functions (Strauss, Carpenter & Bartko, 1974). Negative symptoms denominate an impairment of "normal" emotional responses, thought processes, and behaviors, and are shown in blunting or flattening affect, alogia/aprosody, avolition/apathy, anhedonia, and asociality (Chue & Lalonde, 2014). Schizophrenia as a severe mental disorder means deep suffering for the persons and caregivers affected (Sartory, 2007).

Although schizophrenia has been defined as a clinical entity for over a century, there are still no definite treatments to cure or prevent it (Abayomi et al., 2014) and many aspects of the disease remain not well understood. Despite the improvements in pharmacological treatment and more than 100 years of research, schizophrenia is still one of the most burdensome mental disorders with a high degree of disability (Murray & Lopez, 1997; Rössler, Salize, van Os, & Riecher-Rössler, 2005).

Medical therapy is the central treatment component, and with the discovery of atypical neuroleptics success concerning the reduction of side effects was achieved. Extrapyramidal symptoms are less frequent with the second-generation neuroleptics (Möller, 2003). Antipsychotic medication is successful in treating acute psychotic states and improves positive symptoms in 85% of patients in the early stages of schizophrenia (Lambert et al., 2008). Despite those significant gains in the knowledge of evidence-based pharmacological treatment (Buchanan et al., 2010), negative symptoms are influenced only marginally (Arango, Buchanan, Kirkpatrick, & Carpenter, 2004).

A significant proportion of people with schizophrenia show primary or persistent negative symptoms, which are associated with poor health outcomes and represent an unmet treatment need (Buchanan et al., 2010). The European Schizophrenia Outpatients Health Outcome Study, analyzing 6,642 patients, revealed outcome rates ranging from 33% of long-lasting symptomatic remission (defined as achieving a level of severity that was mild or less in positive, negative, cognitive, and overall severity cores of the Clinical Global Impression–Schizophrenia Scale CGI-SCH; Haro et al., 2003), via 16–23.3% long-lasting functional remission, 27% long-lasting adequate quality of life, to 4% achieved recovery, including all three aspects, within a three-year follow-up period (Novick, Haro, Suarez, Vieta, & Naber, 2008). Andrews and co-workers showed that current interventions could avert only some 13% of the burden of schizophrenia (Andrews, Sanderson, Corry, Issakidis, & Lapsley, 2003). Another problem of the current mainstay of antipsychotic treatment is the heterogeneity in terms of an individual's response to antipsychotic treatment. The subsequent inability to predict response leads to a trial-and-error strategy with respect to treatment choice and a significant number of side effects (Lally & McCabe, 2015).

In consideration of these findings, the great demand for the improvement of intervention strategies in order to meet the needs of persons with schizophrenia is obvious. Thus, we want to provide a new view on body-oriented interventions as embodied psychotherapies with the underlying principle of supporting the mind–body connection. Against the background of embodiment, phenomenological findings suggest a conceptualization of schizophrenia as a self-disorder characterized in terms of *disembodiment* (Fuchs, 2012; Koch et al., 2016). We furthermore refer to findings on emotional comorbidity in schizophrenia and consider well-being as a component of the subjective evaluation of health (Diener & Ryan, 2009) and an important health outcome (Sobel, 1994).

The definition of desirable outcomes is discussed with reference to the biopsychosocial model and a salutogenetic perspective of health promotion (Antonovsky, 1997). Finally, movement therapy as an embodied therapy, covering body-oriented psychotherapy and dance movement therapy, is considered a core treatment for persons with schizophrenia in addressing the challenges of the disorder (Koch et al., 2016; Martin, Koch, Hirjak, & Fuchs, 2016; Röhricht & Priebe, 2006; Xia & Grant, 2009).

Embodied therapies: body-oriented psychotherapy and dance movement therapy

Body-oriented psychotherapy

While body-oriented psychotherapy can be understood as an overarching umbrella term (Röhricht & Papadopoulos, 2010), Loew, Tritt, Lahmann, and

Röhricht (2006) draw a distinction between body-oriented psychological therapies and body therapy. In contrast to body therapies such as massage therapy, physiotherapy, yoga, qigong or t'ai chi, body-oriented psychotherapy always refers to a psychotherapeutic framework, including therapy aims such as enhanced self-awareness, behavior modification, or insight-oriented psychological problem-solving.

Body-oriented methods cover two main practices with different historical roots: While a rich practice of body-oriented psychotherapy leads back to psychoanalysis and is based on theoretic psychodynamic foundation, different forms of movement therapy developed from a reform movement in gymnastics and dance. After Sandòr Ferenczi started to explore gestures and facial expressions, Wilhelm Reich with his character theory, expressed in body postures, certainly had the biggest influence on body-oriented psychotherapy. His work later found much correspondence, such as in Alexander Lowen's Bioenergetic. Elsa Gindler's work as a reform of gymnastics focusing on body awareness further influenced the development of forms such as concentrative movement therapy (Geuter, 2006).

Dance movement therapy

Isadora Duncan's changed conception of dance was taken up in modern dance (M. Graham, Larson) and the German expressive dance movement (Laban, Wigman) in the 1920s. Following this pioneer movement, the dancers Franziska Boas, Marian Chace, Lilian Espenak, Mary Whitehouse, and Trudi Schoop brought dance – as a means of expression – into psychiatry. The use of the expressive function of dance was certainly influenced by the discovery of the unconscious in psychoanalysis, and humanistic psychology supported the development of the dance movement therapy practice (Willke, 1991).

Today the American Dance Therapy Association defines dance therapy as "the therapeutic use of movement as a process which furthers the emotional, social, cognitive and physical integration of the individual" (ADTA, 2015). In relying on the healing factors of the mind–body connection (Koch & Cruz, 2015) and with the assumption that motion and emotion are reciprocally linked (Payne, 2006), dance movement therapy is in many ways related to body-oriented psychotherapies. Additionally covering factors of aesthetics and expressive emotions, it is also defined as a creative arts therapy (Koch & Cruz, 2015). In dance therapy the patients' own expressive impulses unfold in an interactive, improvisatory way. Dance movement therapists follow the clients within their emerging themes (Goodill, 2005). Through continued movements in line with authentic experience, non-rational elements of the psyche are transformed into coherent resources for the conscious self (Caldwell, 2006).

Despite the heterogeneity of different body-oriented methods, common main principles can be found. With its orientation on wholeness, integrating psychological and physical dimensions of human experience, the embodied subjectivity can be seen as a basic axiom of somatic therapies. The therapeutic process can take both directions: reaching from the psychological dimension to a deeper body self-awareness, or start with body sensations leading toward insight into psychological realities. The therapeutic relationship is furthermore reflected in psychological and bodily aspects (Marlock & Weiss, 2006). No matter, whether one starts from a moving/expressing or a sensing side, depending on the professional background, most experienced body psychotherapists balance both sides (Caldwell, 2012).

In the following we will subsume body-oriented psychotherapy and dance movement therapy as movement therapy. Hence, with the elementary assumption that mind is always embedded in a body (Tschacher & Storch, 2012), the embodiment paradigm can serve as a theoretical framework for all body-oriented therapies.

Embodiment and embodied affectivity

The interest in the body–mind connection is certainly not a new phenomenon. It is still a modern tendency of the Western world, historically attributable to Cartesian dualism, to separate mind and body, which eminently influences our way of thinking (Caldwell, 2006). In times of the predominant paradigm of cognitive psychology, however, the embodiment paradigm introduces a necessary differentiation, assuming a fundamental interaction of body and mind. Based on the concept of fundamental corporeality (Fuchs, 2014), it demands consideration of the body in every psychological and cognitive variable (Tschacher & Storch, 2012). The postulation that all human experience is embodied goes way beyond the embedding of cognitive processes in neuronal networks; it rather denominates their origin in the sensorimotor experience of the living organism (Fuchs, 2009).

Assuming grounded cognition and the idea of intelligence emerging from the interaction of an organism with its environment as a result of sensorimotor function (Smith, 2005), the embodiment approach emerged in cognitive science at the end of the last century (Clark, 1997; Varela, Thompson, & Rosch, 1991). With the conceptual metaphor theory, Lakoff and Johnson (1999) offered an explanation of how abstract concepts relate to metaphors for bodily and physical concepts. In contrast to traditional views of cognition as computation of amodal symbols representing knowledge, cognition was viewed as based on bodily states and situated action (Barsalou, 2008). Cognitive processes were regarded as deeply rooted in the body's interaction with the world (Wilson, 2002). Thus, the embodied cognitive science movement is a reaction to the traditional view that human beings as information-processing systems function only in terms of perception–thinking–action sequences (Dawson, 2002).

In recent years, a growing body of research has supported the hypothesis of embodiment and indicated that bodily sensations, body postures, and expressions have an influence on emotional perception and evaluation (Fuchs & Koch, 2014; Koch, 2014). Empirical findings from social psychology revealed how motion influences affect and cognition in the form of bodily resonance including proprioceptive and interoceptive feedback. Social emotion processes seem to involve actual bodily states and simulations of experience (Niedenthal, Barsalou, Winkielman, Krauth-Gruber, & Ric, 2005). For instance, embodiment research indicated that facial expressions modulated emotional experiences (Strack, Martin, & Stepper, 1988), posture influenced emotional memory (Michalak, Mischnat, & Teismann, 2014; Riskind, 1984), and motor processes related to approach or avoidance affected subjects' appraisal (Cacioppo, Priester, & Berntson, 1993). Botox paralysis of the facial frowning muscles influenced the processing of sad or angry emotional content and the understanding of critical texts (Havas, Glenberg, Gutowski, Lucarelli, & Davidson, 2010). A related finding showed that listening to action words evokes brain activities in associated motor regions of the brain (Hauk, Johnsrude, & Pulvermüller, 2004). In addition, nonverbal synchronicity in bodily psychotherapeutic interaction predicted therapy outcomes for schizophrenic patients (Ramseyer & Tschacher, 2011; Tschacher & Storch, 2012).

Fuchs and Koch (2014) provided a model of embodied affectivity to clarify the understanding of the influence of embodiment on the complexity of emotional life. They describe a circular interaction between affective qualities and affordances of the environment and bodily resonance in the form of sensations, postures, expressive moments, and movement tendencies. Feelings are seen as circular interactions or feedback cycles between centripetal *affection* and centrifugal *e-motion*, referring to the Latin *e-movere*, "to move out", implying that every emotion covers a movement potential. Being almost always relational, emotions include embodied action tendencies, in terms of movements toward or against an actual or implicit counterpart (Kafka, 1950). In reference to the model of embodied affectivity, emotions cover different aspects ranging from (a) affective intentionality as an embodied resonance to a situation that mediates its affective appeal, via (b) bodily resonance including all kinds of local or general bodily sensations, (c) action tendencies, as well as (d) function and significance providing a basic orientation to a communicative function. The model is further extended into the social sphere. *Interaffectivity* means a circular interaction covering two dimensions. In terms of self- or individual resonance, our body is affected by the other's expression through our own interoceptive feedback. At the same time, we experience the kinaesthetic aspect and intensity of the opponent's emotions as a dynamic mutual feedback between two bodies. This interaffective system connects two bodies in interbodily resonance or *intercorporeality* (Merleau-Ponty, 1966). While cognitive approaches conceptualize emotions mostly as an act of appraisal, this comprehensive view on emotional experience considers the phenomenal quality by emphasizing the affective concerns of a person. The embodiment of affectivity has important implications for the therapeutic practice, because emotional aspects then can be addressed in two ways: via cognitive modulation, but also via corporeal (or inter-corporeal) modulation.

Since the body may be taken as a mediator of the interaction between the individual and the world, it seems obvious that this interaction also manifests itself in implicit or body memory (Fuchs, 2008). Embodiment theory assumes that all bodily mediated experiences are also stored in our body memory (Koch, Fuchs, Summa, & Müller, 2012). The term refers to all implicit knowledge, capacities, and dispositions that are actualized by the body in pre-reflexive mode (Koch, Caldwell & Fuchs, 2014). This plays an important role for the phenomenological approach to schizophrenia, as will be shown in the following.

Phenomenology and psychopathology: disembodiment in schizophrenia

Despite a strong tradition of literature on anomalous self-experience in schizophrenia from a first-person perspective (Blankenburg, 1971; Fuchs, 2005; Stanghellini, 2004), contemporary research primarily focuses on biological and social determinants of dysfunctions from a third-person perspective and with less consideration of the subjective experience of the persons affected (Lysaker & Lysaker, 2010). In recent years there has been much focus on the apparent heterogeneity of symptoms, and the alteration of the self is rather seen on a par with other characteristics of the disorder such as disturbances in cognition and affect, perception, and beliefs (Sass & Parnas, 2003).

Recent phenomenological approaches following German and French philosophical traditions build a bridge between psychopathology and philosophical anthropology in schizophrenia research. They assume a disruption of basic, pre-reflexive self-experience, thus describing schizophrenia as a self-disorder (Fuchs, 2000, 2005; Sass & Parnas, 2003). This tacit or basic self is also referred to as the "core" or "minimal" self or as "ipseity" (mine-ness) (Nelson, Parnas, & Sass, 2014). Applying a Husserlian approach, Blankenburg (1971), in his seminal work on the "Loss of Natural Self-Evidence," described schizophrenia as a loss of implicit knowledge and "common sense" which finds correspondence in a weakened sense of self. Sass and Parnas (2003) further assumed that the basic self-disorder includes both a diminished self-affection and a form of hyper-reflexivity, expressing itself in a decline of the fundamental sense of existing as a subject of awareness and action, on the one hand, and showing an exaggerated, reflexive awareness of aspects of experience that are normally implicit, on the other hand. Hirjak, Breyer, Thomann, and Fuchs (2013) consider the altered self-experience as a sequence of steps ranging from divergent body sensations to delusion. Fuchs (2012) highlights that from a phenomenological perspective, the slow degradation of self-experience, awareness, and action, which can be traced back to unremarkable prodromal stages and even to the patient's childhood, appears as more relevant to the comprehension of the disorder than the positive symptoms of acute schizophrenia.

In line with the disturbed self-experience, altered body experiences seem to be an additional characteristic of schizophrenia. Affected persons experience disturbances in their body image, such as the enlargement or diminution of certain body parts or unusual sensations of movement in the body (e.g., *my brain always slips down the back of my head*). They may also report phenomena such as not feeling at home in their body, feeling disintegrated or fragmented, for example, as if their body was torn apart. Furthermore, abnormal thoughts and attitudes toward the body and pathological sensory sensations are common. In acute states of schizophrenia, patients moreover show disturbances of body size perception and a lack of control over the body (Priebe & Röhricht, 2001). Thakkar, Nichols, McIntosh, and Park (2011) empirically studied body ownership in schizophrenia patients as a component of self-awareness with the rubber hand illusion. By watching an artificial hand being stroked while one's own unseen hand is stroked simultaneously, a spontaneous out-of-body experience can be induced: The experimental arrangement raises a sense of body ownership over the artificial hand and a shift in perceived position of the real hand toward the rubber hand. Results showed that the illusion is quantitatively and qualitatively stronger in persons with schizophrenia, pointing to a less stable body schema and body integrity.

The most frequently reported abnormal bodily sensations in schizophrenia are: abnormal bodily sensations (cenesthesias), desomatization/depersonalization with boundary loss, subjectively experienced as fear of body loss/disintegration and resulting in reconstructive behavioral efforts such as mirror exposure or compulsive rituals, loss of ego-control over one's body, disturbances of body size perception of peripheral parts of the body, and stereotypical movements with repetitive self-contact (Röhricht & Papadopoulos, 2010).

The alteration of self-experience is accompanied by an alienation of corporeality and can be described as *disembodiment* (Fuchs, 2005; Fuchs & Schlimme, 2009; Stanghellini, 2004). Referring to phenomenological, developmental, and neuroscientific concepts, Fuchs (2012) differentiates between the basic bodily self and the extended reflexive or personal self. The self-disorder in schizophrenia then manifests itself in different aspects: The weakness of the basic bodily self as a disruption of implicit body functions leads to an alienation in perception and action involving the environment, concerning the so-called ecological self. Furthermore the inter-bodily contact with others is impaired, referring to the social self. Eventually there is a disturbance on the level of the personal self, affecting the awareness of boundaries between self and others.

Measuring the outcome: well-being in schizophrenia

Since schizophrenia is a severe mental illness associated with disruptions in cognition, emotion, and psychosocial functioning (Chien, Leung, Yeung, & Wong, 2013), well-being is an important clinical goal and outcome.

Negative symptoms, which are only slightly influenced by antipsychotic medical treatment (Arango et al., 2004), impair functioning and quality of life profoundly (Savill, Banks, Khanom, & Priebe, 2015). They are associated with increased functional disability, increased burden of illness, and poorer long-term outcomes (Chue & Lalonde, 2014), as well as restrictions on social life (Barnes & the Schizophrenia Consensus Group of the British Association for Psychopharmacology, 2011). Suicide rates in schizophrenia are high. Compared to the general population, patients with schizophrenia have an 8.5-fold greater risk of suicide (Kasckow, Felmet & Zisook, 2011). Besides symptomatology, unmet basic and illness-related needs were shown to compromise the quality of life of persons with schizophrenia (Eack, Newhill, Anderson, & Rotondi, 2007). Negative affect additionally plays an important role in schizophrenia. Prevalence of depression in schizophrenia ranges from 22 to 75%, depending on the criteria and the chronicity of the sample (Birchwood, Iqbal & Upthegrove, 2005).

Emotional dysfunction and depressed affect already play a key role in the prodromal stage (Birchwood, 2003): along with negative symptoms, altered affectivity is an early indicator of schizophrenia (Häfner et al., 1998) being mirrored by individual psychotic symptoms being linked to a raised risk for depression (Birchwood et al., 2005). The second generation of factor analytic studies on schizophrenia has yielded further dimensions of depressive and manic symptoms (McGorry, Bell, Dudgeon, & Jackson, 1998; van Os et al., 1999). Birchwood et al. (2005) therefore discuss depression as an inherent part of psychosis and part of the loss of functioning. To improve the understanding of emotional dysfunction, the authors propose a distinction between three pathways, which are not mutually exclusive: (a) depression, which is intrinsic to the psychosis diathesis; (b) a psychological reaction to it; and (c) products of disturbed developmental pathways resulting from developmental trauma and the child antecedents of psychosis (Birchwood, 2003). Depressive symptoms are correlated inversely with a patient's subjective well-being (Mauriño, Sanjúan, Haro, Díez, & Ballesteros, 2011).

Care and outcomes for people with schizophrenia have improved in recent years, but further progress is needed to help more individuals live an independent and fulfilled life (Fleischhacker et al., 2014). The articulation of the biopsychosocial model (Engel, 1977) raised the awareness of the multidimensionality of health and the idea of holism found its way into mainstream health care discussions (Goodill, 2005). For the patients themselves, recovery comprises different dimensions including disease-related, psychological, and social aspects: besides symptom recovery, reconciling the meaning of the illness experience, regaining control, and the acceptance of the treatment seem to be important factors in predicting improvement (Windell, Norman, Lal, & Malla, 2015).

Although the pathogenic, biomedical perspective still has greater influence in health research and health politics, there is a growing interest in the salutogenetic approach (Hartung, 2011). In the World Health Organization's (1946) definition of health as "a state of complete physical, social, and mental well-being and not merely the absence of disease or infirmity," it becomes clear that symptom reduction is only one aspect of health. The salutogenetic view, according to Antonovsky's (1997) concept, is looking for health-promoting and health-preserving factors from a resource-oriented perspective and signifies a shift of attention from disease avoidance toward health promotion. Psychological resources are seen to mediate the interaction with environmental stress factors and seem to cushion the harmful effects of stressful events (Hartung, 2011). Poor health is not necessarily linked to poor quality of life, because some individuals manage to overcome disease-specific limitations, and adapt their lives to pursue their goals (Wikman, Wardle, & Steptoe, 2011).

Psychological well-being seems to have a protective effect. Independent from negative affect, emotional well-being such as positive mood, joy, happiness, vigor, and energy are associated with reduced mortality (Chida & Steptoe, 2008). Furthermore, well-being is one of the major determinants of medical treatment compliance (Naber et al., 2001). Psychological entities can influence the health outcome efficiently and underlying health determinants such as attitude, beliefs, and mood are positive predictors for health (Sobel, 1994).

A successful treatment should include not only symptom reduction, but also subjectively experienced change. Subjective outcome measures such as subjective well-being are important for the evaluation of treatment success. While the pathogenic view created a large number of deficit-oriented methods, resource-oriented methods and instruments are now gaining importance (Singer & Brähler, 2007). To satisfy the treatment needs, beyond the core symptoms, and to optimize the chances of recovery, the incomplete medical knowledge has to be enriched (Buchanan et al., 2010). Schizophrenia needs to be considered as the product of a progressive interaction of the disease process, treatment, environment, and the active role of the affected person (Hopper, Harrison, Janca, & Sartorius, 2007).

Merely measuring symptom reduction fails to provide a wider picture of the subjective impact of the treatment on the patient and only addresses one aspect. Nevertheless, improvement in the psychopathological domain and perceived well-being were so far only shown to be moderately correlated (Fleischhacker, Rabinowitz, Kemmler, Eerdekens, & Meehnert, 2005).

Movement therapy for schizophrenia

Unmet needs of persons with schizophrenia, due to limited effects on negative symptoms and well-being, demand a better understanding of the disease as a requirement for the improvement of treatment. Especially negative symptoms, which are only slightly influenced by the medical treatment, produce deep suffering for schizophrenic persons.

Regarding schizophrenia as a self-disorder, according to phenomenological findings, we assume that a body-oriented psychological method helps to address the needs of persons with schizophrenia. Phenomenologically oriented psychopathology is taking the subjective experience into focus. A deeper understanding of the disorder may help to meet the unmet needs of persons with schizophrenia. Dance movement therapy and body-oriented psychotherapy, subsumed as movement therapy in this chapter, employ the same principles of embodiment and can therefore also be labeled embodied therapies. Methods of improving body awareness and coherence of body experience should support a coherent self-experience. Moving from *disembodiment* to a more coherent experience of the self with an improved bodily and inter-bodily resonance should also result in improved well-being.

Moreover, in movement therapy as a resource-oriented method, principles in terms of general mechanisms of psychotherapy are in operation. Those underlying factors as general health determinants should strengthen the resources of the schizophrenic patient. Besides all other active factors of dance movement therapy (Koch & Eberhard-Kaechele, 2015), resource activation is seen as one of the most important premises and starting points of dance movement therapy (Koch & Eberhard-Kaechele, 2015). By addressing underlying health principles, dance movement therapy particularly aims at improving health-related psychological outcomes, and has been shown to do so for many different populations (Koch, Kunz, Lykou, & Cruz, 2014). Creative aspects inviting the patient to express themselves (Goodill, 2005) are taking the patient as a subject into the focus of the process and support their personal development.

A meta-analysis covering 23 primary trials suggests that in dance and dance movement therapy, positive effects concerning quality of life, well-being, positive mood, affect, and body image, as well as a reduction of symptoms, could be shown across a variety of populations (Koch et al., 2012). Recent RCT studies suggest that body-oriented psychological therapy/dance movement therapy is effective in treating negative symptoms of schizophrenia (Martin et al., 2016; Röhricht, Papadopoulos, Holden, Clarke, & Priebe, 2011; Röhricht & Priebe, 2006) and ego-pathology aspects of the disorder (Röhricht, Papadopoulos, Suzuki, & Priebe, 2009). Besides positive effects on negative symptoms, Lee, Jang, Lee, and Hwang (2015) showed the effectiveness of dance movement therapy on depression, states of anger, and anger control in a schizophrenic sample.

Following these findings, the present study aims to investigate the effects of dance movement therapy/body-oriented psychotherapy on the well-being of patients with schizophrenia. We hypothesize that movement therapy improves psychological well-being compared to a waiting-list control group. Our empirical examination contributes to the growing body of research helping to understand whether and how body-oriented psychotherapy and dance movement therapy can improve the treatment of schizophrenia.

Method

The study was conducted as part of the Marie Curie ITN-Project TESIS ("Towards an Embodied Science of Intersubjectivity," 2012–2014; Fuchs/Di Paolo). Participants were consecutively recruited between 2012 and 2014 from three medical centers: The Center for Psychosocial Medicine in Heidelberg (Setting 1; Therapist Ariane Konrad, DMT, DGT), the Psychiatrisches Zentrum Nordbaden (PZN) in Wiesloch (Setting 2; Therapist Anja Holzinger, DMT, BTD), and the Johannes-Diakonie in Mosbach (Setting 3; Therapist Martina Bopp, DMT, BTD), and cooperating regional clinical and rehabilitation facilities. Data was collected with support from students and interns of the Department of Psychology at the University of Heidelberg, and the Department of Dance Movement Therapy at SRH University Heidelberg. In this randomized controlled multicenter study, patients were randomly allocated to either the treatment or control condition with block randomization of a 2:1 ratio. The study used a two-group repeated measures design comparing the treatment group to a waiting-list control group. Patients met the following inclusion criteria: ICD-10 diagnosis of schizophrenia (IDC-10: F20–22, F24–29), aged between 14 and 65, outpatient, stable medication. Exclusion criteria were: acute psychosis, severe internistic neurological disease with an impact on the ability to move, severe traumatic brain injury in the past, addictive disorder, mental retardation (IQ<70), substance-induced psychosis, and pronounced language barriers. All participants gave their written informed consent and received €20 at the post-test of the control as well as treatment condition.

Sample

A total of 95 patients were referred for inclusion. For not attending baseline assessment, missing information, or not meeting inclusion criteria, 27 patients had to be excluded. Some 68 were randomly allocated to either the treatment condition or control condition. Due to motivational reasons, 14 persons in the treatment condition and 12 persons in the control condition were lost to post-test (see Figure 6.1). A total of $N=36$ individuals with schizophrenia completed their participation in this study, with $N=24$ (13 male and 11 female) participants in the treatment condition and $N=12$ (eight male and four female) in the control condition. The mean age in the treatment condition was $M=42.0$

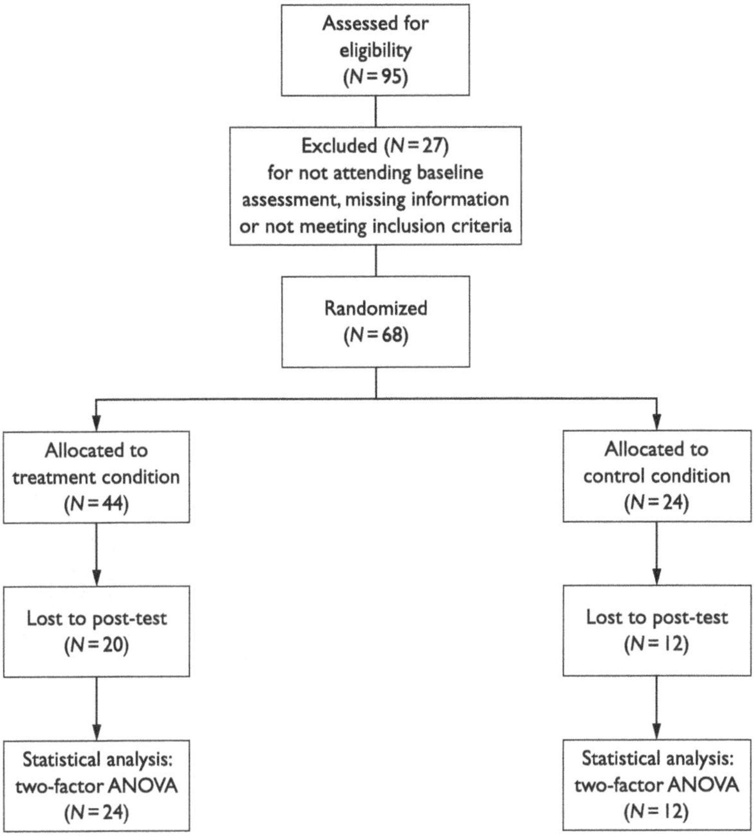

Figure 6.1 **Participant flow diagram.**

(standard deviation $SD=12.29$, *range* 20–63) and $M=35.0$ years in the control condition (standard deviation $SD=7.89$, *range* 18–47). Demographic and clinical characteristics of the study sample are shown in Table 6.1. Participants' education level was mixed and all but five patients were outpatients.

Instruments

Psychological well-being was measured by the 26 unipolar *Heidelberger State Inventory* (*HSI*; Koch, Mehl, Sobanski, Sieber, & Fuchs, 2015; Koch, Morlinghaus & Fuchs, 2007) (Table 6.2) with a range from "1" ("does not apply at all") to "6" ("applies exactly") assessing *tension, anxiety, coping, positive affect, depressed affect, and vitality* (Goodill, 2005). The *HSI* had been constructed for use with clinical patients receiving dance movement therapy and has been tested and factor analyzed in previous studies with bigger samples. The

Table 6.1 Demographic data

		Treatment[a]	*Control*[b]
Gender	Male/female	13/11	8/4
Age	(years)/SD	42.0/12.29	35.0/7.89
Location	Heidelberg	12 (50%)	9 (75%)
	Mosbach	10 (41.7%)	3 (25%)
	Wiesloch	2 (8.3%)	0
Nationality	German	22 (91.7%)	11 (91.7%)
	German and second citizenship	0	1 (8.3%)
	Other	2 (8.3%)	0
First language	German	21(87.5%)	10 (83.3%)
	English	1 (4.2%)	1 (8.3%)
	Italian	0	1 (8.3%)
	Spanish	1 (4.2%)	0
	Other	1 (4.2%)	0
Family status	Unmarried	16 (66%)	8 (72.7%)
	Married	4 (16.7%)	1 (9.1%)
	Widowed	1 (4.2%)	0
	Divorced	2 (8.3%)	1 (9.1%)
	Missing	1 (4.2%)	2 (16.7%)
Relationship	Yes	8 (33.3%)	4 (33.3%)
	No	14 (58.3%)	6 (50.0%)
	Missing	2 (8.3%)	2 (16.7%)
Children	Yes	5 (20.8%)	0
	No	13 (54.2%)	9 (75%)
	Missing	6 (25%)	3 (25%)
Education	No educational degree	2 (8.3%)	0
	Lower secondary education	1 (4.2%)	2 (16.7%)
	Middle school	3 (12.5%)	1 (9.1%)
	Abitur	3 (12.5%)	1 (9.1%)
Treatment	Completed vocational training	10 (41.7%)	4 (33.3%)
	University training	5 (20.8%)	4 (33.3%)
	Day-unit	4 (16.7%)	1 (8.3%)
	Outpatient	20 (83.3%)	11 (91.6%)
Medication	Atypical neuroleptica (Aripiprazol, Olanzapin, Clozapin)	1 (4.2%)	5 (41.7%)
	Dopamine receptor antagonist (Amilsuprid)	1 (4.2%)	0
	Tricyclic antidepressant	1 (4.2%)	1 (8.3%)
	Lithium	1 (4.2%)	0
	SSRI	0	1 (8.3%)
	No medication	1 (4.2%)	0
	Missing	21 (87.5%)	7 (8.3%)

Notes
a $N = 24$;
b $N = 12$.

Table 6.2 Heidelberger State Inventory *HSI*

Heidelberger State Inventory HSI

I am in the following state …	*Does not apply at all*	*Does not apply*	*Does rather not apply*	*Does rather apply*	*Does apply*	*Does fully apply*
relaxed	☐	☐	☐	☐	☐	☐
in a good mood	☐	☐	☐	☐	☐	☐
carefree	☐	☐	☐	☐	☐	☐
enjoying	☐	☐	☐	☐	☐	☐
tensed	☐	☐	☐	☐	☐	☐
in a bad mood	☐	☐	☐	☐	☐	☐
depressive	☐	☐	☐	☐	☐	☐
anxious	☐	☐	☐	☐	☐	☐
lifeless, empty	☐	☐	☐	☐	☐	☐
tired	☐	☐	☐	☐	☐	☐
prepared to deal with the world	☐	☐	☐	☐	☐	☐
full of energy	☐	☐	☐	☐	☐	☐
full of resources	☐	☐	☐	☐	☐	☐
positive	☐	☐	☐	☐	☐	☐
strong, vital	☐	☐	☐	☐	☐	☐
fighting	☐	☐	☐	☐	☐	☐
negative	☐	☐	☐	☐	☐	☐
worried	☐	☐	☐	☐	☐	☐
not prepared to deal with the world	☐	☐	☐	☐	☐	☐
without energy	☐	☐	☐	☐	☐	☐
without resources	☐	☐	☐	☐	☐	☐
weak	☐	☐	☐	☐	☐	☐
not depressive	☐	☐	☐	☐	☐	☐
full of life	☐	☐	☐	☐	☐	☐
not anxious	☐	☐	☐	☐	☐	☐
awake	☐	☐	☐	☐	☐	☐

Sources: Koch et al. (2007, 2015).

internal consistency of the entire scale in previous studies was Cronbach's Alpha $\alpha = .63–.91$ (Koch et al., 2007, 2015). In the present study, Cronbach's Alpha was $\alpha = .94$ for T_0 and $\alpha = .93$ for T_1.

Procedure

Participants were recruited at outpatients' facilities, day-care hospitals, and sheltered housing facilities. Patients were randomly allocated to either the treatment or control condition. All patients were informed of their participation in movement therapy either right after the pre-test or later on after the post-test. All participants gave written informed consent.

Patients of the treatment or the control condition answered the *HSI* before and after the movement therapy sessions or before and after the waiting period accordingly. The movement therapy took place in groups of up to 10 participants in the Center for Psychosocial Medicine in Heidelberg, the Psychiatrisches Zentrum Nordbaden (PZN) in Wiesloch, and the Johannes-Diakonie in Mosbach, each over a period of 20 weeks (one session per week, 20 sessions of 90 minutes).

The movement therapy groups were run by three different dance movement therapists (one for each location) and attended by at least one co-therapist/assistant to allow intensive care. The treatment was mainly manualized using the treatment manual *Body Oriented Psychological Therapy for Chronic Schizophrenia* (Röhricht & Papadopoulos, 2010). Some treatment examples can be seen in the Appendix.

Whenever indicated, the therapists carried out context- or disease-specific modifications. The main goals of the treatment manual were:

1. Body-oriented non-verbal interventions with the aim to reconstruct a basic and coherent ego-structure, strengthen self-referential processes and hence ipseity ("mine-ness") as a pre-requisite for safe social interaction;
2. To widen and deepen the range of emotional responses to environmental stimuli – particularly intersubjective ones – on the basis of enhanced contact with one's own bodily reality with physical anchor points in the external world and other participants/therapists.
3. To help patients explore a range of expressive and communicative behaviors (movement and speech) in order to reduce emotional withdrawal and improve affective modulation.

(Röhricht & Papadopoulos, 2010)

After a first session aiming at familiarization among the participants with each other and with the therapeutic elements, the following sessions contained a repetitive structure (opening circle, warm-up section, structured task section, creative movement section, and closing circle/verbal integration). The last session focused on group closure and options for continuing therapy (Röhricht & Papadopoulos, 2010).

Statistical analysis

Statistical analyses were conducted using SPSS Version 21. At first, descriptive data was evaluated. To confirm a successful randomization, baseline measures were compared using an independent samples *t*-test. Statistical hypothesis testing was implemented by computing a mixed-model design ANOVA. The observations at the two different measurement times (T_0 and T_1) formed the two levels on the repeated-measures factor as the within-subjects factor. The group variable (treatment condition vs. control condition) formed the between-subject factor. Main effects and interactions were calculated.

Results

Descriptive statistics

For participants of the control condition, means of well-being measured with the *HSI* almost did not change from pre-test T_0 (M=4.2, SD=.87) to post-test T_1 (M=4.19, SD=.81). In the treatment group, means changed in the hypothesized direction from measurement T_0 (M=3.54, SD=.96) to measurement T_1 (M=4.0, SD=.82). Figure 6.2 illustrates the change of psychological well-being over time in both conditions (treatment vs. control).

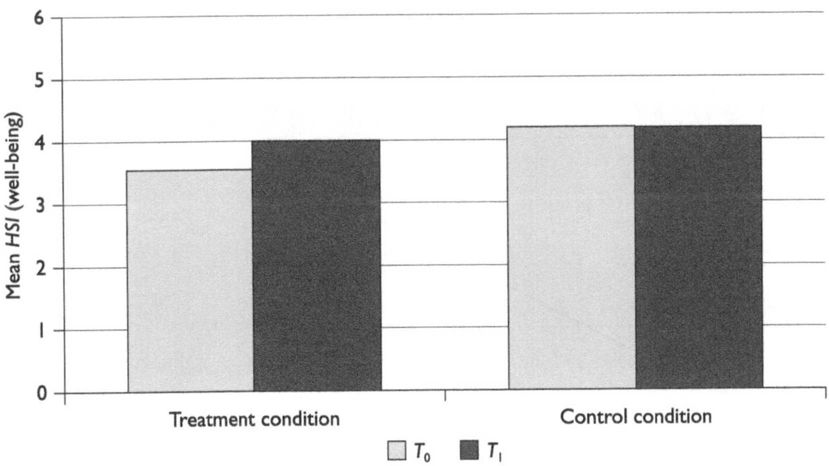

Figure 6.2 Changes of well-being (*HSI*) from measurement time T_0 (pre-test/baseline) to measurement time T_1 (post-test, after movement therapy).

Inferential statistics

The results of the *t*-test comparing the baseline scores yielded no significant differences in well-being at T_0. Multivariate normal distribution and homogeneity of error variances (Levene Test) were confirmed. With only two times of measurement, the assumption of sphericity was also given. Results of the ANOVA revealed a significant main effect of time ($F = 4.98$, $p < .05$) and an interaction effect of time and group ($F = 5.26$, $p < .05$) regarding well-being assessed with the *HSI* with an effect size of $\eta^2 = .13$. For all descriptive and inferential statistics, see Table 6.3. Figure 6.3 illustrates all descriptives and the group × time interaction of the inferential statistics.

Discussion

The aim of the study was to investigate the effects of movement therapy on the psychological well-being of patients with schizophrenia. Three dance movement therapists provided body-oriented psychotherapy (Röhricht & Papadopoulos, 2010) in a multicenter RCT study. Regarding schizophrenia as a self-disorder, methods focused on the reconstruction of a basic and coherent ego-structure, strengthening self-referential processes and therefore ipseity, widening and deepening the range of emotional responses to environmental stimuli, and helping to explore a range of expressive and communicative behaviors (Röhricht & Papadopoulos, 2010). Well-being was operationalized by the *HSI* (Koch et al., 2007, 2015). The analyses revealed a significant group × time interaction in favor of the treatment condition. Psychological well-being of patients in the treatment condition increased

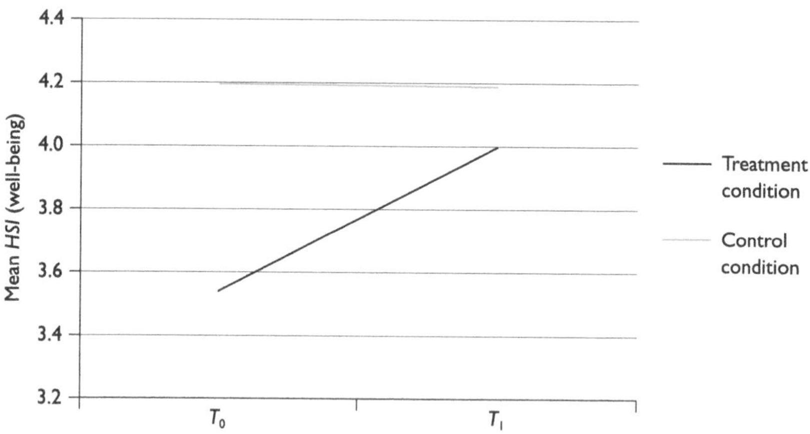

Figure 6.3 Interaction effect group × time from pre-test (T_0) to post-test (T_1) for movement therapy vs. waiting control group; $N = 36$.

Table 6.3 Group differences between treatment and control group ($N = 36$)

Variable	*Group*	*Mean pre*	*Mean post*	SD *pre*	SD *post*	F-*value*		p-*value*		η^2	
						time	*group x time*	*time*	*group x time*	*time*	*group x time*
Psychological well-being assessed with *HSI*	treatment condition ($N = 24$)	3.54	4.0	0.96	0.82	4.98	5.46	0.03*	0.03*	0.13	0.13
	Control condition ($N = 12$)	4.20	4.19	0.87	0.81						

Notes
$N = 36$;
* $p < .05$.

significantly from T_1 to T_2 and differed significantly from the psychological well-being of the control group, which did not change from T_0 to T_1.

In general, new intervention strategies are needed to improve the treatment of schizophrenia because current treatment can only address part of the burden. Recent investigations revealed an effect of body-oriented psychotherapy/dance movement therapy on negative symptoms (Martin et al., 2016; Röhricht & Priebe, 2006). Since subjective well-being is regarded as a relevant outcome measure, quantifying the patient's subjective experience of health, the current findings support the effects of body-oriented interventions for schizophrenia. Mere treatment with medication does not satisfy the idea of the biopsychosocial model and reflects a mostly biomedical pathogenic approach. Biological, psychological, and social aspects should be addressed in treatment as well as in diagnostics.

The results of our study are encouraging. Body-oriented methods improve clinical intervention strategies, and fill a gap toward a more integrative treatment of schizophrenia. Regarding the phenomenological findings of the subjective experience of schizophrenia, they may address unmet needs of the patients. Regarding schizophrenia as a self-disorder characterized by *disembodiment*, dance movement therapy and body-oriented psychotherapy with their interventions on the nonverbal level should be beneficial, complementing cognitive methods, and addressing the characteristics of the aberration of the self.

Further research is needed to determine the underlying factors of the improvement of well-being and to further investigate how embodied therapies could specifically address the unmet needs of schizophrenia patients, which impair their quality of life (Eack et al., 2007). Depressed affect has been shown to play a key role in schizophrenia (Birchwood et al., 2005). From the perspective of embodied affectivity, depression is characterized by a lack of bodily resonance (Fuchs & Koch, 2014). If movement therapy can specifically address the affective dimension of the disorder, this issue needs further exploration. Since negative symptoms were shown to impair well-being by causing a high amount of suffering (Savill et al., 2015), it is likely that a reduction of negative symptoms (Martin et al., 2016; Röhricht & Priebe, 2006) mediates a more favorable psychological state.

Limitations

A number of restrictions of our study should be mentioned. Due to the high number of patient dropouts, only a small sample size ($N=36$) was available for statistical analyses. The dropout rate is attributable to the outpatient setting and to motivational issues related to the disease. Many patients had to travel for a considerable amount of time to reach the location of the therapy, in winter when it was dark outside. In total, we lost about half of the patients. A replication with a bigger sample size could provide validity for the current results.

There is a lot of missing information concerning the psychopharmacological therapy of the participants, which doesn't allow a statement about equal conditions of drug treatment for the two groups compared.

Measuring the momentary state, the *HSI* does not cover a wider timespan and has to be seen as a temporary assessment. Findings therefore could be situational as psychological states can be quite unstable. In order to exclude a limitation to situational aspects and to assume stability of the treatment, it would be preferable to assess well-being in a longitudinal study with more than two times of measurement. Moreover the *HSI* is a self-constructed scale (Koch et al., 2007, 2015). By now it is widely employed, but there has not been a standardization of the instrument.

Conclusion

In conclusion, the current investigation revealed promising findings concerning the effectiveness of dance movement therapy/body-oriented psychotherapy for improving well-being in the treatment of schizophrenia. Besides the benefits of body-oriented interventions regarding negative symptoms (Martin et al., 2016; Röhricht & Priebe, 2006), the current results have a high relevance for understanding and measuring the subjective experience of health. However, further research with a bigger sample size and follow-up measurements is needed to support the findings conclusively. Although it is just one among many methodological possibilities (Koch et al., 2014), randomized controlled trials as employed in the present study are still seen as the gold standard of empirical investigations in clinical contexts and thus contribute to the professionalization of body-oriented therapies and dance movement therapy (Koch & Cruz, 2015). To improve the treatment of schizophrenia, new intervention strategies are needed, particularly for addressing negative symptoms. Embodied therapies can address unmet treatment needs related to affect expression, social interaction, and body distortions in schizophrenia, and promote the development of a more grounded individual and relational self-experience.

Note

1 We would like to thank study therapists Martina Bopp, Ariane Konrad, and Anja Holzinger for their reliability in conducting the movement therapy sessions; Judith Raeke, Laura Mehl, Janna Kelbel, and Christina Gallinat for organizing and coordinating the assessments, data collection, and data entry; Dr. Dusan Hirjak for training and coordination of medical assessments; Laura Galbusera and Max Ludwig for supporting patient access and collection of qualitative data; Lily Martin for corrections; and Rixta Fambach and Waltraud Werkmann for their patience with the turmoil the many helpers of the study sometimes cause in the office. We would like to thank the EU for the Marie Curie ITN grant "TESIS – Toward an Embodied Science of Intersubjectivity" (No. 264828) to Prof. Dr. Thomas Fuchs and Prof. Dr. Ezequiel DiPaolo.

References

Abayomi, O., Amato, D., Bailey, C., Bitanihirwe, B., Bowen, L., Burshtein, S., et al. (2014). The 4th Schizophrenia International Research Society Conference, 5–9 April 2014, Florence, Italy: A summary of topics and trends. *Schizophrenia research, 159*, e1–e22.

ADTA (American Dance Therapy Association). (2015). About dance/movement therapy. Retrieved December 7, 2015 from: www.adta.org/About_DMT.

Andrews, G., Sanderson, K., Corry, J., Issakidis, C., & Lapsley, H. (2003). Cost-effectiveness of current and optimal treatment for schizophrenia. *British Journal of Psychiatry, 183*, 427–435.

Antonovsky, A. (1997). *Salutogenese: Zur Entmystifizierung der Gesundheit.* Deutsche erweiterte Herausgabe von A. Franke. Tübingen: DGVT-Verlag.

Arango, C., Buchanan, R. W., Kirkpatrick, B., & Carpenter, W. T. (2004). The deficit syndrome in schizophrenia: Implications for the treatment of negative symptoms. *European Psychiatry, 19*, 21–26.

Barnes, T., & the Schizophrenia Consensus Group of the British Association for Psychopharmacology. (2011). Evidence-based guidelines for the pharmacological treatment of schizophrenia: Recommendations from the British Association for Psychopharmacology. *Journal of Psychopharmacology, 25*(5), 567–620.

Barsalou, L. W. (2008). Grounded cognition. *Annual Review Of Psychology, 59*, 617–645.

Birchwood, M. (2003). Editorial: Pathways to emotional dysfunction in psychosis. *The British Journal of Psychiatry, 182*, 373–375.

Birchwood, M., Iqbal, Z., & Upthegrove, R. (2005). Psychological pathways to depression in schizophrenia: Studies in acute psychosis, post psychotic depression and auditory hallucinations. *European Archives of Psychiatry and Clinical Neuroscience, 255*, 202–212.

Blankenburg, W. (1971). *Der Verlust der natürlichen Selbstverständlichkeit: ein Beitrag zur Psychopathologie symptomarmer Schizophrenien.* Stuttgart: Enke.

Buchanan, R. W., & Carpenter, W. T. (1994). Domains of psychopathology: An approach to the reduction of heterogeneity in schizophrenia. *The Journal of Nervous and Mental Disease, 182*(4), 193–204.

Buchanan, R. W., Kreyenbuhl, J., Kelly, D. L., Noel, J. M., Boggs, D. L., Fischer, B. A., et al. (2010). The 2009 schizophrenia PORT psychopharmacological treatment recommendations and summary statements. *Schizophrenia Bulletin, 36*(1), 71–93.

Cacioppo, J. T., Priester, J. R., & Berntson, G. G. (1993). Rudimentary determinants of attitudes: II. Arm flexion and extension have differential effects on attitudes. *Journal of Personality and Social Psychology, 65*(1), 5–17.

Caldwell, C. (2006). Bewegung als Psychotherapie und in der Psychotherapie. In G. Marlock & H. Weiss (Eds.), *Handbuch der Körperpsychotherapie* (pp. 430–441). Stuttgart: Schattauer.

Caldwell, C. (2012). Sensation, movement, and emotion: Explicit procedures for implicit memories. In S. C. Koch, T. Fuchs, M. Summa, & C. Müller (Eds.), *Body memory, metaphor and movement* (pp. 255–265). Amsterdam: John Benjamins.

Chida, Y., & Steptoe, A. (2008). Positive psychological well-being and mortality: A quantitative review of prospective observational studies. *Psychosomatic Medicine, 70*(7), 741–756.

Chien, W. T., Leung, S. F., Yeung, F. K., & Wong, W. K. (2013). Current approaches to treatments for schizophrenia spectrum disorders, part II: Psychosocial interventions and patient focused perspectives in psychiatric care. *Neuropsychiatric Disease and Treatment, 9*, 1463–1481.

Chue, P., & Lalonde, J. K. (2014). Addressing the unmet needs of patients with persistent negative symptoms of schizophrenia: Emerging pharmacological treatment options. *Neuropsychiatric Disease and Treatment, 10*, 777–789.

Clark, A. (1997). *Being there: Putting brain, body and world together again*. Cambridge, MA: MIT Press.

Dawson, M. R. W. (2002). From embodied cognitive science to synthetic psychology. In Y. Wang, R. H. Johnston, & M. R. Smith (Eds.), *Proceedings of the first IEEE International Conference on Cognitive Informatics (ICCI'02)* (pp. 13–22). Los Alamitos, CA: IEEE Computer Society.

Diener, E., & Ryan, K. (2009). Subjective well-being: A general overview. *South African Journal of Psychology, 39*(4), 391–406.

Eack, S. M., Newhill, C. E., Anderson, C. M., & Rotondi, A. J. (2007). Quality of life for persons with schizophrenia: More than just symptoms. *Psychiatric Rehabilitation, 30*(3), 219–222.

Engel, G. L. (1977). The need for a new medical model: A challenge for biomedicine. *Science, 8*, 129–136.

Fleischhacker, W. W., Arango, C., Arteel, P., Barnes, T. R. E., Carpenter, W., Duckworth, K., et al. (2014). Schizophrenia: Time to commit to policy change. *Schizophrenia Bulletin, 40*(3), 165–194.

Fleischhacker, W. W., Rabinowitz, J., Kemmler, G., Eerdekens, M., & Meehnert, A. (2005). Perceived functioning, well-being and psychiatric symptoms in patients with stable schizophrenia treated with long-acting risperidone for 1 year. *The British Journal of Psychiatry, 187*(2), 131–136.

Fuchs, T. (2000). *Psychopathologie von Leib und Raum: Phänomenologisch-empirische Untersuchungen zu depressiven und paranoiden Erkrankungen*. Darmstadt: Steinkopf.

Fuchs, T. (2005). Corporealized and disembodied minds: A phenomenological view of the body in melancholia and schizophrenia. *Philosophy, Psychiatry, & Psychology, 12*, 95–107.

Fuchs, T. (2008). Leibgedächtnis und Unbewusstes: Zur Phänomenologie der Selbstverborgenheit. *Psycho-Logik. Jahrbuch für Psychotherapie, Philosophie und Kultur, 3*, 33–50.

Fuchs, T. (2009). Embodied cognitive neuroscience and its consequences for psychiatry. *Poiesis and Praxis, 6*, 219–233.

Fuchs, T. (2012). Selbst und Schizophrenie. *Deutsche Zeitschrift für Philosophie, 60*, 887–901.

Fuchs, T. (2014). Verkörperte Emotionen: Wie Gefühl und Leib zusammenhängen. *Psychologische Medizin, 25*(1), 13–20.

Fuchs, T., & Koch, S. (2014). Embodied affectivity: On moving and being moved. *Frontiers in Psychology* [online]. Retrieved March 21, 2016 from: http://dx.doi.org/10.3389/fpsyg.2014.00508.

Fuchs, T., & Schlimme, J. (2009). Embodiment and psychopathology: A phenomenological perspective. *Current Opinion in Psychiatry, 22*, 570–575.

Geuter, U. (2006). Geschichte der Körperpsychotherapie. In G. Marlock & H. Weiss (Eds.), *Handbuch der Körperpsychotherapie* (pp. 17–32). Stuttgart: Schattauer,

Goodill, S. W. (2005). *An introduction to medical dance/movement therapy: Health care in motion*. Philadelphia, PA: Jessica Kingsley.

Häfner, H., Maurer, K., Löffler, W., van der Heiden, W., Munk-Jørgensen, P., Hambrecht, M., & Riecher-Roessler, A. (1998). The ABC schizophrenia study: A preliminary overview of the results. *Social Psychiatry and Psychiatric Epidemiology, 33*, 380–386.

Haro, J. M., Kamath, S. A., Ochoa, S., Novick, D., Rele, K., Fargas, A., Rodriguez, M. J., et al. (2003). The Clinical Global Impression–Schizophrenia Scale: A simple instrument to measure the diversity of symptoms present in schizophrenia. *Acta Psychiatrica Scandinavica, 416*, 16–23.

Hartung, S. (2011). Was hält uns gesund? Gesundheitsressourcen: Von der Salutogenese zum Sozialkapital. In T. Schott & C. Hornberg (Eds.), *Die Gesellschaft und ihre Gesundheit* (pp. 235–255). Wiesbaden: VS Verlag für Sozialwissenschaften.

Hauk, O., Johnsrude, I., & Pulvermüller, F. (2004). Somatotopic representation of action words in human motor and premotor cortex. *Neuron, 41*, 301–307.

Havas, D. A., Glenberg, A. M., Gutowski, K. A., Lucarelli, M. J., & Davidson, R. J. (2010). Cosmetic use of botulinum toxin affects processing of emotional language. *Psychological Science, 21*(7), 895–900.

Hirjak, D., Breyer, T., Thomann, P. A., & Fuchs, T. (2013). Disturbance of intentionality: A phenomenological study of body-affecting first-rank symptoms in schizophrenia. *PLOS ONE, 8*, e73662.

Hopper, K., Harrison, G., Janca, A., & Sartorius, N. (2007). *Recovery from schizophrenia: An international perspective – A report from the WHO collaborative project, the International Study of Schizophrenia*. Oxford: Oxford University Press.

Kafka, G. (1950). Über Uraffekte. *Acta Psychologica, 7*, 256–278.

Kasckow, J., Felmet, K., & Zisook, S. (2011). Managing suicide risk in patients with schizophrenia. *CSN Drugs, 25*(2), 129–143.

Koch, S. (2014). Rhythm is it: Effects of dynamic body feedback on affect and attitudes. *Frontiers in Psychology* [online]. Retrieved March 21, 2016 from: http://dx.doi.org/10.3389/fpsyg.2014.00537.

Koch, S. C., Caldwell, C. & Fuchs, T. (2014). On body memory and embodied therapy. *Body, Movement and Dance in Psychotherapy: An International Journal for Theory, Research and Practice, 8*, 82–94.

Koch, S. C., & Cruz, R. F. (2015). Reading and evaluating quantitative research in body psychotherapy. *International Body Psychotherapy Journal, 14*(1), 10–19.

Koch, S. C., & Eberhard-Kaechele, M. (2015). Wirkfaktoren der Tanztherapie. Replik auf Tschacher, Munt und Storch [online]. Retrieved March 21, 2016 from: www.researchgate.net/publication/272892640_Wirkfaktoren_der_Tanztherapie.

Koch, S. C., Fuchs, T., Summa, M., & Müller, C. (2012). *Body memory, metaphor and movement*. Philadelphia, PA: John Benjamins.

Koch, S. C., Jünger, J., Kelbel, J., Kolter, A., Sattel, H., & Fuchs, T. (2016). (Dis-) embodiment in schizophrenia: Effects of mirroring on self-experience, empathy, and wellbeing in a pilot study. In S. Oliver, V. Karkou, & S. Lycouris (Eds.), *The Oxford handbook of dance and wellbeing*. Oxford: Oxford University Press.

Koch, S. C., Kunz, T., Lykou, S., & Cruz, R. F. (2014). Effects of dance movement therapy and dance on health-related psychological outcomes: A meta-analysis. *The Arts in Psychotherapy, 41*, 46–64.

Koch, S. C., Mehl, L., Sobanski, E., Sieber, M., & Fuchs, T. (2015). Fixing the mirrors: A feasibility study of the effects of dance movement therapy on young adults with Autism Spectrum Disorder. *Autism, 19*(3), 338–350.

Koch, S. C., Morlinghaus, K., & Fuchs, T. (2007). The joy dance: Effects of a single dance intervention on patients with depression. *The Arts in Psychotherapy, 34*, 340–349.

Koch, S. C., Ostermann, T., Steinhage, A., Kende, P., Haller, K., & Chyle, F. (2015). Breaking barriers: Evaluating an arts-based emotion regulation training in prison. *The Arts in Psychotherapy, 42*, 41–49.

Lakoff, G., & Johnson, M. (1999). *Philosophy in the flesh: The embodied mind and its challenge to Western thought*. New York: Basic Books.

Lally, J., & McCabe, J. H. (2015). Antipsychotic medication in schizophrenia: A review. *British Medical Bulletin, 114*, 169–179.

Lambert, M., Naber, D., Schacht, A., Wagner, T., Hundemer, H.-P., Karow, A., et al. (2008). Rates and predictors of remission and recovery during 3 years in 392 never-treated patients with schizophrenia. *Acta Psychiatrica Scandinavica, 118*, 220–229.

Lee, H.-J., Jang, S.-H., Lee, S.-Y., & Hwang, K.-S. (2015). Effectiveness of dance/movement therapy on affect and psychotic symptoms in patients with schizophrenia. *The Arts in Psychotherapy, 45*, 64–68.

Loew, T., Tritt, K., Lahmann, C., & Röhricht, F. (2006). Körperpsychotherapien – wissenschaftlich begründet? Eine Übersicht über empirisch evaluierte Körperpsychotherapieverfahren. *Psychodynamische Psychotherapie, 5*, 6–19.

Lysaker, P. H., & Lysaker, J. T. (2010). Schizophrenia and alterations in self-experience: A comparison of 6 perspectives. *Schizophrenia Bulletin, 36*(2), 331–340.

Marlock, G., & Weiss, H. (2006). Einführung: Das Spektrum der Körperpsychotherapie. In G. Marlock & H. Weiss (Eds.), *Handbuch der Körperpsychotherapie* (pp. 1–16). Stuttgart: Schattauer.

Martin, L., Koch, S. C., Hirjak, D., & T. Fuchs (2016). Overcoming disembodiment: The effect of movement therapy on negative symptoms in schizophrenia – A multicenter randomized controlled trial. *Frontiers in Psychology* [online]. Retrieved April 10, 2016 from: http://journal.frontiersin.org/article/10.3389/fpsyg.2016.00483/full#.

Mauriño, J., Sanjúan, J., Haro, J. M., Díez, T., & Ballesteros, J. (2011). Impact of depressive symptoms on subjective well-being: The importance of patient-reported outcomes in schizophrenia. *Patient Preference and Adherence, 5*, 471–474.

McGorry, P. D., Bell, R. C., Dudgeon, P. L., & Jackson, H. J. (1998). The dimensional structure of first episode psychosis: An exploratory factor analysis. *Psychological Medicine, 28*, 935–947.

Merleau-Ponty, M. (1966). Phänomenologie der Wahrnehmung. In C. F. Graumann & J. Linschoten (Eds.), *Phänomenologisch-Psychologische Forschungen* (pp. 75–518). Berlin: de Gruyter.

Michalak, J., Mischnat, J., & Teismann, T. (2014). Sitting posture makes a difference: Embodiment effects on depressive memory bias. *Clinical Psychology and Psychotherapy, 21*, 519–524.

Möller, H.-J. (2003). Antipsychotische Wirksamkeit des atypischen Neuroleptikums Amisulprid auf Positiv- und Negativsymptomatik. In H. Hippius (Ed.), *Universitätskolloquien zur Schizophrenie* (pp. 293–313). Darmstadt: Steinkopff.

Murray, C. J., & Lopez, A. D. (1997). Global mortality, disability, and the contribution of risk factors: Global burden of disease study. *The Lancet, 349*, 1436–1442.

Naber, D., Moritz, S., Lambert, M., Rajonk, F., Holzbach, R., Mass, R., et al. (2001). Improvement of schizophrenic patients' subjective well-being under atypical antipsychotic drugs. *Schizophrenia Research, 50*, 79–88.

Nelson, B., Parnas, J., & Sass, L. A. (2014). Disturbance of minimal self (ipseity) in schizophrenia: Clarification and current status. *Schizophrenia Bulletin, 40*, 479–482.

Niedenthal, P. M., Barsalou, L. W., Winkielman, P., Krauth-Gruber, S., & Ric, F. (2005). Embodiment in attitudes, social perception, and emotion. *Personality and Social Psychology Review, 9*, 184–211.

Novick, D., Haro, J. M., Suarez, D., Vieta, E., & Naber, D. (2008). Recovery in the outpatient setting: 36-month results from the Schizophrenia Outpatients Health Outcome (SOHO) study. *Schizophrenia Research, 108*, 223–230.

Payne, H. (2006). Tracking the web of interconnectivity. *Body, Movement and Dance in Psychotherapy, 1*(1), 7–15.

Priebe, S., & Röhricht, F. (2001). Specific body image pathology in acute schizophrenia. *Psychiatry Research, 101*, 289–301.

Ramseyer, F., & Tschacher, W. (2011). Nonverbal synchrony in psychotherapy: Coordinated body movement reflects relationship quality and outcome. *Journal of Consulting and Clinical Psychology, 79*, 284–295.

Riskind, J. H. (1984). They stoop to conquer: Guiding and self-regulatory functions of physical posture after success and failure. *Journal of Personality and Social Psychology, 47*, 479–493.

Röhricht, F., & Papadopoulos, N. (2010). *A treatment manual: Body oriented psychological therapy for chronic schizophrenia*. London: Newham Centre for Mental Health.

Röhricht, F., Papadopoulos, N., Holden, S., Clarke, T., & Priebe, S. (2011). Clinical effectiveness and therapeutic processes of body psychotherapy in chronic schizophrenia: An open clinical trial. *The Arts in Psychotherapy, 38*, 196–203.

Röhricht, F., Papadopoulos, N., Suzuki, I., & Priebe, S. (2009). Ego-pathology, body experience. *Psychology and Psychotherapy, 82*(1), 19–30.

Röhricht, F., & Priebe, S. (2006). Effect of body-oriented psychological therapy on negative symptoms in schizophrenia: A randomized controlled trial. *Psychological Medicine, 36*, 669–678.

Rössler, W., Salize, H. J., van Os, J., & Riecher-Rössler, A. (2005). Size of burden of schizophrenia and psychotic disorders. *European Neuropsychopharmacology, 15*, 399–409.

Sartory, G. (2007). *Schizophrenie: Empirische Befunde und Behandlungsansätze*. Heidelberg: Spektrum-Elsevier.

Sass, L. A., & Parnas, J. (2003). Schizophrenia, consciousness, and the self. *Schizophrenia Bulletin, 29*(3), 427–444.

Savill, M., Banks, C., Khanom, H., & Priebe, S. (2015). Do negative symptoms of schizophrenia change over time? A meta-analysis of longitudinal data. *Psychological Medicine, 45*(8), 1613–1627.

Singer, S., & Brähler, E. (2007). *Die "Sense of Coherence Scale": Testhandbuch zur deutschen Version*. Göttingen: Vandenhoeck & Ruprecht.

Smith, L. B. (2005). Cognition as a dynamic system: Principles from embodiment. *Developmental Review, 25*(3–4), 278–298.

Sobel, D. S. (1994). Rethinking medicine: Improving health outcomes with cost-effective psychosocial interventions. *Psychosomatic Medicine, 57*, 234–244.
Stanghellini, G. (2004). *Disembodied spirits and deanimated bodies: The psychopathology of common sense*. Oxford: Oxford University Press.
Strack, F., Martin, L. L., & Stepper, S. (1988). Inhibiting and facilitating conditions of the human smile: A nonobtrusive test of the facial feedback hypothesis. *Journal of Personality and Social Psychology, 54*(5), 768–777.
Strauss, J. S., Carpenter, W. T., & Bartko, J. J. (1974). The diagnosis and understanding of schizophrenia: Part III. Speculations in the processes that underlie schizophrenic symptoms and signs. *Schizophrenia Bulletin, 1*, 61–69.
Thakkar, K. N., Nichols, H. S., McIntosh, L. G., & Park, S. (2011). Disturbances in body ownership in schizophrenia: Evidence from the rubber hand illusion and case study of a spontaneous out-of-body experience. *PLoS ONE*. Retrieved March 21, 2016 from: http://journals.plos.org/plosone/article?id=10.1371/journal.pone.0027089.
Tschacher, W., & Storch, M. (2012). Die Bedeutung von Embodiment für Psychologie und Psychotherapie. *Psychotherapie, 17*(2), 259–267.
van Os, J., Gilvarry, C., Bale, R., van Horn, E., Tattan, T., White, I., & Murray, R. (1999). A comparison of the utility of dimensional and categorical representations of psychosis. *Psychological Medicine, 29*, 595–606.
Varela, F. J., Thompson, E., & Rosch, E. (1991). *The embodied mind: Cognitive science and human experience*. Cambridge, MA: MIT Press.
Wikman, A., Wardle, J., & Steptoe, A. (2011). Quality of life and affective well-being in middle-aged and older people with chronic medical illnesses: A cross-sectional population pased study. *PLoS One*. Retrieved March 21, 2016 from: http://journals.plos.org/plosone/article?id=10.1371/journal.pone.0018952.
Willke, E. (1991). *Tanztherapie – Theorie und Praxis. Ein Handbuch*. Paderborn: Junfermann.
Wilson, M. (2002). Six views of embodied cognition. *Psychonomic Bulletin & Review, 9*(4), 625–636.
Windell, D. M., Norman, R., Lal, S., & Malla, A. (2015). Subjective experiences of illness recovery in individuals treated for first-episode psychosis. *Social Psychiatry and Psychiatric Epidemiology, 50*, 1069–1077.
World Health Organization. (1946). *Constitution of the World Health Organization*. Retrieved September 27, 2017 from: www.who.int/governance/eb/who_constitution_en.pdf.
Xia, J., & Grant, T. J. (2009). Dance Therapy for Schizophrenia (review). *The Cochrane Library*. Retrieved March 21, 2016 from: http://onlinelibrary.wiley.com/doi/10.1002/14651858.CD006868.pub2/abstract.

Appendix

Some examples of interventions – excerpts from *A Treatment Manual: Body Oriented Psychological Therapy for Chronic Schizophrenia* (Röhricht & Papadopoulos, 2010).

1 An excerpt from "The opening cycle: focusing on body-self and engagement"

3.2.1 Introduction to sessions including function of the group

Each group begins with a ceremonial/ritual activity to demarcate the transition from the ordinary everyday world into the therapeutic space. Participants are asked to take off their shoes and to sit in a circle either on chairs or on the floor. The group starts with an opening "ceremony", allowing each individual participant to settle safely within the physical and social environment. In the first session the therapist will explain some basic principles of the therapeutic intervention, introduce rules and give very simple and clear instructions. At this stage of the group the therapist is as re-assuring as possible.

2 Excerpts from "Warm up and grounding: techniques to promote self-awareness, emotional stimulation and reality-testing through the body"

3.3.3 Self-explorage of body surface

Participants explore in a number of direct physical ways the actual boundaries and surfaces of their own body; this is achieved through gentle tapping with the hands or more powerful clapping against the different parts of the body. This exercise is sometimes extended to include quite strong tapping against the chest with an accompanying voicing of the breath. Additionally, "bean bags" are used to add weight to specific body parts as well as to tap against body parts to bring attention through visual, auditory and sensory stimuli. Verbalizations regarding the quality of the physical sensation, the experience of body/skin boundaries and body dimensions in space are encouraged throughout whilst the therapist may draw specific attention of individuals to their observed reactions.

3.3.6 Exploring natural rhythms

Pulse, breathing and rhythm also play a fundamental part in the warm-up. In addition to attending to breathing rhythms, participants may be asked to clap or walk the rhythm of their own heart beat, and experience the tempo of other group members' pulse rhythms.

As the treatment program progresses a fuller range of warm-up activities are included in the sessions.

3 An excerpt from "Structured tasks: strategies to address dysfunctional self-regulation and body image aberration"

3.4.2 Ipseity/mine-ness, social withdrawal

A range of mirroring techniques is used in this part of the session to strengthen the sense of self, and more specifically to demarcate where "I" end and the "other" begins. Mirroring can be limited to gestures, or posture and gestures, or it can also include locomotion of the whole body. Empathy can be stimulated through the mirroring exercises.

Examples: Participants are asked to pair up and face each other. One person (A) will take the lead and the other (B) will follow. First A improvises a movement phrase with or without music, either staying stationary and moving with gestures in one's own kineasphere, or travelling from one place in the room to another, and B attempts to mirror this movement as precisely as possible. Later the leadership is transferred from A to B. Variations on dyad mirroring include group mirroring based on free improvisations or themes such as sporting gestures. Here, one member of the group will suggest a movement pattern such as the serving action in a game of tennis and the other group members will mirror it; each person in the group will have an opportunity to take the lead and share a movement pattern that they create. This can be done with or without music.

4 An excerpt from "Creative movements: expressing emotions, working with self-potentials"

- Creative mirroring to a diverse range of music (according to individual preferences, patients are encouraged to bring their own music to sessions).
- Creating a group collage: one at a time and without discussion each member is invited to add material (e.g. cloths, feathers, balls etc.) to create a group image on the floor. This is followed by a discussion in which each participant would say something about how they saw the

image evolving, what they "saw" as the final image or theme and how it felt to have their contributions altered or added to by the other members.

- Encouraging creative movement with different effort qualities
- Exploring states: two efforts together, i.e. awake/dream…

5 An excerpt from "The closing cycle: verbalization and integration of experiences"

Finally, in this part of the session participants are being supported to gradually disengage from the group process and each other and return to themselves. Usually specific body-oriented exercises are suggested including guided relaxation, self massage, deep breathing, polarity exercises. In addition in the closing circle participants are encouraged to reflect on all the events of the group including the aspects that they have enjoyed and those that they have found difficult. This includes reflection on individual problems in relation to the various areas of psychopathology, depending on group dynamics and introspective abilities of participants. Group members are informed that this feedback is important in the planning of future sessions so that they can begin to take some responsibility for the contents of the sessions.

Chapter 7

Adapting Winnicott's squiggle technique in group art therapy to a psychotic population undergoing a psychosocial rehabilitation programme

Alice Reid

Introduction

To understand the scope of this study fully, it is important to clarify the context in which this experiment took place before describing its protocol and results.

This research was carried out to prepare a dissertation in order to complete a master's degree in clinical psychology. Students were required to demonstrate that they were able to conduct an innovative experiment that could raise new questions in a given field. Therefore, the researcher (myself) at that time was a graduate student intern. However, in preparing my master's dissertation, I was rigorously supervised by Elizabeth Stone, art therapist and psychoanalyst, whose advice strongly influenced the way the experiment was conceived and conducted.

We initially wished to work on the link between depression and creativity. We wondered whether the creative process could boost a depressed patient's vital energy and help the patient to understand his or her pathology and whether depression necessarily implied the impossibility of being involved in a creative process. We intended to use several forms of mediation to compare them, but one procedure was particularly intriguing: Donald Woods Winnicott's Squiggle game. While the materials are easily accessible and the instructions are simple to understand, the squiggle and scribble techniques are known to be very useful tools that can serve different purposes in art classes, psychotherapy and art therapy. Not only do they encourage the release of spontaneous imagery, thereby enabling creativity and unconscious contents to be expressed, they can also play an important role in the early stages of a diagnosis and the building of a therapeutic relationship. We therefore decided to determine whether the squiggle was a useful tool to help depressed patients connect with their creative process.

As we already had access to a psychotic population undergoing a rehabilitation programme having been there as an intern, we decided to adapt the experiment to this population. Our goal was to show that even when using a "regressive tool" such as the squiggle, cognitive and social skills can be improved and a sense of self strengthened.

What was particularly attractive about the squiggle technique was its analogy with problem solving. The same squiggle can suggest many answers and many ways of using it: some subjects might add only a few elements to it, others might add many more features to make it part of a bigger picture, whereas others might use only one part or a few parts of the squiggle. It had to be versatile enough for each person to react differently to it and to solve it in his or her own way. Fostering a patient's ability to solve problems is central in psychosocial rehabilitation. Once the patients return to living outside hospital again, it is important for them to recover as much autonomy as possible. Artwork in general is a great tool for practising different ways of solving a problem rather than enacting them prematurely in real life. The squiggle demands of the subject an ability to mentally perceive answers that could adapt to the lines. This type of exercise requires flexibility and alternative thinking, two abilities that are sometimes fraught with difficulty in psychotic patients.

Another dimension upon which the use of the squiggle can shed light is self-cohesion. It can be challenging to use the different parts of a continuous squiggle but it can be even more challenging to use different parts of a discontinuous squiggle. Both continuous and discontinuous squiggles can help a therapist to measure a subject's degree of cohesion in the way he organizes his drawing and in the words he uses to talk about it.

Moreover, as patients undergoing a rehabilitation programme can sometimes still be fragile, paranoid and inhibited, the squiggle seemed to be an appropriate means to encourage playfulness among subjects. It allowed them to express themselves without feeling directly exposed to external judgement. Random line(s) on a blank page ready to be completed constituted a form of mediation which was both a constraint and an opportunity for free expression. When a subject wonders what a given squiggle might represent, a minimum of tolerable frustration would incite the subject to look for answers. At the same time, the stimulus-squiggle mustn't hint at a sole solution. It must be neutral and vague enough to evoke personal and subjective associations. If the squiggle is challenging enough but not too limited in its suggestions or not unsolvable, play is likely to be observed. A patient's ability to play is a strong indication that he or she feels safe in engaging in a therapeutic process and in self-exploration.

One illustration of this is pioneering American art therapist Elinor Ulman's "joint family scribble," a technique that encourages family members to complete their own individual scribbles before completing a scribble together as a group (Ulman, 1975). In her practice, she observed that parents who thought they wouldn't enjoy drawing were sometimes more enthusiastic than they expected to be. They felt less shame and guilt drawing images that showed affect often socially repressed. The fact that they were asked to draw starting from tangled lines helped to reduce the feeling of being responsible for the imagery and affect that emerged. The focus was not on the choice of imagery or on its conscious or unconscious meaning but on how to make something from/with the squiggle ("What could it be?"). Moreover, the perceived pressure to produce something aesthetically pleasing or "correctly drawn" was usually diminished by techniques such as the squiggle and scribble because the hazardous lines often implied a necessary distortion of what the patients chose to draw. The patient did not feel that having artistic skills was necessary to complete a squiggle. Overall, one of the advantages of the squiggle was that inhibitions were removed, which helped to create a favourable environment for more open discussion.

Our focus

All these attributes of the squiggle technique led us to think that the squiggle could be an appropriate therapeutic means to create a secure environment to study whether greater flexibility, adaptation and self-cohesion could result. Why focus on these three dimensions? First, because enhancing problem-solving capacities and adaptation abilities are central in a rehabilitation programme. The patients are meant to recover and develop skills that will be useful in everyday life when they are living on their own again. Facing problems alone and adapting to the constraints of the outer world are daily preoccupations. However, many experiments (such as those referred to below) have shown that psychotic patients lack cognitive flexibility, a mental ability crucial to problem solving and adaptation. Flexibility implies finding a new solution adapted to a problem that was previously thought unsolvable. In 2004, Daniel Freeman conducted an experiment in which he concluded that psychotic patients with delusional disorders had difficulty in finding alternative solutions to their thoughts and problems (Freeman et al., 2004). Moreover, Moez Bejaoui and Jean-Louis Pedinielli also carried out an experiment showing that some symptoms in schizophrenia were linked to a deficit in task switching (Bejaoui & Pedinielli, 2010). Therefore, it is essential to help a patient change his strategies to find another one more adapted to a given situation. As for self-cohesion, in psychosis and particularly in schizophrenia, a disorganized self can be observed through a disordered speech, jumbled thoughts and incoherencies between affects and behaviours. The lack of a unified sense of self is at the root of extreme anxieties (such as fear of annihilation or fragmentation) and often results in the impossibility of expressing oneself and communicating as one would wish to.

Our group adaptation of the squiggle technique: methodology

To specifically try to improve adaptation, flexibility and self-cohesion using the squiggle technique, we imagined a way of adapting it to a group by inventing a particular system: Before each session, three or four different members (subjects of the group and supervisors) would design a squiggle for the group. We made sure that different types of squiggles were drawn (some with curves, some with dots, some with straight lines and some that mixed all three) so that each participant wouldn't remain stuck on one squiggle. They could choose to complete the ones that seemed the most appealing. Three or four different types of squiggles were then photocopied on thick paper and given to all the members of the group. The subjects were then allowed 40 minutes to complete as many "ready-made" squiggles as they wished using various materials. The squiggles that were finished were then posted on a wall and each subject was invited to discuss his or her squiggles. The discussion also lasted 40 minutes. In short, the technique chosen was to give the same squiggles to all the members of the group. The next step was to discuss what each subject "saw" in the squiggle and how he or she proceeded to solve it. We thought this method could be interesting for several reasons: First, because we thought it could help the subjects to realize that many solutions could be found to the same problem. This could therefore increase alternative thinking. Second, we hoped that starting each session with the common goal of solving the same problem could help create bonds among the group members. We also wondered if it would help to reinforce a sense of agency, as a patient might think or say, "This is how I dealt with the problem." Similarly, we wondered if it would help to reinforce a sense of relatedness, such as interest in each other's work; a patient might think or say, "How did you solve the problem? What did you imagine?" Moreover, according to Elizabeth Stone, creating individually in a group is an effective way to work on boundaries ("What belongs to me? To you? To the group?") (Elizabeth Stone, personal communication). Many people asked us why we didn't choose to make all the subjects work on the same squiggle together. We had decided not to because inner/outer world boundaries in psychosis are usually fragile and paranoid subjects could have felt intruded upon or could have had the impression that they didn't have enough space for their own individual expression. At the end of the experiment when we asked the subjects what they had thought of proceeding that way and if they would have liked to all work together on a mural squiggle, for example, all of them said that they had enjoyed working on their own squiggle and were pleased to share what they had to say about it. Only one subject said he would also have felt comfortable working with other members of the group. Furthermore, our method encouraged the participants to talk about themselves (or talk about their creation) to a group that demanded many social and communicative skills, abilities that were targeted in psychosocial rehabilitation programmes. The possibility of performing a creative act on one's own and then sharing the creation with a group is a particularly efficient way to become aware of one's sense of self through the graphic organization of the drawing (how the subject used the different parts of the squiggle). The links the participants made between the product, process and themselves served to strengthen sense of self, leading to a feeling of self-cohesion.

Goals of the experiment

Many interesting hypotheses could have been posited by our group adaptation of the squiggle technique, but as narrowing down the focus of our study was necessary, we chose to concentrate on the following main question: *Is this group adaptation of the squiggle technique a therapeutic tool and can it be a relevant tool in a psychosocial rehabilitation programme?*

The two main working hypotheses on which we based our study were as follows:

Hypothesis number 1: This group adaptation of the squiggle technique enables participants to gain cognitive flexibility needed when facing situations that require adaptation or problem solving.

Sub-hypothesis 1.1: We expect to observe an improvement in the ability to give several answers to the same problem (to improve alternative thinking).

Sub-hypothesis 1.2: We expect to observe diversity in the ways used to solve or adapt to a problem.

Hypothesis number 2: This group adaptation of the squiggle technique strengthens self-cohesion. This phenomenon can be observed via:

Sub-hypothesis 2.1: An enhancement of graphic cohesion (how the different parts of a squiggle interact together).

Sub-hypothesis 2.1: An enhancement of the level of verbal symbolization that is attributed to elaboration of content within the product.

Sub-hypothesis 2.3: Both previous dimensions interact together: When graphic cohesion improves, verbal symbolization improves.

We will now describe how we proceeded to validate (or not) these hypotheses.

Description of the experiment

The study took place in a psychiatric hospital. The experiment was open to all the inpatients and outpatients (living in a home or living on their own) who were part of a psychosocial rehabilitation programme. Age and gender were not controlled. Even though the goal of this study was to focus on the enhancement of capacities and characteristics that are particularly fragile in schizophrenia, subjects with other mental disorders were invited to participate in the squiggle group too. The choice of a wider spectrum of mental disorders enabled us to have a more extensive view of the impact of the squiggle technique in a psychiatric field. However, the group was open chiefly to schizophrenic patients (diagnosed according to DSM-IV) who had experienced or who still experienced hallucinations, delusions and disorganized speech and thoughts. To be selected for the experiment the subjects had to be patients who needed to or wanted to work on one or several of the following capacities: flexibility, fluidity (in thought processing) and insight. We wished to recruit participants who were attracted by the prospect of working with art materials and were willing to work in a group (as many had already been overwhelmed with art workshops and some were too paranoid or were uneasy about sharing their artwork in a group).

As most patients had already tried free drawing workshops, they found the concept of the squiggle group innovative and interesting. Unfortunately, many of them had other groups on the same day. After several explanations of what the group would involve, 10 subjects agreed to participate and signed a consent form. However, the final results took into account the data covering nine subjects as one subject left the rehabilitation centre. To be able to interpret the results, the subjects needed to have taken part in at least five squiggle sessions and both (before and after squiggle group) test sessions. As the conditions would not have been optimal in a group of 10 (there would have been neither enough space nor enough time for all the subjects to express themselves), we divided the group in two: a subgroup of six subjects with sessions held in the activities room of the home where they lived and another group of four subjects with sessions that took place in an activities room in the main hospital. The division of the subjects was as shown in Table 7.1 (the names and ages have been changed).

The experiment took place as follows: First, a meeting was arranged in which various aspects of the study were explained. The subjects interested in participating in the squiggle group were interviewed individually to discuss their specific goals and motivations. Once the consent forms were signed, a first test session was organized with the whole group. Two exercises were given:

- A free drawing task to observe how each of them reacted to a blank page and how they reacted to art materials.

Table 7.1 Division of the groups and presentation of the subjects according to their age, diagnosis and their place of residence

Home group			*Hospital group*			
Name	*Age*	*Diagnosis*	*Name*	*Age*	*Diagnosis*	*In/out patient*
Kieran	21	Schizophrenia	Nathan	31	ASD	Outpatient
Tommy	25	Schizophrenia	Jeremy	28	ASD	Inpatient
Alan	40	ASD	Vincent	56	Schizophrenia	Inpatient slowly integrating
Outpatient unit						
Fanny	41	Bipolar disorder	Esther	32	Schizophrenia	Inpatient
Sylvain	31	Bipolar disorder and ADHD				
Martin (left the home)	28	Schizophrenia				

Note
None of the subjects knew what a squiggle was before attending the group. However, Nathan regularly went to art groups and Esther had done part of her schooling in different art schools.

- A sub-test from the EPOC "Evaluation du Potentiel Créatif" (Hogrefe, 2015), a graphic divergent thinking task. The EPOC is an assessment tool originally designed to measure and portray a child's (4–12 years old) creativity. Therefore, we had to adapt the scoring of the sub-test to our population and to our goals. We will explain in more detail how it worked in the next section.

In the next stage, each group participated in weekly squiggle sessions for seven weeks. At least one nurse assisted in running the sessions to help coordinate the group. During the post-squiggle discussion time, the nurse(s) would also write down all the comments made by the participants while the researcher (myself) focused on asking questions. This element is not to be neglected, as the progress in the comments and interactions of the group depended on the questions and the comments made by the researcher. A list of standardized questions designed to encourage speech was drawn up. The first rule was that the researcher had mostly to ask open-ended questions that could be answered by yes or no, so that participants wouldn't feel ill at ease if they couldn't find an answer to the questions (e.g. Can you say more about this object? Is it somewhere? Is something going to happen to it?). The questions asked by the researcher to help a participant complete his squiggle (if a subject asked for help during the drawing part of the session) were also standardized as far as possible.

After the seventh squiggle session, a second test session was set using the same tasks to see if any changes could be observed. A few weeks later the subjects were then interviewed individually again, using standardized questions to know more about what they had thought of the squiggle group and what they had experienced.

Measuring the results

For each hypothesis we tried to create a method to measure our results.

To determine whether the participant's divergent thinking had improved (*hypothesis 1.1*) we used a sub-test from the EPOC before and after the squiggle sessions.

A graphic stimulus (Figure 7.1) was given to the participants and they were asked "What could it be?" They had 10 minutes to draw as many answers as possible from the same stimulus.

We looked at the evolution of fluidity and flexibility, fluidity being the number of answers given and flexibility being the number of different ideas given. We only counted the answers that were adapted to the stimulus and had a clear shape. However, we distinguished three types of differences: flexibility in themes, flexibility in objects and flexibility in the way of using the stimulus.

Kieran's divergent thinking tasks were a good example to illustrate the three categories of flexibility (see Figure 7.2). On the left, the answers given

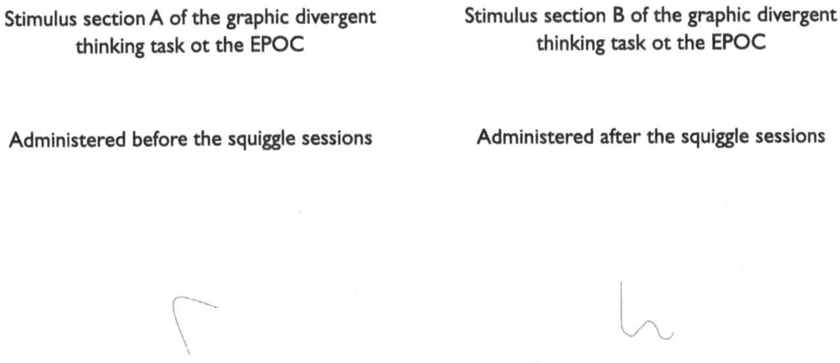

Figure 7.1 Graphic divergent thinking task of the EPOC.

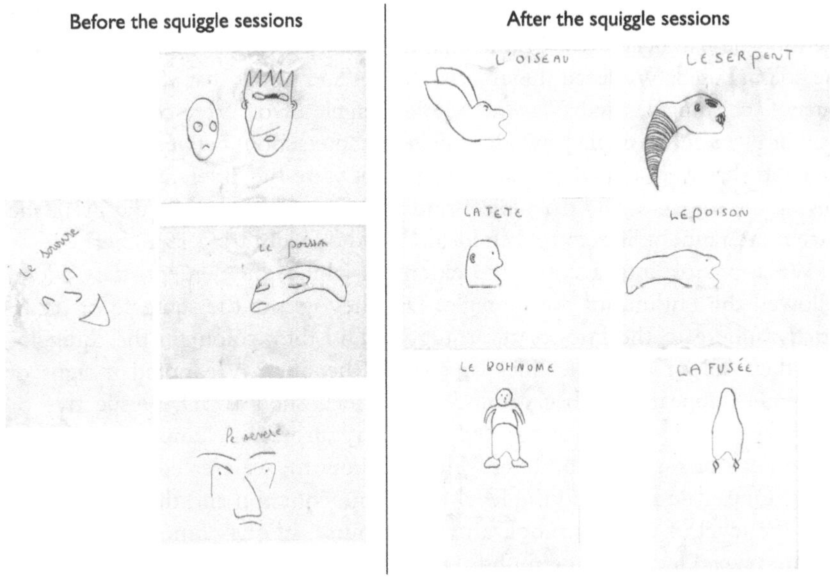

Figure 7.2 Kieran's divergent thinking tasks.

to stimulus A before the squiggle sessions can be seen; on the right, the answers given to stimulus B done after the squiggle sessions can be seen.

On the left, we can observe that Kieran was already at ease in using the stimulus in different ways: to form a human mouth, a human nose, human eyes and a fish's head. However, we can note that out of four drawings, Kieran drew three human faces. So we could only count two different objects (one for the fish and one for the human faces). We could also count only two different themes, human beings and animals.

After the squiggle sessions, Kieran did not improve his flexibility in using the stimulus in different ways, as we could see that he used the stimulus the same way to make the mouths of the fish, the snake, the human face and the bird. However, we observed that he expanded the number of objects he drew (pair of trousers, rocket, bird, fish, snake, human face) as well as his number of themes (human beings, animals, clothes, technology).

The results were then depicted in graphs: one graph for each patient, one graph for each type of mental disorder (i.e. bipolar disorders, schizophrenia and ASD). Another graph depicted the results of the whole group.

To observe more closely whether the participants could change their ways of adapting or solving the squiggle (*hypothesis 1.2*), we created a codified table for each subject with each line showing how we analysed the way in which one squiggle had been completed. This table helped to distinguish more easily whether or not strategies were modified throughout the experiment. We compared the choice of squiggle (dotted, straight lines, curvy lines, mixed), whether the squiggle had been turned on its side or upside down, the materials used and the colours used. We listed the objects, themes and stories that were drawn, the parts of the squiggle used: Was the whole squiggle used? Were only a few parts used or even only a single part? How were the interactions between the different elements that were drawn characterized? What were the different steps taken in solving the squiggle: Did the subject find an idea straight away or did he or she trace more random lines to find an idea? Or did one idea trigger another?

We also took into account the extent to which the elements they added followed the outlines of the squiggle: Did they ignore the squiggle or try to strictly adhere to the lines of the squiggle? Did they colour in the squiggle? Did they colour over the lines or around the lines? We noted if signs of movement appeared, if backgrounds and effects such as 3D, perspective or depths were used and we also jotted down any surprising elements.

To test our second hypothesis (on self-cohesion), we created two different scales. One scale measured the level of graphic cohesion and the other measured the level of verbal symbolization. Of course, in one comment or in one picture several levels can be found. However, the scale was used to see which was the highest level attained.

Graphic cohesion scale (for hypothesis 2.1)

0 = The participant was unable to complete the squiggle or drew next to it or over it.

0.5 = The participant only coloured in the squiggle.

1 = The participant linked different parts of the squiggle together.

1.5 = The participant drew abstract shapes using the squiggle.

2 = The participant drew several objects but they were incongruous.

2.5 = The participant drew several objects, some of which formed a congruous group and some of which did not.

3 = Several objects were drawn as variations on a theme. Or, one entire and coherent object was drawn.

4 = Two or more objects were drawn and interacted together coherently.

5 = Several objects contributed to creating a scene.

6 = A story is represented.

Verbal symbolization scale (for hypothesis 2.2)

0 = The participant was unable say anything about his or her product.

0.5 = The participant only made an irrelevant or judgemental comment about his/her work.

1 = The participant only named and designated the elements drawn or described his emotional state without linking it to his or her product.

2 = Only a factual description of what was represented was made; or only the different steps of a process were described; or the participant only explained his intentions, difficulties, abilities.

3 = Links were made between the product and cultural references or objects in the world; or a description of the product was made with the emergence of narration, causality, staging; or emotions are attributed to characters.

3.5 = Links were made between the product and beliefs or a description is made of how it felt to complete this particular squiggle.

4 = A story was told with intelligible temporality, but no links were made with the participant's personal life.

5 = The participant linked the product to an experience or a personal situation that he or she had undergone or thought or wished to go through in the future. Or the participant explained the link between the product and an emotional state.

6 = A better understanding of oneself was achieved based on the product or the emergence of meta-thoughts was observed.

The scores were then displayed in graphs to determine whether or not there was evidence of an evolution. It particularly helped us to see if verbal symbolization relied on graphic cohesion or not.

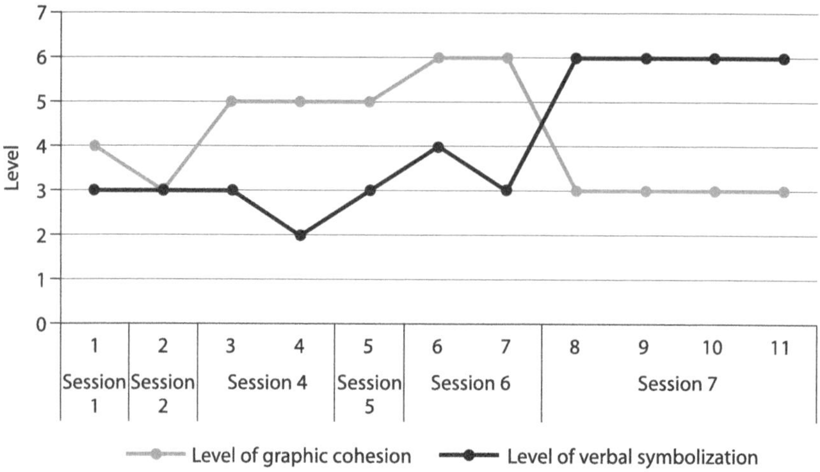

Figure 7.3 **Comparison between the variation in the level of complexity of verbal symbolization and the variation in the level of graphic cohesion in Tommy's squiggles throughout the sessions.**

Figure 7.3 reveals Tommy's results throughout the sessions. The dark line shows the evolution of his graphic cohesion, the light line shows the evolution of his verbal symbolization. We observed that better graphic cohesion does not necessarily generate better verbal symbolization.

Results of the experiment

The results of the experiment varied significantly from one participant to another. Therefore, it was difficult to validate or invalidate our hypotheses. However, some results were clear:

As we can observe in Figures 7.4–7.7, on average, the group adaptation of the squiggle technique helped the subjects (all different mental disorders combined) to improve their fluidity and flexibility in divergent thinking tasks. The light lines represented the average scores before the squiggle sessions and the dark lines represented the average scores after the squiggle sessions. From top to bottom we can see their scores for Theme Flexibility, Object Flexibility, Stimulus Flexibility and Fluidity. We observed that their scores doubled or tripled (especially for the schizophrenic subjects). The group adaptation of the squiggle technique seems to be a relevant means to start working on alternative thinking with psychotic patients (*hypothesis 1.1*).

Unfortunately, the limited number of sessions did not enable us to confirm that the squiggle group helped to find different ways of adapting to a

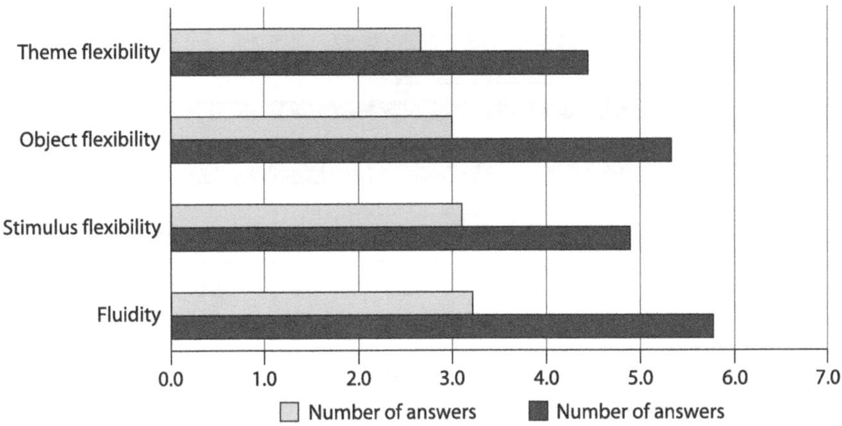

Figure 7.4 Overall average of the graphic divergent thinking task scores before and after the experiment for all subjects combined.

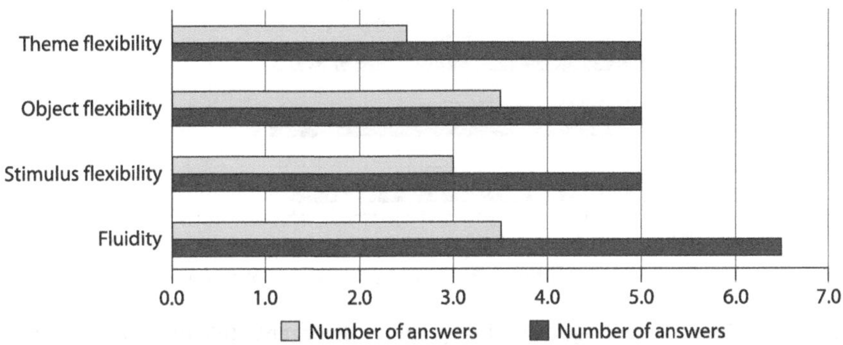

Figure 7.5 Overall average of the graphic divergent thinking task scores obtained by the bipolar subjects before and after the experiment.

problem. We did observe that some participants sometimes managed to completely change their ways of modifying the squiggle but the grid we used helped to observe change and not to quantify it. Many more sessions would have been needed to obtain a broader overview of a subject's ways of adapting to a squiggle and to determine whether a subject's strategies of resolution had become more flexible (*hypothesis 1.2*).

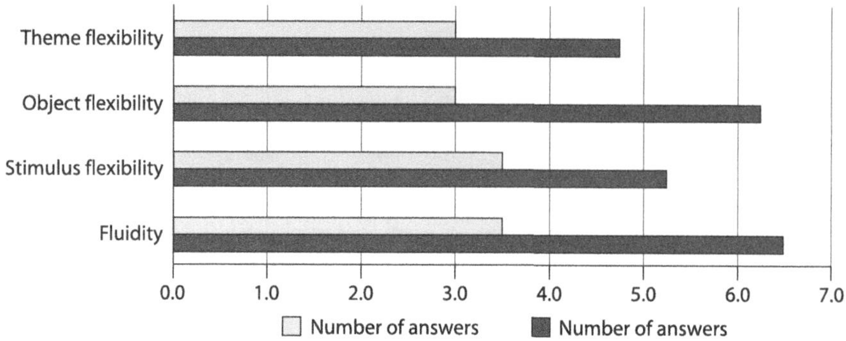

Figure 7.6 Overall average of the graphic divergent thinking task scores obtained by the schizophrenic subjects before and after the experiment.

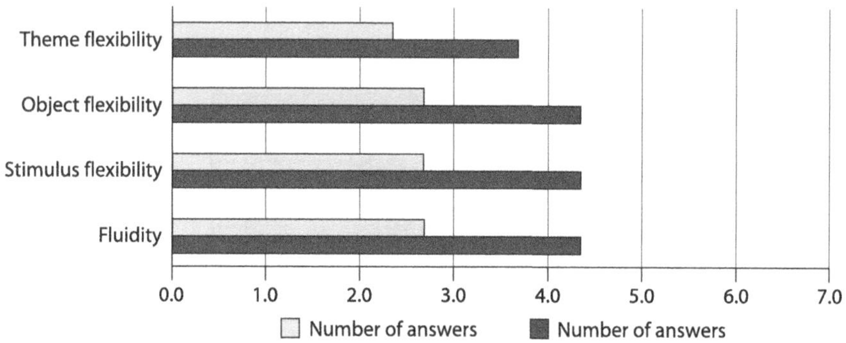

Figure 7.7 Overall average of the graphic divergent thinking task scores obtained by ASD subjects before and after the experiment.

Kieran

The following is an example of a subject who suddenly and radically changed his way of using the squiggle: Kieran, a man in his 30s, was described by the nurses as being shy and paranoid. Very little was known about Kieran's personal story except for one thing: when Kieran was four years old, his mother had been murdered by her boyfriend, who stabbed her several times. It was not clear whether Kieran had witnessed the murder or not. Yet, in the free drawing tasks and during some squiggle sessions, Kieran could only draw very threatening faces (Figure 7.8, drawings 1a, 1b and 1c). This was a constant source of puzzlement for him. He often stated that he wished that he could understand

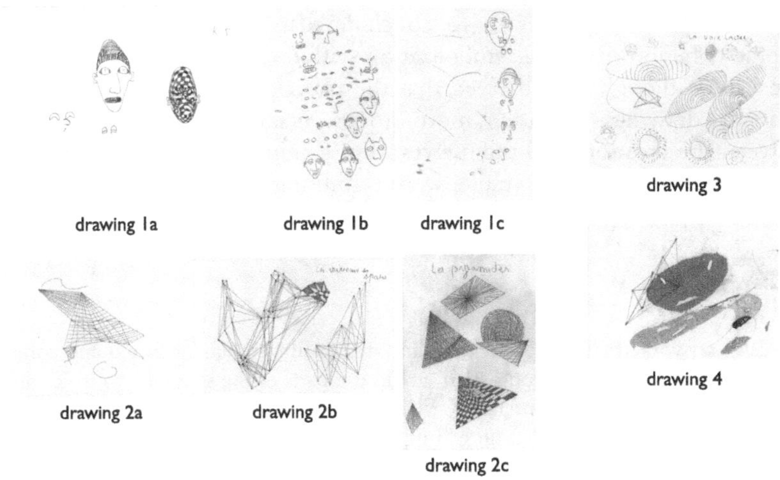

Figure 7.8 Kieran.

why he only drew faces. All the members of the group were very surprised and impressed by Kieran's drawing skills and they therefore encouraged him to share his creations. During the first sessions, Kieran linked all the different parts of the squiggles together with a ruler, producing highly structured black-and-white objects in 3D such as pyramids and spaceships (2a, 2b and 2c). He randomly traced straight lines and then asked himself what they could represent. He would usually only name the object and state that he hadn't thought of anything while drawing it. Gradually, he changed his way of working and started to draw differently.

As we can see on the right, in his picture of the Milky Way (drawing 3), he started drawing curves and a background. This picture was the first one to trigger a conversation and discussion of a common interest shared with the other group members, namely manga stories which took place in space. Drawing 4 is Kieran's last squiggle drawing. We can observe that he started to draw in his usual way linking dots with straight lines. Then he interrupted his work to draw colourful ghosts with different facial expressions swirling in the air. This was the first time Kieran had used colour. He had applied an idea to the squiggle rather than drawing randomly until he asked himself what it could represent. Though the drawing may have appeared to be less elaborate, it helped Kieran to talk about something personal about himself for the first time: his belief in ghosts. He was also particularly pleased with the ghost (top-right image in drawing 4) because for once he had managed to draw a friendly face. In this example we can see how change in artwork offered Kieran the possibility to talk about himself and deal with anxiety by, first, mastering his artwork with a ruler and then being able to make his characters convey different emotions.

It was also difficult for us to conclude that there was an evolution in graphic cohesion or verbal symbolization within the group in only seven sessions. Even though we observed that the participants were producing more elaborate drawings, narrating more stories, making more and more links between the creations and themselves, thus gaining a better understanding of how they functioned, the results were promising but too uneven to validate *hypotheses 2.1* and *2.2*.

Alan

Alan's artwork (Figure 7.9) clearly illustrated an improvement in graphic cohesion. During the first sessions, Alan would use parts of the squiggles to make different objects that didn't interact together or were not part of a same context. He would then simply list what he had drawn. For example, in drawing 1 he commented: "It's a smile, a carrot, a trowel and lightning." As the weeks went by, Alan was finding ways of bringing the different parts of the squiggles together and would sometimes even start narrating a story. The picture of a man smoking (drawing 2) is "Lucky Luke who has put on weight." Alan commented,

> It was difficult for me to find the face. I had to turn the squiggle round several times. I drew a cigarette because Lucky Luke smokes. He's in Nevada, and he's angry because he weighed himself and has put on weight so he lit a cigarette.

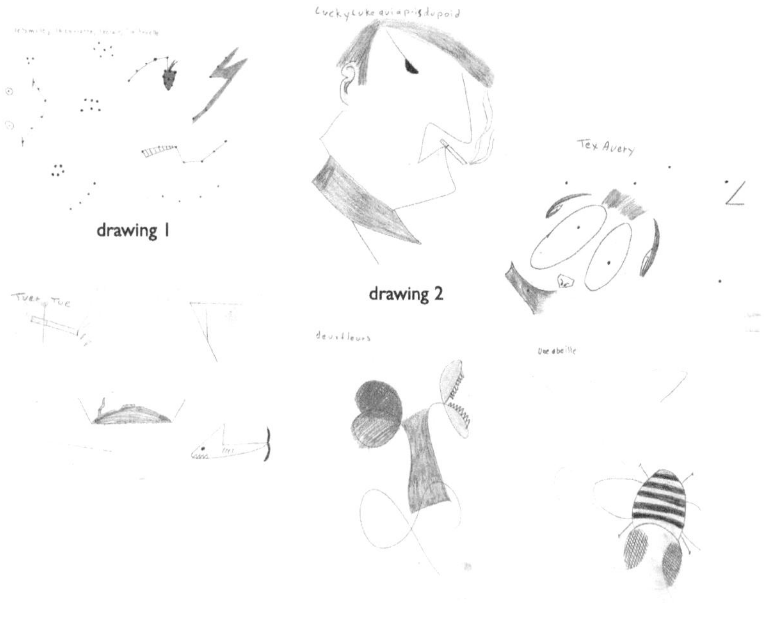

Figure 7.9 Alan.

His story made the whole group laugh. At that time, Alan was a heavy smoker and his psychotropic treatment had caused him to put on weight. As Alan was not a talkative person, the nurses were impressed to see that he could create a comic book character from the squiggle and use it to express his anger. In this particular example we can see that a stronger graphic cohesion triggered a more structured and developed narration.

Tommy

Tommy would also often attribute his feelings, doubts and dreams to the characters he drew from the squiggles (in the upper line of drawings). However, he would do so without ever mentioning the links between his story and his characters' stories. During the first sessions, Tommy would hesitate for 20 minutes before drawing anything. He wanted his ideas to be fun and original. His characters played the role of protective masks behind which he could talk about himself without revealing himself. However, as the sessions went on, Tommy was becoming more and more spontaneous. He would find ideas in a split second. The lower line of Tommy's drawings displayed those he produced at the last squiggle session. He used the squiggles to write the names of all the characters he had drawn. He gave them old-fashioned names that made him laugh a lot. But for the first time, doing so enabled him to explain that his funny characters made it easier for him to express himself. He was then starting to understand his own patterns of thoughts.

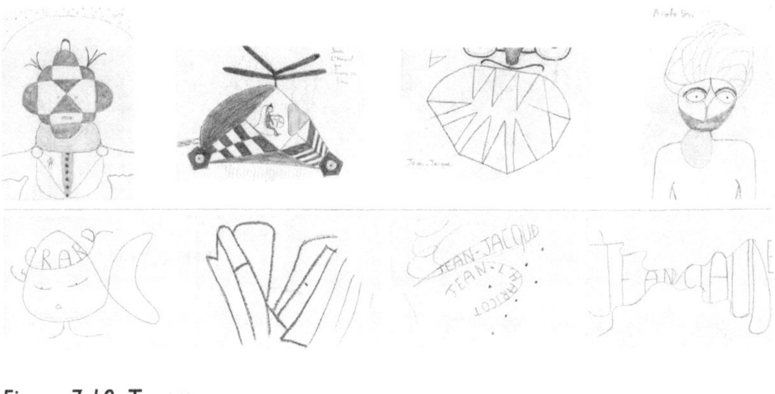

Figure 7.10 Tommy.

A result of the experiment that seemed to be clear was that the level of verbal symbolization did not necessarily depend on the level of graphic cohesion (at least not with the scales we made). Some products showing graphically elaborate characters and settings did not always lead to a high level of verbal symbolization. On the other hand, we observed that creations that contained a low level of graphic cohesion were sometimes made with more spontaneity which triggered deeper levels of introspection and more elaborate comments (*hypothesis 2.3*).

Esther

We can see in drawings 5 and 6 of Figure 7.11 how elaborate Esther's free drawings were, yet she would usually offer only a factual description of them. Esther went to art school for several years. She was very nostalgic about her life before entering the psychiatric hospital. She used to attend art classes, go to work, take care of animals and be teased by her parents. The picture of the dog (drawing 2) reminded Esther of when she used to take care of her animals. She especially focused on the eyes of the dog, saying that he often gave her a teasing look. She regretted the fact that her parents had stopped teasing her since the appearance of her illness. Esther also used the squiggles to challenge herself and to create things she enjoyed in the past. The sketch of the roll of film (drawing 1) represented one of the first objects she drew using perspective. In drawing 3, the patches (coloured pink in the original) represented a show she enjoyed on TV but also an exercise in drawing depth in field that she used to do at art school. The pink patches were supposed to look as though they were jutting out more than the white patches. Her squiggle drawings were less sophisticated and more spontaneous than her free drawings. These squiggle drawings helped

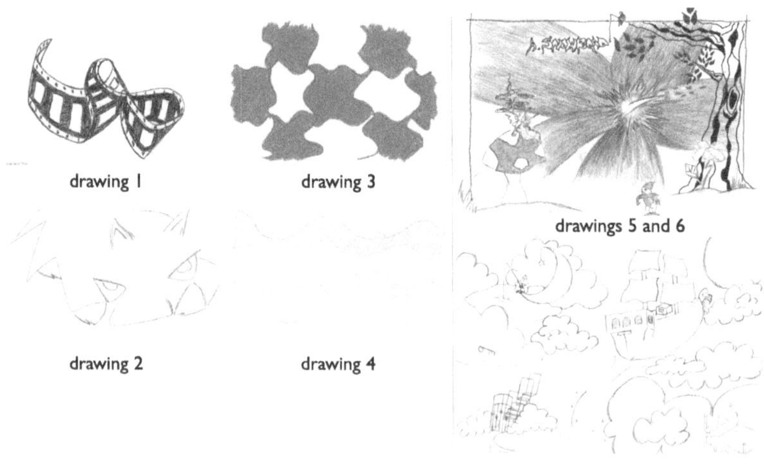

Figure 7.11 Esther.

her to express herself about painful subjects that she wouldn't usually discuss. The sketch of the waves (drawing 4) represented the sea, which in French is pronounced the same way as the word "mother" ("la mer" and "la mère"). This picture triggered a long explanation of all her worries and anxieties concerning her mother. She said she wanted to live with her again but that the nurses were preventing her from going back to her home because they wanted to steal her house from her. Esther had never talked about her interpretation of the situation. It was a very paranoid and defensive interpretation of reality as the truth was unbearable: in fact, it was her mother who didn't want Esther to live with her any more.

Vincent

Another example that clearly showed that very basic artwork could lead to a high level of verbal symbolization was Vincent's drawing. Vincent suffered from a highly disorganized type of schizophrenia that sometimes prevented him from making full intelligible sentences. In this picture we can see that he simply had connected all the dots randomly. Yet, once he had posted it up for the discussion, he realized that it looked a lot like a flower. More associations sprang to his mind: It looked like the rose he had given his mother in hospital a few days before her death.

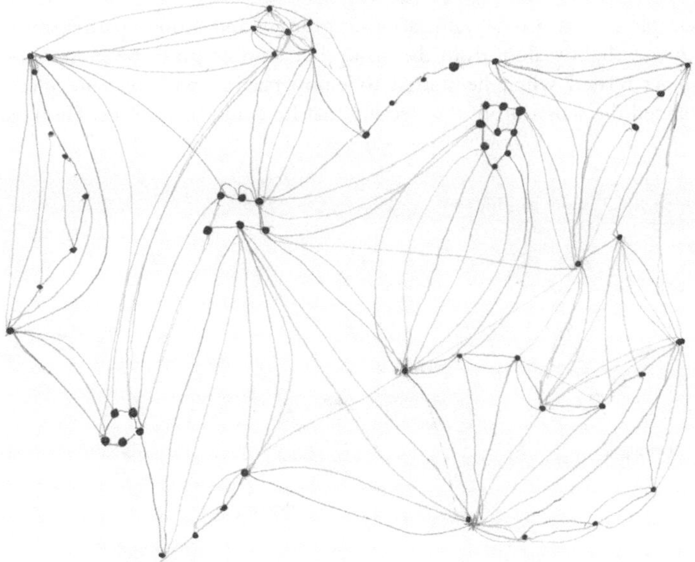

Figure 7.12 Vincent.

Moreover, many unintended outcomes were observed but we could not provide any objective measurements or proof of what we noticed. Most patients stated that they had the impression that this form of art demanded that they mobilize their cognitive resources (they often said, "*It makes our brain work*"). They also described a feeling of achievement after finding a way to complete the squiggles. Furthermore, the other members' reactions (often very positive reactions) contributed to increasing the subjects' sense of self-esteem. Most participants shyly commented on their products during the first sessions but gradually gained confidence and would share their creations with enthusiasm. The observations described by other authors and therapists who worked on the squiggle have been borne out by our experiments. The fact that the squiggle is a co-construction (one member draws the squiggle and the other member completes it) makes it more difficult to respect the shapes and proportions one would draw by copying a model. The hazardous lines that we needed to take into consideration sometimes made distortion and exaggeration part of the game. This seemed to reduce the anxiety about not drawing skilfully or of being judged. The "rules" of the squiggle technique seemed to encourage the participants to play and therefore to be more spontaneous and natural.

Sylvain

An example of this was Sylvain, a rather grumpy and moody participant who liked to stay slightly aloof from the group but who began to be more cheerful and object-related when he started to enjoy playing with his squiggles. He experienced the sensation of discovering that he could be creative. He liked to

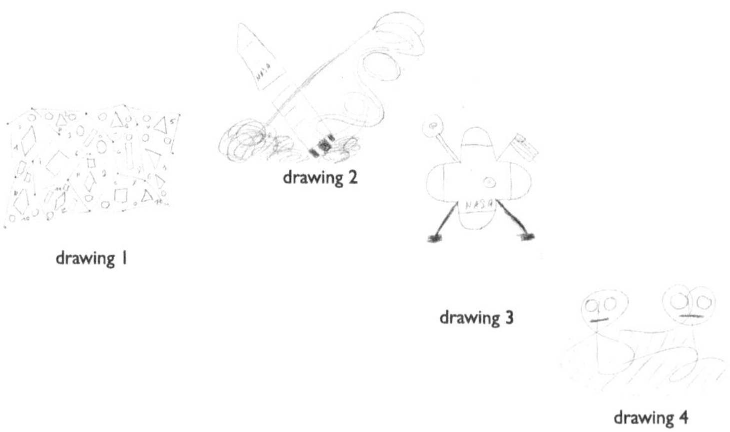

Figure 7.13 Sylvain.

challenge the group or tell them stories using his squiggles. Drawing 1 was a puzzle that he created for the group that hid his pseudonym. Drawings 2, 3 and 4 were three squiggles that formed a story.

> It's a rocket taking off. It's going to Mars. It's following the Earth's curve. Then Mars 1, the rocket's capsule, lands on Mars, but its flag isn't French, it's American, it's NASA's. And here you can see the Martians, the "little grey men" from Spielberg's series. The three squiggles go together. The rocket takes off in the atmosphere, it continues to fly to Mars. The capsule lands with the Americans inside it. They have portholes, flags and can live inside it. Then they find two Martians, the "little grey men."

The nurses were very surprised by how little time it would take for the participants to settle down and concentrate and how long they managed to concentrate. Most of them described a state of flux in which they couldn't see time going by and were completely absorbed in their artwork. Another effect that we weren't expecting to be so striking was the interest that the participants showed in each other's work. They were very curious to know what the others had drawn or how they had solved their squiggles and they were eager to listen to each other's stories and comments. They gradually dared more and more to ask questions about each other's squiggles. At the end of the sessions the researcher almost no longer needed to ask questions or intervene because the participants would ask the same types of questions and the group would regulate itself. This phenomenon also pushed the participants to develop their comments and broaden their imagination or specify their explanations. Before starting the group, some nurses were worried that the patients would copy from each other. They were very surprised to see that the participants did glance at their neighbour's work sometimes to see if they could find a bit more inspiration, but that they were determined to draw something different from the other members' drawings. They wanted their product to be unique, which enabled them to work on differentiation and on their sense of agency, but it also trained their flexibility as they would give up on one solution to try to find another one of their own.

Some other findings that were noteworthy concerned the subjects' relationship with the squiggle. We realized that the majority of their creations scrupulously followed the outlines of the squiggles. Delusions and hallucinations often made us characterize a psychotic patient as someone disconnected or non-adapted to reality. Yet, when it came to the squiggle, the subjects seemed to be "relying on reality." Moreover, when they drew the squiggles (as the bases of all the imagery produced) we realized that they were in difficulty. They seemed frightened to be spontaneous as if they were afraid of doing something wrong. Their squiggles were often quite simple, linear or very structured. However, this must be left open to conjecture.

Unfortunately, like every experiment, our pilot study had its limits and biases. The researcher, the intern-therapist, the examiner and the person who invented the scales and the tables were one and the same person. So the results could have been induced by the way the experiment was conducted and by the belief in the project. The results also greatly depended on the setting, the group dynamics and how the sessions were carried out. The EPOC sub-test, being very similar to the squiggle, was not necessarily the most relevant test to use. We would have needed to use more flexibility tests to determine whether the participants' achievements were transposable to other tasks and fields other than art. As mentioned above, more sessions and more subjects would have been needed to confirm some of our hypotheses.

Conclusion

We would like to conclude somewhat unconventionally by quoting a participant's comment about the squiggle group that summarized, better than our own words could, all the different aspects that the squiggle group stimulated, including flexibility, subjectivity, self-esteem, social skills, expression and narration. It was also a relevant answer to our question: Is the group adaptation of the squiggle technique a therapeutic tool and is it coherent to use it in a psychosocial rehabilitation programme?

> It made me use my creativity. It can help in everyday life. For example, if we want to make a meal, we can improvise, we have a basis and we create more on top of it, like the squiggle! There are plenty of jobs in which we need to use our creativity. In my job I need to draw plans and I can bring a bit of personal touch to them. This group helped me because I used to only copy out creations but with the squiggle I realized that I could imagine things on my own. I always wanted to find a funny story to tell, I wanted to create a good atmosphere in the group. I wanted my drawings to be nice to look at and I especially wanted my explanations to make sense. At first I used to look at all the drawings the others made and compared them to mine thinking that mine weren't great, that they could be better. Then I stopped looking at the others' work because I wanted to have my own ideas. Little by little my own ideas came up more easily. The squiggle helps to trigger the imagination; it isn't really a constraint. It's a little constraint that releases free expression.
>
> (Tommy)

References

Bejaoui, M. & Pedinielli, J.-L. (2010). Flexibilité cognitive, attention sélective et fluidité verbale sémantique dans trois dimensions de schizophrénie: Psychotique, négative et de désorganisation. *Pratiques psychologiques, Septembre, 16*(3), 259–272. doi:10.1016/j.prps.2009.04.007.

Cane, F. (1951/1983). *The artist in each of us*. Craftsbury Common, VT: Art Therapy Publications.

Freeman, D., Garety, P. A., Fowler, D., Kuipers, E., Bebbington, P. E. & Dunn, G. (2004). Why do people with delusions fail to choose more realistic explanations for their experiences? An empirical investigation. *J Consult Clin Psychol, 72*(4), 671–680. doi:10.1037/0022-006X.72.4.671.

Hogrefe. (2015). EPOC: Evaluation du potentiel créatif des enfants. In Hogrefe (Ed.), *Récupéré sur Hogrefe*. Retrieved from: www.hogrefe.fr/produit/epoc-evaluation-du-potentiel-creatif-desenfants/#information.

Lubart, T., Besançon, M. & Barbot, B. (2011). *Manuel: Evaluation du Potentiel Créatif.* Paris: Hogrefe.

Ulman, E. (1975). *Art therapy in theory and practice*. New York: Schocken Books.

Winnicott, D. W. (1971). *La Consultation Thérapeutique et l'Enfant*. Paris: Gallimard. (Original work published as *Therapeutic consultations in child psychiatry*. London: Karnac Books)

Chapter 8

The borrowed image in art therapy with psychiatric patients

The internalization process

Elizabeth Stone

This chapter offers an exploration and reflection from clinical practice about the role of the borrowed image in art therapy, something that may lead to a qualitative research project in the future. Based upon clinical observation, I argue that the use of the borrowed image promotes the developmental process of internalization and contributes to strengthening psychic structure.

Many years ago as a young art therapist, I had observed that quite a few adult psychiatric inpatients seemed to benefit from having an image outside of themselves from which to borrow or copy subject matter. Surprisingly, these "borrowed images" seemed to facilitate creativity rather than hamper it. The patients with whom I was working were often less confident about creating purely from imagination, feelings or personal life stories. Yet, when they had an image before them, whether from an art reproduction, a photo or actual life (a person, object or landscape), a reduction in anxiety was clearly discernible. Less hesitant, they drew with greater ease. Yet, in spite of my keen interest in the role of the borrowed image, I do not especially promote borrowing imagery over any other means of expression in my own practice; all patients have the freedom to choose the medium and form of expression that fit their needs.

The central premise for this pilot study has been incubating throughout most of my career as an art therapist (Stone, 1981). My curiosity was first sparked during my work with adult psychiatric patients in the 1970s and early 1980s.[1] At the time, I knew that a greater spectrum of clinical vignettes would help me flesh out my ideas. Since then, I have amassed many such vignettes, too numerous to be included here.

This chapter will offer a taste of clinical vignettes from psychiatric patients and my theoretical hypothesis about the nature of borrowing and its developmental antecedents. One caveat: I do not prescribe borrowing or copying as a singular art therapy directive. My approach is to take my cues from my patients while providing a range of basic art materials. They are free to create imagery that is important to them without prompting from me.

Over the years I accumulated a large collection of art reproductions that contain a wide variety of themes. Patients have freely perused them when unsure of how to begin or in search of an image with which to connect on an affective level. The images provide structure when patients feel empty of ideas or images of their own. Among the patients with whom I have worked, certain reproductions were chosen more frequently than others. A separate chapter would be needed to analyze why this was so. Suffice it to say, each patient interpreted even the more frequently chosen reproductions in his or her unique way. Some patients have told me that they chose images that were "easy" to draw. However, by the time they finished their drawing, they had become able to articulate some personal connection to it. Finding meaning is particularly important when working with psychiatric patients, even if the connection is on the baseline sensory level of the art-making process (i.e., the colors, the movement, or even something humorous). Often, patients are able to make an affective connection with the mood of the artwork or feelings embodied in a character's expression or gesture. Such connections occur during the sharing time, arising out of the back-and-forth dialogue with the art therapist, and possibly the other patients, if in group art therapy. It is important to discuss the artwork only after completion so as not to interfere with the unfolding of the creative process. However, when a patient is stuck during the art-making process, discussing the problem is always helpful.

Even before my ideas about borrowing began to form, during my apprenticeship in child psychiatry with the pioneer art therapist Edith Kramer, I realized just how valuable her voluminous encyclopedia of animal photos was for these children. As a handy reference for a child who needed help to conceptualize an image or clarify anatomical detail, the child became able to bring his/her animal to life rather than create a generic or oversimplified facsimile. The animal encyclopedia helped children who were too empty to summon up any form of mental imagery on their own. Looking through these photos enabled an idea to eventually click. The child then created a drawing, painting or sculpture based upon what the animal evoked in him/her. The way he/she positioned it reflected something about the child's inner world. Other elements were added that included characters, settings and narratives. The art reproduction has functioned similarly for my adult patients.

Borrowing, copying and appropriation

Copying in art has traditionally held a position of low esteem. Nevertheless, all art develops from artists borrowing from each other to some extent. Today, contemporary art criticism has elevated the art of appropriation, yet "borrowing" in therapy has had more negative connotations and less therapeutic value than imagery created entirely from the inner subjective world. Borrowing or copying has been thought to conceal personal imagery that would arise from fantasy. Traditionally, therapy has been thought of as a means to break down defenses to attain more authentic functioning. Disallowing copying was part of that effort. I support the position that ego defenses are necessary for healthy mental functioning. Our job is to encourage adaptive and flexible defenses to eventually replace rigid ones. The more damaged the individual, the more rigid the defense. We cannot break these defenses down because they are what the fragile patient has to hold him or herself together. I work toward strengthening ego defenses when they are inadequate. I take the non-judgmental position that anything a patient creates is really about him or herself, whether or not the image is borrowed. Finally, I suggest that the time has come to widen the lens through which the borrowed image is viewed in art therapy; its usefulness has become more than apparent.

Examples of borrowing in psychotic patients

Patients in all diagnostic categories with whom I worked found portraits by Amadeus Modigliani intriguing and powerful and frequently selected them. Figures 8.1–8.4 reproduce images drawn by four different patients that were based upon Modigliani's "Portrait of Anna" (reproduction not shown). Each reflects something unique about the patient. We will return to these drawings later.

In the light of the richness and evocative power that borrowed imagery brought to the work of my patients, I reconsider the need to copy or borrow. I will now share an extract of the session that first galvanized my interest and offered me a clue as to how to understand the role and relevance of "borrowing" and its connection to the psychoanalytic concept of internalization (Blanck & Blanck, 1994; Blatt & Blass, 1990, p. 118; Hartmann, 1958; Jacobson, 1964; Meissner, 1981). In doing so, the direction of my thinking began to take shape. Instead of viewing borrowing as a problem to overcome, I came to see it as a potentially useful therapeutic support.

Abigail, in her mid-50s, was hospitalized on a short-term psychiatric unit. Attempting to draw a landscape from her imagination, she became increasingly agitated by her own psychotic delusional processes. She could neither control her body nor stop herself from talking aloud. Disturbing other group members, her difficulty remaining connected to her drawing infused her imagery with turbulence and regression, depleting the talents of this intelligent woman who had briefly attended an art school as a young woman (Figure 8.5). The questionably personified tree, along with the jagged, repetitive and intrusive lines of her landscape, appear as menacing forces. A darkened shadow-like couple stands beneath birds and an enormous but empty sun. The flock of birds looks like wavy extensions of the sun's rays.

Once Abigail finished drawing, she chaotically rushed to begin another when I intervened. In an attempt to rechannel and help her focus her energies, I suggested that she draw a portrait of the nurse in the room. Although my approach is usually non-directive, this spontaneous intervention was designed to contain Abigail, to create ego boundaries and diminish her confusion.

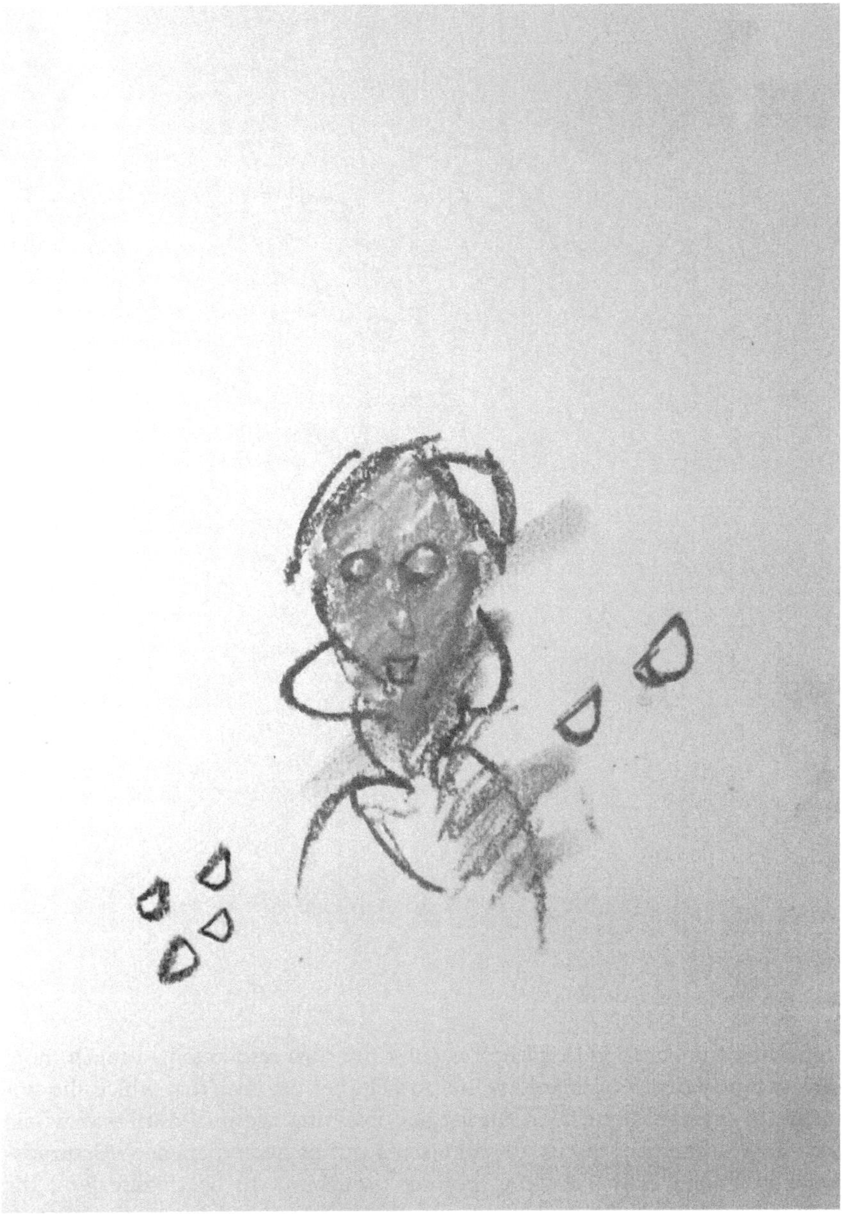

Figure 8.1 After *Anna*.

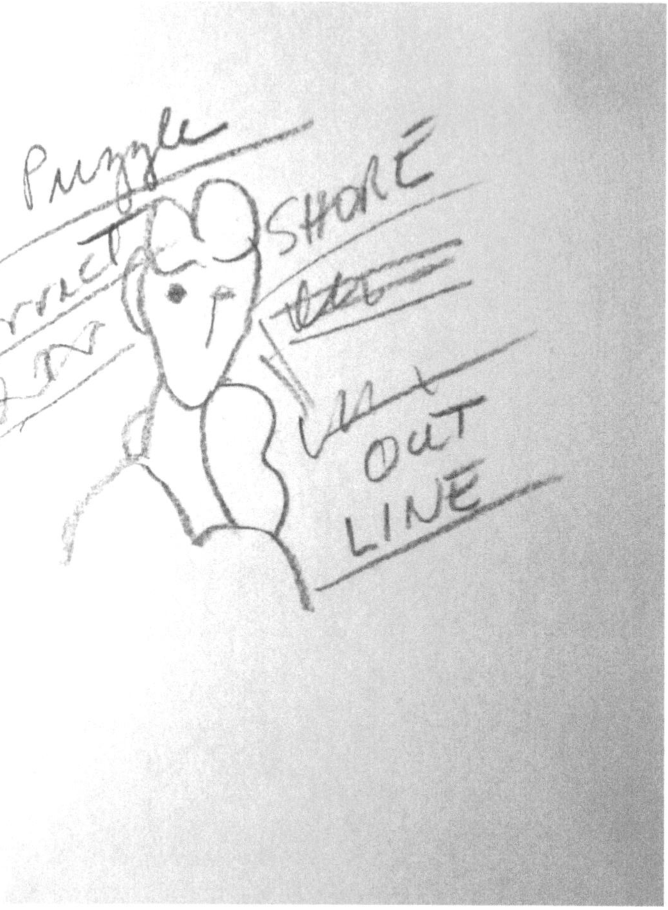

Figure 8.2 After *Anna.*

Implicitly, I understood that I had to enlist my own resources in a much more directive way than I ordinarily would to help her organize that which she was unable to organize herself. To engage her observing ego in a visual way would activate her internal capacity to make sense out of her experience. As surprisingly structured as the resulting portrait turned out to be (Figure 8.6), the process by which it occurred was as remarkable. She later drew a series of other patients on the unit. The difference in her affect and behavior was as striking as the relatedness emanating from the portraits she drew. Her drawing style had taken a leap from a rigid cartoon-like pictogram to an alive and communicative graphic expression. She thanked me warmly for the session, telling me how much better she felt.

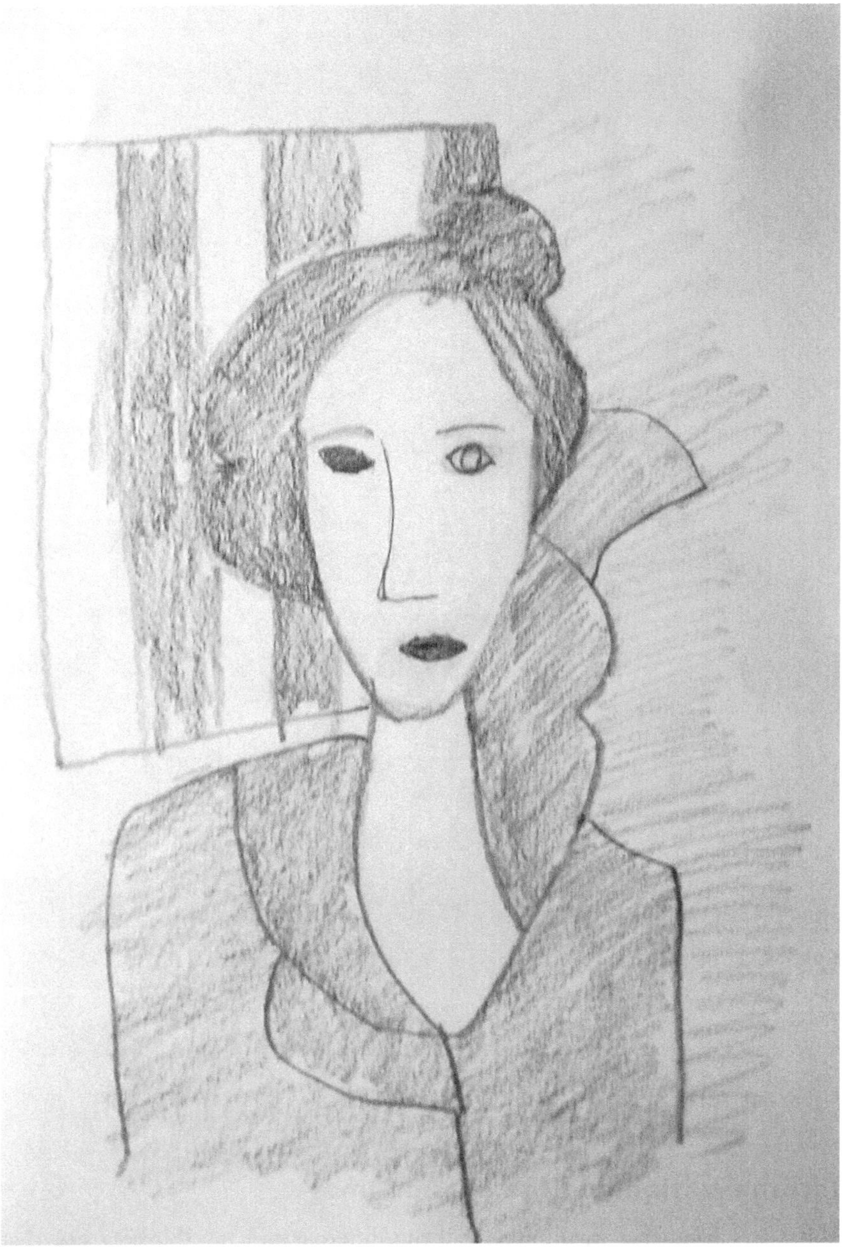

Figure 8.3 After *Anna*.

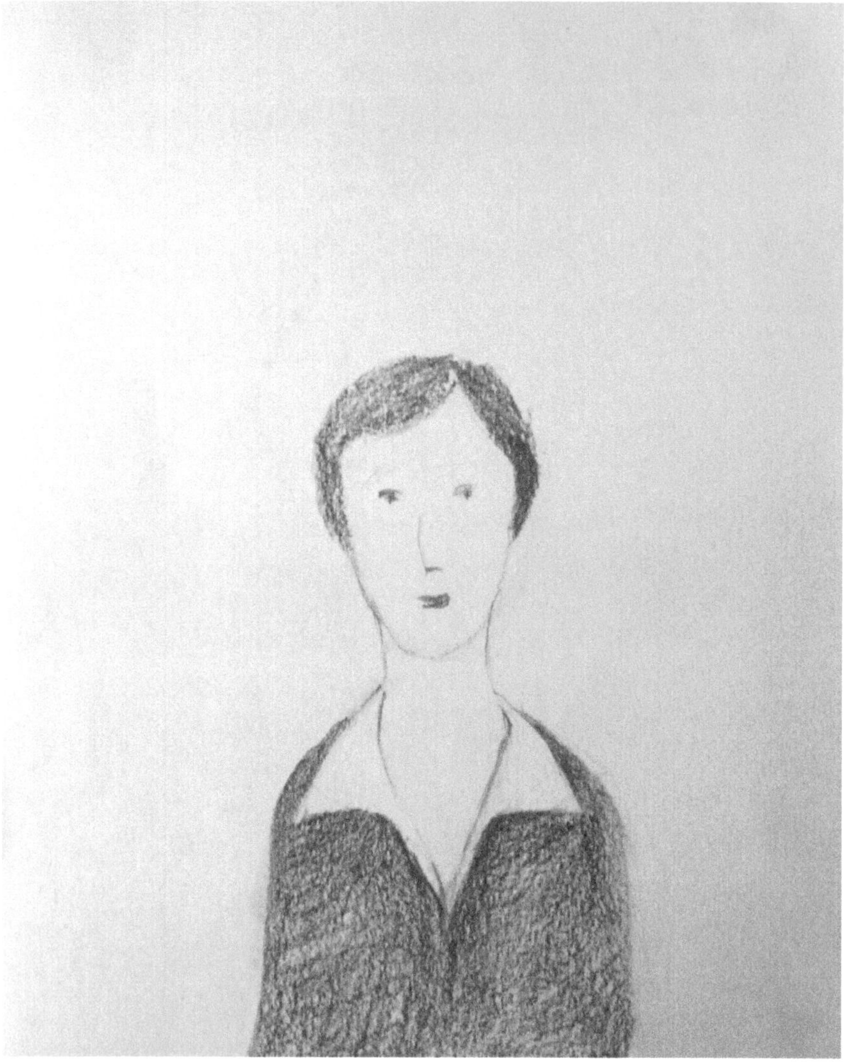

Figure 8.4 After *Anna.*

Internalization and the outside image

What I realized that finally made all the difference in my thinking was that having a live person as an outside image provided her with an object in the sense of an "object relationship." She thus "peopled" her internal world, which had been impoverished due to regressive psychotic processes. The nurse functioned as more than just herself, enabling Abigail to make an

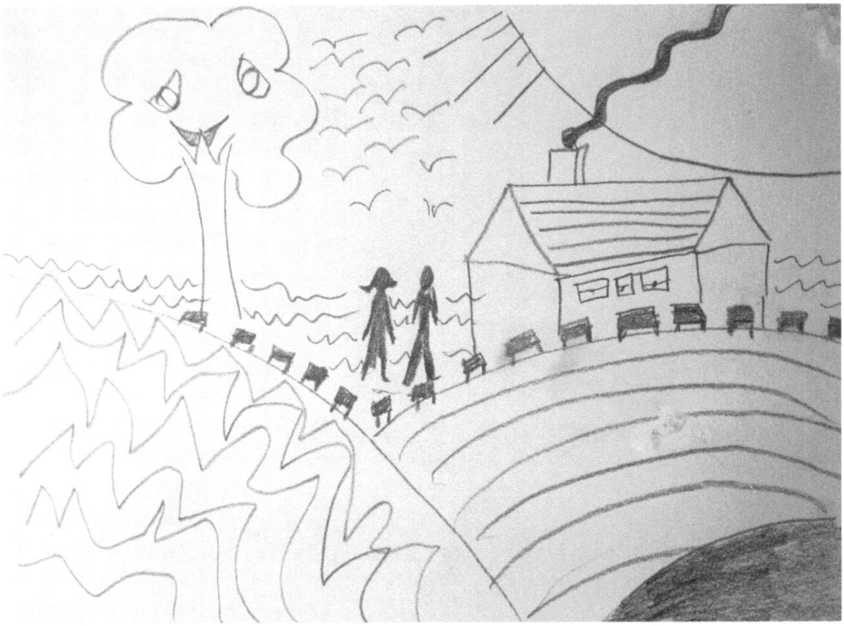

Figure 8.5 Early drawing by Abigail.

internal affective object connection. My intervention provided her with a beacon of orientation to help her organize her resources. This was reminiscent of the mutuality of connectedness that was once a part of the earliest good-enough mothering experience. It is what enables the infant to derive a feeling of well-being that will lead to a capacity for self-regulation. Described by many mother–infant observers (Beebe, Cohen, Lachmann & Yothers, 2016; Mahler, Pine & Bergman, 1975; Winnicott, 1953), the affective process of taking in an "object" experience and making it part of the self is what Heinz Hartmann referred to as *internalization* (Blanck & Blanck, 1974; Hartmann, 1958; Jacobson, 1964). Hans Loewald, as quoted in Blatt and Blass (1990, p. 118), defined internalization as "the process by which interactions within the original mother-child psychic matrix, and later between the growing individual and his environment, become transmuted into internal interaction constituting the individual psyche and creating, maintaining and developing an internal world." Blatt and Blass (1990, p. 118) continued: "Loewald's definition highlights that it is not the image of the object but the nature of the interaction with the object that is internalized."

For many disorganized patients such as Abigail, comfortable taking-in experiences may not have been frequent enough, consistent enough, or may have been ill-timed or unattuned to the young child's needs. Of course, an

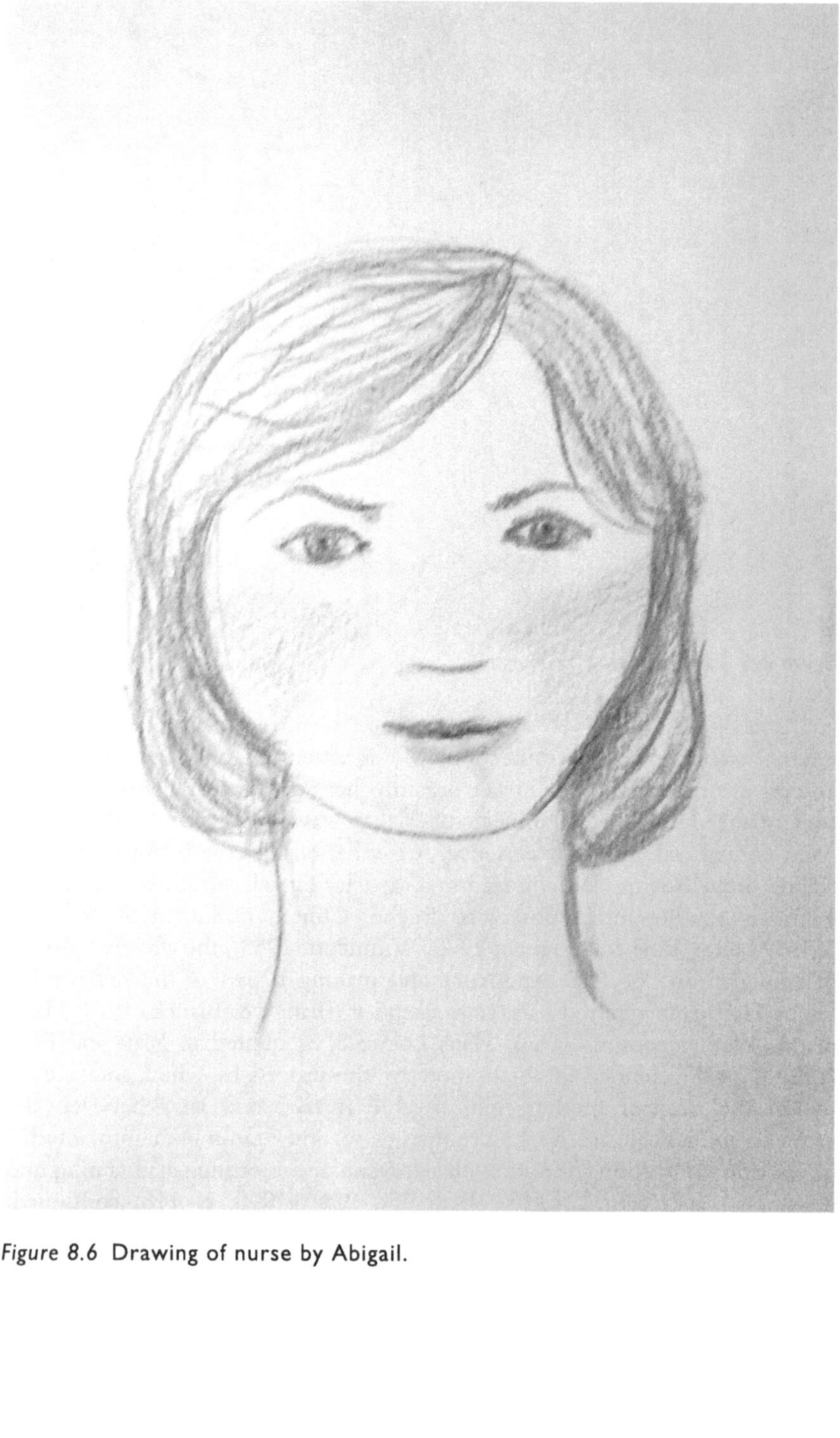

Figure 8.6 Drawing of nurse by Abigail.

early infant/mother history cannot be extrapolated without extensive details, and even then we must be careful. However, when insufficient affective nurturance has been organized into a nascent ego organization, the result can be a deficit of inner equipment to hold onto an internal image of the other (mother). Such deficit impedes the creation of a fledgling sense of self. Only when the child has developed an internalized sense of a dependable mother will he or she feel sustained in her absence (Mahler et al., 1975). We refer to this internalized sense of mother as *mental representations*. When this taking-in process has not occurred predictably, distortion and deficit become part of the early ego organization (other genetic factors also must be considered in discussing origins of schizophrenia). Where Abigail had been floundering at the mercy of her internal chaotic processes, lacking the inner ability to organize her own resources, she was able to use the nurse as an external object along with the "holding environment" I provided to feel her impulses safely contained. "As with other psychoanalytic propositions concerning processes of internalization and structure formation, it is assumed that the psyche can preserve a lost maternal function because of its inherent endowment" (Tolpin, 1971, p. 343). The therapeutic containment I offered activated this lost maternal function. I find it timely to refer to Jacques Luis Borges, who wrote that after Socrates' death, Plato invented the Platonic dialogue so as to hear his master's voice once again. He did so "to have the illusion that, in spite of Socrates having taken hemlock, he was still accompanying him (Plato)" (Borges, 1967–1968, pp. 22–23), wrote Maria Cristina Melgar (2009). Melgar was referring to traumatic object loss.

Organizing process: the role of the ego

In practical terms, mid-20th-century psychoanalytic theory declared that engaging the ego as organizing process remained a fundamental therapeutic aim in working with many patients with less than neurotic structures (Hartmann, 1958). The therapist contained and strengthened the fragile or insubstantial ego capacities of the disorganized patient through the therapeutic alliance. This referred to that part of the therapeutic relationship that was reality-based and relatively neutral in nature, that is, not overwrought with transference implications. Recent research today has shown that psychological health arises through the interactional system inherent in the dyad and continues as such throughout development (Beebe & Lachmann, 2003; Beebe, Cohen, Lachmann & Yothers, 2016). Put another way, the ripening of the interactional framework enables internalization to flourish. Understanding that development arises out of the continuous interactional nature in the developing infant/mother dyad helps to bridge certain inconsistencies in the earlier developmental models.

How creativity functions as part of the organizing process within the therapeutic relationship to promote psychic healing and further development forms a central postulate of this chapter. Why some people seem to have greater access as well as a fuller range of creative functioning, despite elements of psychopathology, has puzzled researchers because other gifted people seem quite unable to rescue their creativity from regressive forces and other fluctuations of their psychic organization. For those whose egos have been impoverished through trauma, loss, or insecure or disorganized attachment patterns, the experience of inner emptiness is often too painful to summon up enough inner resources to produce "original" work. Therefore, rather than to intimate that the borrowing or "copying" is linked directly to psychopathology, we need to understand its broader role in facilitating creativity and infusing it with meaning.

The transitional object and transitional phenomena

The concept of the transitional object as formulated by D. W. Winnicott (1953) and elaborated upon by many other authors (Abram, 2013; Deri, 1978; Kaminer, 1978; Metcalf & Spitz, 1978; Saragnano & Seulin, 2015) has relevance as a prototype for the borrowed or copied image in art therapy. The transitional object (i.e., security blanket, teddy bear or other similar physical object used by a baby for self-soothing) has become not only part and parcel of our contemporary conceptual therapeutic framework, but is integrated into today's lay language. While not exactly a substitute for mother, the transitional object can be irreplaceable for a child in a moment of need. It functions as the baby's first creation because the baby endowed it with meaning that the blanket soothes (Kaplan, 1978; Winnicott, 1953/1958). It represents the child's ability to internalize the mother's soothing ministrations. To paraphrase Kaplan, the transitional object, unlike a real mother, never lets the baby down; it is always there for him, in contrast to mothers of reality who may not always be present at a moment of need (Kaplan, 1978). However, the transitional object can never become more important than a child's actual mother. The capacity for self-soothing underpins the formation of the cohesive self (Tolpin, 1971). Without sufficient cohesiveness in the self-representations, the capacity for self-regulation is compromised, leading to various forms of severe intrapsychic damage. Whereas Winnicott believed that the transitional object eventually lost meaning and did not "go inside," Marion Tolpin argued that once the object itself is no longer needed, its soothing functions do indeed go inside as mental structure (Tolpin, 1971, p. 321).

Again, Tolpin continues, "the soothing functions of the transitional object have entered into the formation of the matrix of the child's ego" (1971, p. 324). Tolpin's implications lend credence to my hypothesis about the borrowed image. I argue that just as the blanket acquires inner regulatory functions for the infant, so the borrowed image serves a regulatory function for the individual creating artwork.

Susan Deri (1978) emphasized that the transitional object represents an illusion of the merged self-object, protecting connectedness while simultaneously preserving a measure of autonomous functioning. For her, the illusion of connectedness allowed for a feeling of unity between inner and outer, the dream and reality, a reconciliation of opposites. Therefore, the child's capacity to foster an illusion through the transitional object served as a precursor to symbol formation (Deri, 1978). The implications for the fostering of creativity are enormous.

Whereas the transitional object is considered phase-specific to toddlerhood, *transitional phenomena* can persist throughout life and take different forms. Transitional phenomena operate in an interim territory between fantasy and reality in an out-of-phase way that militates against anxiety. An amulet, special song or other artifact can soothe and be experienced as necessary, even to an adult. How often have we heard of wearing a special "good luck" outfit for a job interview or first date? Therefore, the soothing function, when needed, can be projected upon myriad phenomena throughout the life cycle. The transitional object is a prototype for the later acquisition of evocative memory. Borrowing imagery similarly nurtures the individual's internal psychic reality through the process of internalization. The outside image represents the simultaneous illusion of a me- and not-me image. Therefore, the transitional object can be seen as a template for the outside image in art, whether it is borrowed, copied or interpreted from life.

The process of internalization strengthens the ego, and does so by quickening the ego functions. Such activation of ego functions is particularly important with a psychiatric population. Abigail's session exemplified such activation of the ego functions perception, affect, delay and object relations. The art therapist's role as "quickener of ego functions" has largely been underestimated in our field, overlooked amid the errant dichotomy between psychoanalytic and cognitive behavioral approaches. Yet, unless the ego is activated into agency through strengthening the ego functions, focusing upon affect or object relations alone will be without balustrades. Only when ego functions are activated and strengthened can the patient integrate affect, relationships and cognition, psychically.

Components of internalization

Copying and imitation form the underpinnings of childhood developmental passages that have been well documented as fundamental to identity formation. Children's art from all over the world bears witness to this notion. Incorporation, considered the earliest form of internalization, is related to body-based or biological swallowing. Understood metaphorically as a means of taking in the object without mediation or discrimination, we are familiar with the term "swallowing the object whole." Imitation, next along the internalization continuum, is hastened by repetition, taking in parental attributes. The toddler shakes his head back and forth in imitation of the "no-saying" mother. We are quite familiar with babies who reproduce parents' facial gestures by imitation, yet profound internal psychic processes are at work (Blum, 1986). Also known as delayed imitation, such similar non-sequentially parental gestures or behavior can appear later. Introjection appears after incorporation. Whereas imitation has been considered a conscious form of interaction, both introjection and identification are unconscious. Introjection is thought to reside in parts of the ego structure that have remained unassimilated into the entirety of the self-image (Akhtar, 2009). *Selective identification, existing at the upper end of the internalization continuum*, presupposes a certain amount of self and object differentiation as well as the acquisition of a sense of agency. The internalization process is navigated by all of us, psychiatric patients or not. Generally, disturbances in identifications skew the development of a sense of cohesive self in psychiatric patients. Yet, disturbed identifications affect non-psychiatric patients as well. One difference is that psychiatric patients will have more difficulty functioning in life with severely damaged identifications whereas non-psychiatric patients often have other resources for coping.

The process of internalization in artistic creation cannot instantly provide an internal object or object relationship where one barely existed before. Abigail appeared at first as if in an objectless delusional state. It was not easy to predict that she could have so easily become object-related through her portraiture. One explanation of how she had become able to organize is the following. Since internalization is at its height developmentally in the first few years of life, I posit that remnants of *existing object representations* become vitalized so that new self and object images can be gradually built up. We have the advantage of having witnessed a magnified version of the metaphorical internalization process in art therapy through the example of Abigail, and we will see others.

Creativity and the conflict-free ego sphere

The use of the outside image has yet another function. Becoming able to borrow often pulls creativity, or the creative ego function, out of the arena of intrapsychic conflict. Borrowing equips it with some defenses and brings it into what Heinz Hartmann called the *conflict-free ego sphere* (Hartmann, 1958). When embattled or compromised by conflict, trauma or loss, the creative function is freed up and rescued from regressive forces when the outside image is introduced. Freeing up creativity can open doors for the exploration of other kinds of personal meaning. A pivotal aspect of our role as art therapists is to enable the patient to bring creativity out of conflict into the conflict-free ego sphere. Infusing an element of play tacitly into the fabric of the art therapy experience beckons a freeing up of conflict and aggressive superego forces that otherwise disrupt the capacity to engage creativity. The capacity to play underpins our therapeutic endeavor (Winnicott, 1971).

Case vignette: Sumi

Sumi, at age 22, was referred for art therapy upon discharge from a 6-week hospitalization after a diagnosis of paranoid schizophrenia. In a fearful and almost inaudible voice she told me that she enjoyed drawing when she was younger. Having grown up under frightening circumstances in a remote village of a developing Southeast Asian country, Sumi suffered multiple abrupt, untimely and ultimately permanent abandonments by her mother. She then immigrated to the United States with her violent father, who forced her into an arranged marriage to an older man who cared only minimally about her.

My interest in her artwork provided an opportunity for sharing that Sumi otherwise lacked. I had to be careful not to encourage premature closeness for she would have been only confused and panicked; she could not have withstood true closeness. Toward the end of our 10 months of work together, she asked to paint my portrait. Too frightened to look at me directly, Sumi could not paint me from life. Instead, she asked me to bring in a photo of myself that she would copy while I sat beside her (author's replica, due to slight damage to original slide: Figure 8.7). This situation nicely described Winnicott's concept of the "capacity to be alone." Based upon the paradox of being alone in the presence of the mother as a precondition for development to proceed adequately, my role as art therapist became such an "ego-supportive environment" (Winnicott, 1953/1958).

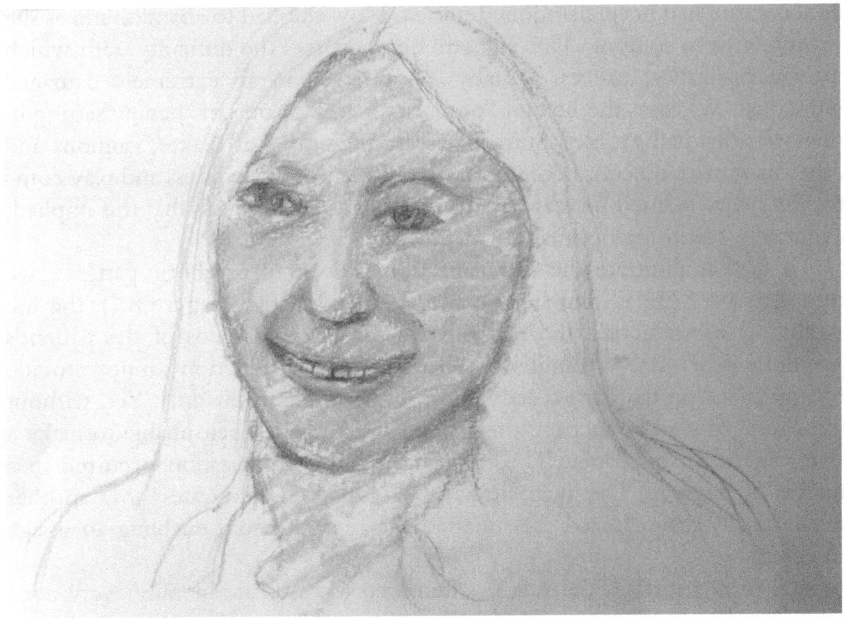

Figure 8.7 Drawing of the author by Sumi.

However, after sketching in my face, she suddenly switched media from paint to pastels. The pastels, however, did not adhere well to the tooth of the canvas board. Yet, Sumi refused to change media to make the job easier. Pastel granules kept falling agonizingly from the canvas board. During the four sessions that she worked on my portrait, she rubbed on more color as the dust slid off. Too arduous a task, Sumi did not complete it.

How can we understand what happened? Sumi feared losing her already fragmented identity by too much closeness with me. The photo functioned to provide a safe psychical distance between us, also known as "optimal distance" (Bouvet, 1955; Mahler, 1967). This early developmental concept aptly describes the way a mother naturally positions herself to be physically and psychically available. Careful not to overwhelm, she allows the developing child to feel both separate yet connected to her affectively. Too much distance impedes the experience of connectedness leading to object loss; too much closeness can be experienced as intrusively stifling of development. At either extreme, a child would have difficulty developing a stable sense of identity. As therapists, we pay attention to how much closeness or distance optimizes the therapeutic action in the therapeutic relationship. My photo enabled Sumi to feel safe in my presence and take a few tentative steps toward internalizing the attentiveness I had shown her during the previous 10 months.

I understood her borrowing of my photo as a version of imitation along the internalization continuum. Yet ultimately, Sumi left the portrait abandoned as she had been abandoned herself. Now she had to abandon me as she withdrew from sessions. This vignette demonstrates the difficulty with which the internalization process actually can proceed in an extremely damaged individual. Whereas the benign "potential space" of our art therapy setting in prior sessions had enabled Sumi to create sculptures of snakes, cannons and other inanimate objects, her longing to represent me as witness and play companion overwhelmed her capacity to withstand the closeness that this implied, eventually collapsing optimal distance.

To further illustrate the internalization process in psychotic patients, we return to the "Anna" drawings seen earlier. In the first (Figure 8.1), the use of the art reproduction did not obviate the internal chaos of the patient's psychotic processes. We understand that an art reproduction cannot provide ego organization that far exceeds all capacities of that individual. Yet, without the Modigliani reproduction, this patient would have been unable to make a single mark on his paper. The resulting graphic organization occurred in a matter of degrees. The next drawing (Figure 8.2), illustrates how another psychotically disorganized patient used the reproduction, enabling an image to emerge.

The third patient (Figure 8.3), attempted to re-create literally every concrete detail that was part of Modigliani's original portrait, a process akin to object incorporation where thinking does not mediate that which is selected on the paper. Although Modigliani blackened the right eye totally in his own painting of Anna, we notice it as an oddly astonishing afterthought in an already somewhat abstracted portrait. We experience this aberration as a fully integrated stylistic distortion that adds expressive punch to his work. For a very concrete individual such as the patient just described, such an incomprehensible detail as the blackened eye was taken literally in attempt to create a full-fledged human being, and then replicated as though it made sense. A detail, no matter how distorted, was reproduced as though thinking about it was no longer necessary. Modigliani did the thinking for the patient. The mental operation of *thinking* and *reality testing* were suspended because they had been pre-digested by the "artist," and thus absorbed by the patient as if they were metaphorically of one mind.

Another view of similar phenomena can be explained by Hanna Segal's concept of how symbols form in psychosis. She introduced the term *symbolic equation* whereby a symbol is *equated* with the thing symbolized, as opposed to a non-psychotic symbolic capacity to utilize abstraction (Segal, 1957, 1979b, in Hinshelwood, 1991). Segal's concept bears exquisite relevance for psychotic patients' representations of imagery in artwork, as revealed in the above example.

Even for patients who copy artwork exactly, symbolic expression can be quite varied. Both psychotic and non-psychotic patients in my experience have sought to produce artwork with as much verisimilitude as possible. Replicating imagery from reproductions does not necessarily "categorize" a patient diagnostically. Selective identification occurs as the image to borrow resonates and is chosen. Most patients who are relatively stable psychologically do attempt to "correct" artistic distortions in borrowed imagery such as giving Modigliani's Anna two "seeing" eyes. In my experience, those with markedly compliant personalities repeatedly defer judgment to the "artist authority."

The patient used the fourth portrait (Figure 8.4), as a vehicle to transform Modigliani's Anna into an ordinary woman. She was no longer a stylized version of a woman as portrayed in the original; rather a most conventional or commonplace figure. The patient was able to create the kind of woman whom he might know, possibly as a mother or other benign presence in his life. He used his ego as agency to create a meaningful portrait that mirrored his own object world.

Case vignette: Phyllis

Phyllis was in her mid-50s, divorced with grown children, when I began to work with her as an outpatient at a community mental health center. Having spent several years in and out of psychiatric hospitals and diagnosed with paranoid schizophrenia, she was not stabilized on medication. Arriving unfailingly early for each session, Phyllis greeted me with a big smile. However, during the two years of our work together, her affect remained largely flat. She usually relied upon art reproductions to stimulate imagery. One day, she decided to reproduce the animals in Franz Marc's painting, *Sleeping White Bull*, in clay (we both thought it was a cow). Pleased with her sculpture, Phyllis created an identical second piece. This time, she modeled it after the first rather than the original Marc painting. Her way of "taking in the image" was by *imitation*. Pleased again with her outcome, she replicated it until she had finally sculpted an assembly line of six. Yet, each iteration involved minor unintended distortion until the sixth was devoid of all vitality; it survived as a sum of its most recognizable body parts. The initial structure and position of the animal remained intact only in the most concrete way. Phyllis imitated her own creations to shore up and celebrate her fragile sense of agency. Yet, her accomplishment was transformed into progressively automatic or robotic acts. She created *symbolic equation*, in Segal's sense. Phyllis's own sense of agency devolved as she suspended "thinking" about the animal she was creating. Similar to other psychiatric patients' concrete acceptance and replication of Modigliani's blackened eye that we had seen earlier, Phyllis's use of the reproduction permitted only an inchoate sense of agency. Her attempt to "hold onto the object" transmuted into the loss of its robustness, with only the animal carcass enduring.

Toward the end of our work, Phyllis sketched Rembrandt's portrait of his sleeping wife, Saskia (*c.*1638). Afterwards, she realized that it reminded her of sleeping with her own grandmother when she visited her farm in the countryside as a young girl. These visits were her happiest memories. They permitted her an experience of more closeness than any other relationship. Now she was able to infuse her drawing with some vigor. She reclaimed remnants of her own inner object world through identification with the sleeping Saskia. Her identification underscored a strengthening of confident expectation and functioned on a more complex personal level than her creations of cows/bulls due to the enduring and remembered mutual affective connection. Her sketch spoke of salient affective memories that served an organizing function in her development. It was not a strong enough one, however, to have averted later psychosis.

Case example: Sybil

In the next vignette I describe Sybil, aged 47. She had undergone several psychiatric hospitalizations for severe depression with persisting suicidal ideation and actual attempts before her cancer diagnosis. Divorced with teenage children, she did not shield them from her rage and desire to abandon them to suicide. I met her on the oncology unit during her cancer treatment after which she entered my women's outpatient cancer group. The other women became visibly uncomfortable hearing Sybil's denigration of both herself and her children when the extent of her pathology became apparent.

Strikingly, Sybil believed that copying an image from an artist would ensure the achievement of a perfect likeness in aesthetic terms. She experienced me as artistically omnipotent and able to guarantee that "success" of a creation would follow, as if by magic. Sometimes, furiously, she berated herself when disappointed with her creations, unable to understand why another patient was more able to obtain a desired result. Apparently, until adolescence she had been an excellent student, albeit with minimal effort. Once effort was required in middle school, her performance fell drastically. Nonetheless, she lacked a sufficient sense of agency to invest herself more fully, in spite of desiring better results.

Though I offered technical help when she felt stuck trying to recreate a fiery Georgia O'Keeffe's 1924 abstract, entitled *From the Lake*, she instantly gave up once I walked away. Having seen another patient in the group, Arielle's precise replica of this painting (Figure 8.8), Sybil compared it unfavorably to her own. No amount of help short of my drawing for her, which I would not do, would have assuaged her sense of frustration. In her disappointment, she turned her drawing sideways, enabling an embryonic bird to eventually become visible to her. She allowed it to emerge. When the group looked at the outcome of her drawing during the sharing time, we realized

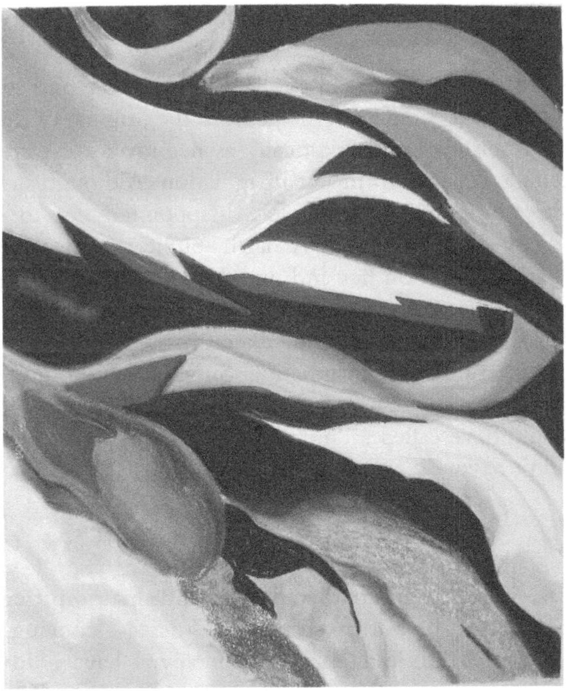

Figure 8.8 Recreation of O'Keeffe's *From the Lake*, by Arielle.

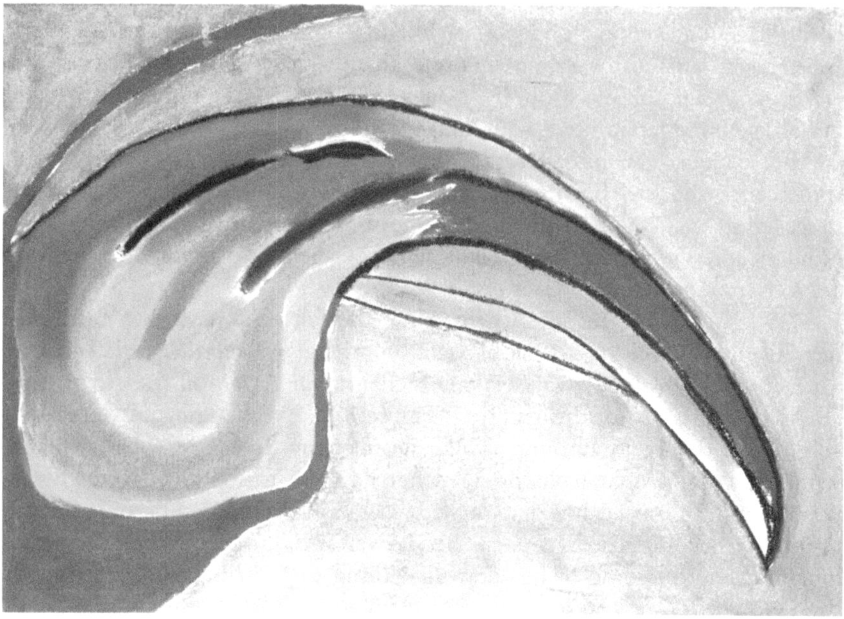

Figure 8.9 Reimagining of O'Keeffe's *From the Lake*, by Sybil.

that the original cave-like abstract form had evolved into a fierce bird with a large beak (Figure 8.9), an entirely different image from the original O'Keeffe. Members of the group responded enthusiastically as her image was created partly from the O'Keeffe and partly from her imagination. Although she felt pleased with the positive response, she still felt disappointed not to have reproduced a carbon copy of the original. A harsh, punitive and primitive superego continually inflicted pain on her and, in turn, upon those closest to her. Creating her bird had been possible due to the repeated influence of other members of my cancer group who freely experimented when borrowing imagery or playfully creating from imagination. Sibyl witnessed this, even as she clung to her wish to replicate by magic. Her painting is reminiscent of what Edith Kramer would have called a "miracle," a painting that came into being but nearly shouldn't have.

Conclusion

Through a series of case vignettes in art therapy with psychiatric patients, I have introduced the concept of the borrowed image. Whereas "copying" has traditionally held a position of low esteem in art therapy, I have illustrated that it is worthwhile for art therapists to examine its role and therapeutic usefulness.

The concept of the transitional object is seen as a prototype to the borrowed image in furthering the internalization process by stimulating creativity. Emphasizing parallels with the role of the transitional object in normal child development, I described how the borrowed image performs a similar function in stimulating creativity in the art therapy process. Psychotic patients previously unable to create or whose creations were disorganized could create with far less internal conflict when borrowing imagery. Artistic imagery, therefore, can function as a catalyst that rescues creativity from conflict. Thus, borrowing helps the patient to enter what Hartmann described as the "conflict-free ego sphere." Imagery can be created with far less anxiety, emptiness and sense of loss. Indeed, patients often expressed feeling better after having used the borrowed image. In my patients, ego organization was strengthened, especially in the cases of severe pathology that were described here. The borrowed image helped to promote a sense of agency, and thus aided self-regulation.

I have argued that the borrowed image holds a similar function to the transitional object in that it provides the means for strengthening the benign and soothing representational object world. The creative and therapeutic experience became meaningful in new ways for many psychiatric patients who previously lacked sufficient internal resources to rely upon their imaginations alone without uncomfortable chaotic expression or uncontrollable regression. This does not obviate the ability of many psychiatric patients to rely upon their imaginations without borrowing from outside. On the whole, they used the borrowed image in the existential sense, to enable their creative expressions to exist at all. Therefore, for the multifaceted reasons I have discussed, the use of the borrowed image can be said to extend the therapeutic process.

Follow up

Further qualitative research studying the borrowed image in psychiatry is needed to affirm its place as a therapeutic tool in art therapy with psychiatric patients. Such research would hopefully confirm the prototype for the borrowed image as the transitional object or transitional phenomena and would stand as a contribution to theory building in art therapy. An examination of the use of the borrowed image with other clinical populations, both children and adults, would help broaden research findings and guide eventual clinical application.

Note

1 Since then, I have also studied the work of children and adults in non-psychiatric populations.

References

Abram, J. (Ed.). (2013). *Donald Winnicott today*. London: Routledge.

Akhtar, S. (2009). *Comprehensive psychoanalytic dictionary*. London: Karnac Books.

Beebe, B., Cohen, P., Lachmann, F. M. & Yothers, D. (2016). *The mother–infant interaction picture book: Origins of attachment*. New York: W. W. Norton & Co.

Beebe, B. & Lachmann, F. M. (2003). The relational turn in psychoanalysis: A dyadic systems view from infant research. *Contemporary Psychoanalysis, 39*, 379–409.

Blanck, G. & Blanck, R. (1994). *Ego psychology: Theory and practice* (2nd ed.). New York: Columbia University Press.

Blatt, S. J. & Blass, R. B. (1990). Attachment and separateness: A dialectic model of the products and processes of development throughout the life cycle. *Psychoanalytic Study of the Child, 45*, 107–127.

Blum, H. P. (1986). On identification and its vicissitudes. *International Journal of Psycho-Analysis, 67*, 267–276.

Bouvet, M. (1955). Technical variation and the concept of distance. *International Journal of Psycho-Analysis, 34*, 211–221.

Deri, S. (1978). Transitional phenomena: Vicissitudes of symbolization and creativity. In S. A. Grolnick, L. Barkin & W. Munsterberger (Eds.), *Between reality and fantasy: Transitional objects and phenomena* (ch. 4). New York: Jason Aronson, Inc.

Hartmann, H. (1958). *The ego and the problem of adaptation*. New York: International Universities Press.

Hinshelwood, R. D. (1991). *A dictionary of Kleinian thought*. New York: Jason Aronson, Inc.

Jacobson, E. (1964). *The self and the object world*. New York: International Universities Press.

Kaminer, H. (1978). Transitional object components in self and object relations. In S. A. Grolnick, L. Barkin & W. Munsterberger (Eds.), *Between reality and fantasy: Transitional objects and phenomena*. New York: Jason Aronson, Inc.

Kaplan, L. (1978). *Oneness & separateness: From infant to individual*. New York: Simon & Schuster.

Loewald, H. (1980). Attachment and separateness: A dialectic model of the products and processes of development throughout the life cycle. *Psychoanalytic Study of the Child*, 45, 107–127.

Mahler, M. S. (1967). On human symbiosis and the vicissitudes of individuation. *Journal of the American Psychoanalytic Association, 15*, 740–763.

Mahler, M. S., Pine, F. & Bergman, A. (1975). *The psychological birth of the human infant*. New York: Basic Books, Inc.

Meissner, W. (1981). *Internalization in psychoanalysis*. New York: International Universities Press.

Melgar, M. C. (2009). Mourning and creativity. In L. Glocer Fiorini, T. Bokanowski & S. Lewkowicz (Eds.), *On Freud's "Mourning and Melancholia"*. London: Karnac Books.

Metcalf, D. & Spitz, R. (1978). The transitional object: Critical developmental period and organizer of the psyche. In S. A. Grolnick, L. Barkin & W. Munsterberger (Eds.), *Between reality and fantasy: Transitional objects and phenomena*. New York: Jason Aronson, Inc.

Saragnano, G. & Seulin, C. (Eds.). (2015). *Playing and reality revisited: A new look at Winnicott's classical work*. International Psychoanalytic Association's Psychoanalytic Classics Revisited Series. London: Karnac Books.

Stone, E. (1981). Some thoughts on the role of copying in art therapy. *American Art Therapy Association Conference Proceedings*. 12th Annual American Art Therapy Association Conference, Philadelphia, PA.

Tolpin, M. (1971). On the beginnings of a cohesive self: An application of the concept of transmuting internalization to the study of the transitional object and signal anxiety. *Psychoanalytic Study of the Child, 26*, 316–352.

Winnicott, D. W. (1958). Transitional objects and transitional phenomena. In *Through Paediatrics to Psycho-Analysis* (pp. 229–242). London: Hogarth Press. (Original work published 1953.)

Winnicott, D. W. (1971). *Playing and reality*. New York: Basic Books.

Further reading

Bollas, C. (1987). *The shadow of the object: Psychoanalysis of the unthought known*. London: Free Association Books.

Freud, A. (1936). *The ego and the mechanisms of defense*. New York: International Universities Press.

Kohut, H. (1971). *The analysis of the self*. New York: International Universities Press.

Nicolo, A. M. (2015). Playing. In G. Saragnano & C. Seulin (Eds.), *Playing and reality revisited: A new look at Winnicott's classical work*. International Psychoanalytic Association's Psychoanalytic Classics Revisited Series. London: Karnac Books.

Rubin, J. A. (2011). *The art of art therapy*. New York: Routledge.

Sandler, J. & Rosenblatt, B. (1962). The representational world. *The Psychoanalytic Study of the Child, 17*, 128–148.

Schaefer, R. (1968). *Aspects of internalization*. New York: International Universities Press.

Chapter 9

Longing for belonging

Zuzana Vasičáková Očenášová and Iveta Koblic Zedková

What are the possibilities, challenges and limits of using Slovak folk dances as a potential therapeutic substrate in dance movement therapy (DMT) when working with clients experiencing psychiatric disorders? In Slovakia, a pilot research aimed at Laban Movement Analyses of five selected Slovak folk dances has been conducted for potential use in dance art and DMT. The initial research question was: What is objectively used and what is negated in terms of movement qualities in Slovak folk dances? The initial research was conducted through video recording of five main types of regional Slovak folk dances demonstrated by professional dancers, and analyses of these recordings through the method of Laban Movement Analysis (LMA). Within each dance type, there was a block of solo dances and pair dances. Five regional folk dances of Zemplín Horehronie, Goral, Podpoľanie and Myjava underwent the basic LMA looking at the four elementary categories of body, effort, shape and space. The project was dedicated to all ancient Slovak dancers whose art has not reached the archival footage of ethnographers, but has survived in living dance.

Expressive therapies (or creative arts therapies) in general add a unique dimension to psychotherapy and counselling because they have several specific characteristics not always found in strictly verbal therapies, including, but not limited to, self-expression, active participation, imagination and mind–body connections (Malchiodi, 2005). In DMT specifically, it is possible that the body–mind connection will evolve and be realized directly in the physical world. Moreover, the majority of psychiatry settings are historically and functionally focused on illness and pathology. DMT enables psychiatric patients to connect to their healthy parts instead, inviting body and movement to serve as a safe bridge to them. The richer the individual movement vocabulary and repertoire of cultural dance metaphors of the dance movement therapist, the better he or she is prepared to follow the unique body–mind process of each patient.

Representing and expressing the cultural and social contexts of the bodily self, folk dances can be seen as a valuable resource for therapeutic interventions. The actual applied follow-up research questions that create a mental frame for this text are: How can we use the insights into the spectrum of the movement qualities of Slovak folk dances to assess them as a potentially therapeutic substrate for DMT? Additionally, based on the analysis carried out, the risks, limits and drawbacks of the application of the elements of Slovak folk dances in DMT will be discussed.

Dance movement therapy is an autonomous holistic psychotherapeutic approach that uses movement and dance in order to achieve emotional, cognitive, social, behavioural and physical integrity in the individual. It operates within the concept of constant interaction of body and mind. DMT is founded on the principle that movement reflects an individual's patterns of thinking and feeling. Through acknowledging and supporting clients' movements, the therapist encourages the development and integration of new adaptive movement patterns together with the emotional experiences that accompany such changes. It is a relational process in which client/s and therapist engage creatively using body movement and dance to assist integration of emotional, cognitive, physical, social and spiritual aspects of self. The philosophical orientation is based on the intrinsic belief in the interrelationship between psyche, soma and spirit as evidenced in the potential held in creative processes. The theoretical background of DMT consists of knowledge of developmental movement patterns, movement analysis and process dynamics. Each individual's nonverbal movement style becomes the fundamental communicative tool. Each individual's personal movement style is made up of a unique organization of these qualities. One of the key therapeutic principles in the field of DMT is observing the expression of the person's movement qualities. The dance therapist aims to help individuals use their bodies through dance and movement to express their experiences of relating to and developing within their surroundings.

One of the key instruments of dance movement therapy is Laban Movement Analysis – a sophisticated, generally applicable complex system that allows the observation and analysis of movement, based on objective concepts. It supports the therapist to see the movement in all its various levels and sub-channels and, as such, avoid rapid interpretations. LMA in DMT can be used as an assessment tool and as a tool for developing and specifying therapeutic interventions. LMA has four main categories also known by the acronym BESS: body, effort, space and shape. Through BESS we can systematically analyse the movement of the human body from both functional and expressive points of view.

Within the "body" category, we tend to ask: Which part of the body initiates the movement? How does the movement continue? Which body parts are connected through the movement? Where in the body is movement supported? How do shifts in body weight happen? Which developmental patterns does the movement refer to? Observing "effort" qualities, we ask: How is the movement executed? What is the intention? What are the dynamics of the movement? Dynamics of work with weight is observed and analysed on a scale of strong–light; the relationship of movement to space on a scale of direct–indirect; the relationship of movement to time on a scale of deceleration–acceleration or quick–sustained; the flow of movement on a scale of bound–free. In "space", we are curious: What is the kinesphere (the sphere around the body whose periphery can be reached by easily extending limbs, without stepping away from that place which is the point of support) of the movement? Which tracks does the movement draw? How does the moving person use his or her internal space? What is the relationship of the moving body to the positioning in space? Within the "shape" category, we ask: What form and what relationships create the moving body? How does the shape change and what is the main element that affects the process of change? Is the change in body shape motivated from internal or external stimuli? In this category we are working with subcategories of shape-flow (one-dimensional relationship to self), directional shape (arch-like or spoke-like two-dimensional relationships to the external environment) and shaping (three-dimensional active relationship with self and the environment).

Slovak folk dances through the lens of LMA

The initial research was conducted under the institutional roof of Laban Atelier Bratislava (www.labanbratislava.sk) through video recording of five main types of regional Slovak folk dances and analyses of these recordings through the method of LMA. The recordings were conducted in cooperation with three professional Slovak folk dancers and a folk dance expert from S UK – Slovak Folk Art Ensemble. Within each dance type, there was a block of solo dances and pair dances. The analysis was conducted for each dance type and block separately – concentrating on the one hand on movement preferences, but also looking at the less or never used movement qualities lying in the "movement shadow". The first-level analysis was outlined during the real-time "life" observation including mirroring and conscious kinesthetic resonance of the researcher as a source of information. The second-level analysis was based on the video recordings. Consequently, a comparative analysis was carried out to see common patterns in either movement preferences or movement qualities in the "shadow". The analysis was focused on the four main LMA movement categories: body, effort, shape and space.

The analyses brought up common movement patterns, shadow movement qualities, movement shifts from authentic folk dancing of the 19th century to its theatre stage modifications of the 20th century and community use in the 21st century, as well as differences in movement choices of men and women. The prevailing common movement choices were indicated.

The following is a summary of the LMA outcomes focusing on common movement patterns of Slovak folk dances:

Verticality

Movement in a vertical direction prevails. Verticality in movement is expressed in the movement upwards–downwards. Developmentally it refers to the connection of head and coccyx ("head–tail connection") and to the pattern of yielding and pushing – as seen in crawling toddlers. In the vertical dimension movement generally takes on a dynamic of effort in the scale from strong movement downwards to light movement upwards. LMA experts may connect the use of the vertical dimension and the use of weight stating they are linked to representing the "self" – the self-consciousness of man.

Stable upper part and active lower part of the body

Unlike the movement and body settings in manual labour with the hands or in verbal communications, in Slovak folk dance the upper body provides stability, while the lower body is active and communicating. The upper body is active but not mobile. It creates a symbol of self-representation, which is not ready to communicate with the outside world because it acts as a stabilizer, as a support for active feet. A homologous developmental pattern prevails.

Free flow of the lower body

In the mobilized lower part of the body, free flow of movement prevails. It brings themes of playfulness, improvisation. What is seen less is the bound flow of the movement connected to the quality of conscious processing, of reflection and of control.

Direct relationship to space

Especially in the movement of male dancers, direct relationship to space prevails, which may be related to the theme of concentration on a single goal and to the theme of decision making. Women are more likely to alternate between a direct and indirect relationship to the space in movement. The quality of an indirect relationship to space is, for a female dancer in Slovak folklore, often necessary in turning or in pair situations where she has to perceive the environment and be ready to follow stimuli from the outside – from the partner. The woman in a pair follows the man in tracks, motives and rhythm changes.

What remains in the movement shadow?

LMA is a tool for naming what is used within the possibilities of our movement scales – what movement choices have taken place. However, to understand the observed movement, it is equally important to see which parts of the movement scales are not used at all or which are used just marginally. What remains in the shadow is often the key. Remaining in the shadow of the movement in Slovak folk dances is the mobility of the upper body and hands; the connection between the centre and upper limbs; the full use of the horizontal space; sustained movement, indulging the quality of time; three-dimensional shaping in movement; contralateral movement across the body axis and transverse movement direction within the kinesphere; the use of anatomically sequential movement and Laban "space" category itself remains hidden.

In other words, someone performing a Slovak folk dance communicates more inwardly; concentrates rather than perceives the outer world; takes less space; reflects less; plays more. Action dominates over recuperation. There is more sorting and less context-making.

Slovak folk dancing creates a scene where a passionate love and hate story between man and the earth takes place. The earth is more explicitly important than heaven and the world around.

Relationship between the landscape and the dance

In the northern mountainous regions, more stamping in the dance style occurs, connected to which is direct strong weight up and down, as well as softer and lighter "ornamental" feet (Goral, Horehron). Towards the less mountainous south (Zemplín, Myjava), the kinesphere of the movement increases and more jumps and a wider range of footwork occur.

Movement differences in male and female dancing

If the Slovak folk dances are an image of the life of men and women living in rural Slovakia in the 19th and early 20th centuries, then what can be seen in movement? Differences are apparent in all categories of BESS. Women use less hip mobility (which is in contrast with typical female physiology of higher mobility in joints and tendons). Men are more mobile in the limbs, often touching their bodies with strong weight effort and direct relationship to space, for example, when dancing "čapáše". Women are relatively more likely to use lightness in footwork, indirect and free-flow movement in pelvis rotation. Women use more of the horizontal direction of movement, but they take less operational space using a smaller kinesphere. They rarely dance solo and use a narrower and a less articulated motif repertoire. Men also widen their kinesphere through the opening of their hands. Women hold their hands mainly on their hips or waist. Men largely shape their movement in two-dimensional space, whereas women's movement sometimes reaches into a three-dimensional sphere. Men disclose more of their physical possibilities of self-expression. Opportunities for self-expression through movement for women remains largely in the movement shadow.

For further information on LMA outcomes on particular types of folk dance from five regions in Slovakia, we refer the reader to the DVD/publication "Come on, Mr. Laban!" published by Laban Atelier Bratislava.

Slovak folk dances in dance movement therapy?

The data material has the potential to be further developed in the area of DMT in the following general directions:

- as a reservoir of set movement metaphors – framed movement material to be therapeutically experienced and worked in addition to improvised dance where different specific themes can be precisely addressed;
- as material for the exploration of patterns of collective nonverbal metaphors and access to re-ownership of the individual–collective roots;
- as a substrate for the specified work with dyads on the themes of relations, partnership and gender;
- as a space for relating and enabling a sense of belonging to emerge.

For the specific psychiatric patient population, therapeutically highly relevant clusters were identified in the research data material:

- the individual level: safety and boundaries in the psychiatric setting (safely bounded repeatable movement material can be provided to be therapeutically worked on where different specific themes can be pointed out and precisely, but safely, addressed);
- the social level: socialization and belonging to the larger community (of a psychiatric patient) in a destigmatizing context (as material to explore patterns of collective nonverbal metaphors and to create access to re-ownership of the individual–collective roots; enabling a sense of belonging to emerge);
- the relational level: dyadic relationships as a source of self–other reconnection and a support (a substrate for specified work with dyads on the themes of relations, partnership and gender; space for relating), connecting to the past.

Slovak folk dances as a treasure chest for individual work in a psychiatric setting

Folk dances in general present a rich source of set, predictable movement metaphors (Capello, 2007) in different anthropological kinesthetic models bound to different cultural areas. Folk dances tend to be familiar in the given community, and therefore their use fluidly supports the therapeutic process.

For example, looking at Indian folk dances, the fast footwork of Kathak dance (Chatterjee, 2013) helps to release anger and tension. Manipuri dancers make rounded movements and avoid any jerks, sharp edges or straight lines. It gives them an undulating and soft appearance, proper body control and peace of mind.

In Slovak folk dances, the prevailing common movement choices were indicated within the cited pilot LMA analyses (Vasičáková Očenášová, 2012) – where further therapeutic effect can be presumed: verticality (sense of self); upper–lower body connection, with upper body stable while lower body half is active (stability/mobility principle); use of flow (creativity and support of spontaneity); strong effort and direct relationship to the space (supporting concentration and decision making).

According to Parvia (Capello, 2007), most DMT students seem to have trained in post-modern dance forms that give ample freedom for moving, experimentation and expression. She feels, however, that there continues to be something missing: a centre to work from, a source of strength, varying use of energy, or, perhaps, a deeper commitment to dance and a fuller understanding of the possibilities of dance in therapy. As a dance movement therapist, Parvia believes it is more important to learn the movement qualities appropriate for the skill level of the client, and the basis of the psychological needs of the client's culture.

Given that DMT is aimed at supporting the integration of the whole scale of movement opportunities for the patient, and taking into account the therapeutic theme of borders as a cross-cutting theme across the variety of diagnoses in a psychiatric setting, then expressing through fixed sets of movement variations that present a collective movement metaphor might strongly support therapeutic processes, add to the feeling of basic safety and open the way for safe movement visits to alternative modes of personal reality and problem-solving for the patient.

We can say that, to learn and dance a folk dance, fixed metaphor means to perform intentional, conscious, ego-directed movement. Intentional, conscious movement includes every conscious deliberate physical action. Voluntary aspects of our gestures, work actions and play involve the intentional use of time, weight and flow (Chodorow, 1995).

One way of approaching the movement material within safe boundaries, rather than (or before) (the aspect of freedom?) working freely, especially in psychiatric settings, is to use the unique source of folk dances' movement variations – presenting safely bounded repeatable movement material which can be provided to be therapeutically worked on, while different specific themes can be pointed out and precisely but safely addressed.

Another possibility of the usage of LMA-analysed Slovak folk dances in individual therapeutic work in psychiatric settings is through drawing on a knowledge of typical movement characteristics of psychiatric disorders and supporting the process of widening the movement repertoire of the patient. This approach aims to match and use precisely the folk dances' variations that correspond, but also go slightly beyond, the nonverbal status quo of the patient.

According to Martha Davis (1981), schizophrenia, major depression and bipolar disorder reflect in movement in flat affect, psychomotor retardation and motor stereotypes. It has been documented for over a century that certain characteristics of physical movement relate to specific mental illnesses (Rennie, 1941; Wittenborn, 1962; both cited in Davis, 1981). The "waxy flexibility" of the catatonic patient, the grimacing of a hebephrenic, the sluggish, heavy manner of someone in severe depression, are symptoms often noted when the disorders are described. Reich (1949, cited in Davis, 1981) and Lowen (1967, cited in Davis, 1981) presented rich clinical descriptions of individual patterns of muscle armouring and physical constriction as they relate to psychopathology. Condon (1968, cited in Davis, 1981) described in detailed film analysis the lack of self-synchrony in the movement of schizophrenic patients. The dance therapist in a hospital setting knows perhaps better than anyone else how movement patterns reflect the patient's psychiatric states.

According to Davis, before linking the movement patterns too irrevocably to traditional psychiatric diagnoses, it would be better at this stage to evaluate the findings of the conducted studies by staying closer to the movement dimension itself. It seems premature to tightly define movement types, in an attempt to approximate traditional psychiatric categories. Where movement could uniquely contribute to the understanding of behaviour would be distorted or missed.

What is important to add, as Davis (1981) writes, is that mapping the typical movement profiles of people suffering different diagnoses focuses on movement pathology which does not do justice to the richness and complexity of the patient's movement patterns nor to the patient as a person. Indeed, in DMT, we do not need to eliminate the movement expressions of the mental disorder – we should rather honour it as a valuable current survival strategy and just offer new movement possibilities to those existing – to ease the suffering through strengthening the ability of self-regulation and widening the scope of alternative ways to deal with life. Here, usage of dance (including folk dances) and DMT is not only a healing mode but also a preventive intervention to be thought of in more general terms.

From our roots in dance we know that the emotions motivate and shape the way we move (Chodorow, 1995). According to Chodorow, there are seven fundamental emotions: joy, interest, surprise, grief, fear, anger and disgust. Each is described by many terms that express a continuum of intensity, from mild to extreme. An emotion is at once somatic and psychic. Somatic means here the bodily innervations and expressive physical action. Trying to define the psychic aspect of emotion, Chodorow writes about associated images and ideas. In the depths of the unconscious, it is emotions that mediate between the realms of body and psyche, instinct and spirit.

One possible approach in using folk dances' fixed movement metaphors in DMT in a psychiatric setting is first to offer the patient different types of movement variations of folk dances. The next step would be to observe where the patients' strongest process appears. The hypothesis here would be that the strongest process appears in the movement material shaped in the very type of emotion that wants to be expressed and the nonverbal channel might be a safe way of communicating this. What are we trying to create space for in DMT using folk dances' fixed movement metaphors? It is nothing less than a safe connection with the emotions, access to which is rather complicated or blocked due to the constellation of the inner censor, the psychiatric disorder itself or emotional dystrophy caused by medication in the psychiatric setting.

From what we have learned in DMT, it also functions the other way round – not only do emotions shape the way we move, but also the way we move influences our emotions and overall psychological states. After creating a safe space for the client, further work can be done through introducing more directly selected movement metaphors inspired by the folk dances' movement material, which allow the client to experience movements and emotions which are hidden in his/her movement shadow (the movement qualities that are not used). The ultimate therapeutic aim here (as elsewhere) would be wholeness – complex psychological, emotional, social and physical integration.

Slovak folk dances as the path to belonging

Folk dances (Capello, 2007) can be seen as a source of collective memory, tying together generations, giving meaning to the movement and serving as the objective of groups, which permit the beginning of the feeling of "belonging" and reinforcing socio-cultural identity. Bednarova (Capello, 2007) believes that structures of folk and community dances mirror the typical essential functioning of human society, giving the dancers an opportunity to learn to cope with situations they may encounter in their everyday lives. Bednarova gave an example of how a Czech folk dance called the Beseda might be utilized in a DMT session. The Beseda is a collection of seven folk dances created in the 19th century at the time of the national revival and independence movement. It became the symbol of national roots and is still danced today. Mapping the use of folk dances in DMT worldwide (Capello, 2007), similarities became apparent in the use of traditional folk dances, particularly those in circle formations and the cross-cultural experience of simple, repetitive communal movements. Essential to the sacred origin of circle dances was the importance of the circle and the centre (Serlin, 1993) (e.g. ring dances in the Mediterranean, Greek orpheotelestale, Middle Eastern and midsummer dances in Scandinavia, and in Slovakia, the women's circle dance of Kari ka, danced originally without music, using group weight support, repetitive steps and acceleration of the tempo, which brings up the theme of trance in folk and community dances). The circle is still used extensively in

DMT to start group sessions, to give participants a sense of boundary and inclusion, to provide closure. Groups, which are cohesive, can form circles and often do so spontaneously; groups which are fragmented form circles with difficulty.

Mary Whitehouse (Chodorow, 1995) was the first dance therapist who described movement from the perspective of conscious and unconscious. Janet Adler (1987, cited in Chodorow, 1995) differentiates between movement patterns that can be traced to personal history and those that seem to come from a transpersonal source. Here, the post-experience verbalization and education around the transpersonal part of fixed folk dances' movement metaphors can bring relief from the notions of individual guilt and individual responsibility to patients in psychiatric settings.

Obviously, there are different challenges and opportunities behind the use of folk dances of the clients' country of origin in comparison with the use of folk dances from different cultures. While the first case would be more aimed at interconnecting the client with his or her transpersonal level of collective patterns and unconsciousness, the second case would presumably bring insights into moving and experiencing his or her or the group's movement shadow (movement qualities not used in the movement choices of the individual or the group). In psychiatric settings, the first alternative can enrich the theme of belonging and integrating, but also can bring a risk of re-traumatization in the cases of wounds in cultural memory or if there are old, unprocessed experiences of violent separation.

Looking at Slovak folk dances' potential for DMT in the psychiatric setting, another type of challenge and risk emerges – related to the acknowledgement of gender differences in movement variations. Connection with the male or female inner and interrelational sources would be the benefit. Risk of re-traumatization of the individual and cultural wounds around male–female polarization, violence, oppression and power conflicts is, however, something to be taken into account as well. According to the LMA analyses of the five selected Slovak folk dances cited in this text, opportunities for self-expression through movement for women remains largely in the movement shadow in comparison with male dancers in Slovak folk dances.

The cultural unconsciousness may express an ongoing stream of the mythic imaginary (Chodorow, 1995). The expressive actions of the cultural unconscious are not planned; rather they emerge: over time, many of these unprompted expressions have entered the cultural collective as a ceremonial act of prayer, and worship dance steps and poetical movements that mirror the beauty of nature and social customs that mediate human relationships. Movements from the cultural unconsciousness are our bridge to mythic images.

For modern dance movement therapists, the understanding of healing practices is enriched with echoes of ancient images and performances (Serlin, 1993). These echoes provide both humility and perspective to a practice carried out in mental health clinics, nursing homes or schools. Early dance suggests a time when thinking was not yet separated from feeling and from action. This form of knowing is ecstatic and involves cyclical rather than linear time, a reverie state and transformation (Serlin, 1993). The inability to connect to these unconscious or immediate forms of knowing characterize the symptomology and alienation of much of the psychic distress of the modern and post-modern age. DMT plays an important role in recovering the intuitive and imaginative powers to make the person whole again.

The following attachment is a shortened version of the concrete Laban movement analyses of each of the five selected Slovak folk dances. It might be interesting specifically for colleagues already working with LMA one way or another and for folk dancers.

Appendix: Laban movement analyses of folk dances from the five regions of Slovakia

Excerpt from the DVD/publication "Come on, Mr. Laban!"

Concept, text: Mgr. Zuzana Vasičáková Očenášová
Analysis: Mgr. Zuzana Vasičáková Očenášová, Doc. Marta Poláková, ArtD
Expert consultations: Mgr. Art. Stanislav Marišler, ArtD
Project partner: SĽUK – Slovak Folk Art Ensemble
The research project was supported by the Ministry of Culture of the Slovak Republic
The English version was supported by the Education and Culture Lifelong Learning Programme GRUNDTVIG.
Published by: Laban ATELIÉR BRATISLAVA (www.labanbratislava.sk).

Zemplín pair dance

Within the body category, homologous and homolateral developmental movement pattern prevails. The body is supported through triangles of head–shoulder blades; tail bone–heels and tailbone–seat bones. The movement begins in the pelvis and is carried on in the vertical direction.

In the effort category, the use of weight varies: from strong weight by stamping, to light by turns. The following action drives are frequent: punch, dab, slash and, in turns, glide. Quality of weight and time are dominant – an inner rhythm state is present. The passion transformation drive prevails – one can see flow, time and weight; relationship to space remains on the margin.

In the category of space, a small kinesphere appears, magnified only in the parts when "čapáš" is performed. A two-dimensional movement shape prevails.

Zemplín woman

A homologous developmental pattern prevails in the ring. In the final solo it is transformed into the homolateral pattern with an arm raised high, but the head facing down. Horizontal space is in use, while the movements return to the vertical plane in skipping and rotations.

There is more indirect relation to space – direct relation to space remains in stamping and in the movement towards the centre of the circle. Especially in the beginning, there is more bound flow and more sustained time than in pair dancing. In the effort category of time and weight there are a lot of changes on the scales of acceleration–deceleration and light–strong. When using strong weight, forward–backward sagittal plane movement is in use. In the solo significant weight shifts appear, with free flow in hips and pelvis: the hips' movement subsides to the end, not stopping abruptly, as it does in the pair dance. The action drives of dabbing, punching, floating and gliding are visible.

Work with space is significant – tracks in a circle, an ellipse, movement forwards and backwards (into and away from the centre of the circle), changing rotation tracks in the solo.

Zemplín man

There is high mobility of the pelvis and legs with a wide movement range up to hip joints, verifying the physical boundaries through touching, slapping at the dancer's own body. The body is supported through the firm torso. Homolateral developmental pattern prevails, changes into contralateral in skipping. Movements interconnecting the upper and lower limbs through the centre of the body and, occasionally, a navel radiation movement pattern.

In the effort scale of movement qualities, indirect space prevails, interchanging with the direct space; strong weight while clapping and stamping with light weight in skipping. Interestingly enough, the dancer uses the sagittal forward–backward plane especially for recuperation after exertion. Action drives of punch, glide, slash, dab appear, always using either direct relation to space or strong weight. The dancer uses a larger kinesphere (see above for a definition of the term) than in a pair dance. Continuing shape-flow happens, expanding and narrowing the movement in the horizontal plane. Sometimes, directional shape of movement appears relating towards the audience or the band. Sometimes we also see three-dimensional shaping (in strikes while kneeling, in vaults).

Horehronie pair dance

In the man's movement, homolateral shifts of body weight in horizontal dimension are seen. The woman remains in the vertical plane. The pelvis rotates around the vertical axis, more visibly in women's movement with the support of external rotation of the feet and soles. The body is supported by the connection of the bony landmarks between the head and hands on hips with the woman, and the head and hands resting on the sacrum bone with the man.

For the recuperation, in the formation of a half-opened pair of dancers, the sagittal forwards–backwards direction functions again. Use of the strong weight in the downwards direction varies: stamping alternates with lighter steady steps. In quick sequences of stamping, accelerated time quality and free flow are in use. When a man claps his hands, the woman turns around and changes the effort quality from direct relation to space in the vertical plane to indirect in the horizontal plane.

The upper body moves in bound flow, while the lower body moves in free flow. In the moments when the pair holds both hands face to face, rare free flow in upper body appears as well. In addition to the prevailing inner rhythm state, while turning around, the woman transverses into an inner dream state of movement with significant qualities of weight and flow in movement.

In stamping, the woman remains at the periphery of the kinesphere. The man uses also upwards direction and movements traversing the kinesphere. The movement paths of the woman are shorter and accented. The connection between the male and female dancer while turning with light weight steps alters with disconnection of partners when moving through sequences of stamping with stronger weight.

Horehronie man

Looking at the body category, arms serve as support and stabilization for mobile legs and feet. The body base is wider – and it is getting narrower while stamping. The upper part of the body is, in comparison with Zemplín dances, more stable. We observe rotation in the hips with a hint of contralaterality. Jumping movements are initiated from the chest. In the effort category, we see more of sustained time and upwards-accented light weight. Movement doesn't risk much – there is more control and more of the bound flow. Legs and feet traverse in diagonals through the kinesphere, directed from the outside inwards. When stamping, shape-flow prevails. When using pull-like steps, movements shift towards a directional shape.

Horehronie woman

The body of the female dancer has a narrower body base, upper limbs stabilize the body through holding hips, arms are opening while turning. Upper limbs are opening and palms are rotating when significant pelvic rotation by stamping happens. Homolateral head movement is observable. We see action drives of dabbing by stamping and gliding by turns. Interestingly, the female dancer almost doesn't use movement in space at all – she never changes the space paths.

Goral pair dance

Movement lacks grounding in the earth, which is compensated in wider body bases by the man and constant weight shift in a quick series of steps by the woman. The woman also compensates for lack of grounding in earth by firm holding hands on hips with wide open firm elbows. There is also stabilizing interconnection of the bony landmarks of head and seat bones. While the activity of legs and feet goes on, the male upper body rotates through contralateral shifts of hands. Female movement remains in the vertical plane, with the centre of gravity shifted upwards. The woman doesn't use the whole surface of her soles, she doesn't repose on the heels at all. The man works with upper limbs in large gestures of opening and closing with hands clapping.

The woman doesn't use the upper limbs at all. Stamping runs in an alternating contralateral and homolateral pattern, while rotation is visible in either the upper or lower part of the body. There is very quick changing of light and strong weight, while the strong weight gravity is, particularly with women, weakened by bound flow and the need to use indirect relation to space when she captures leading signals from the male partner. However, when she repeats the rhythmic stamping of the partner, there is a strong weight without compromising. In the category of space, the man circles around the woman. When the pair positions face each other, sagittal backwards–forwards path prevails. In the category of shape, with the female dancer one-dimensional inwards, oriented shape-flow prevails, interrupted only by the male's leading signals. With the male dancer, two-dimensional directional shape prevails. Both partners strictly respect each other's personal spaces, with no touching. The interconnection happens mainly through male leading signals of hand clapping and stamping, echoed or mirrored by the woman's reaction.

Goral woman

In this region, a woman does not dance alone.

The woman in the couple dances follows these rules:

- keep your shoulders parallel with man's shoulders;
- react when the man stamps, while the movement of the male partner doesn't stop, it continues;
- turn around on the hand-clap signal.

Goral man

In the body category, a left–right homolateral pattern prevails. Body support lies on the triple connection of feet and head, in squatting on the connection of pelvis and arms, one arm holding a valaška (a traditional axe-like stick). Movement work with levels in space through deep squats and high jumps and turning is significant. Rare movement of using recession steps – movement in a backwards direction appears.

Podpoľanie pair dance

Movement brings less rapid changes, less time quality contrasts, more steady speed, fluidity and release. Movement of women is more equal in terms of the richness of the movement material and freedom of decision making over the selection of motifs. In the body category, vertical upper–lower rhythmical suspension and homolateral pattern is seen. The man's arms are raised and held in upper space around the head, sometimes touching the back of his head. The woman's palms are directed down. Upper limbs bend at the elbow simultaneously with a bending of the knees. In the context of Slovak folk dances a rare anatomically sequential movement appears, which is highly articulated. Movement is initiated in the feet and soles, in the pelvis or in the palms. The body is supported via connection of the blades and tail or the pelvis. The upper body stays open.

In the effort category we see indirect relation to space and bound flow more frequently. There is more light weight in a downward direction together with sustained time. Movement is happening in phrases, with the weight emphasis on the first rhythm accent. We see rocking as movement action. A remote inner state of movement prevails with emphasis on the relationship to space and flow. At the end of the sequence, the transformation vision drive appears. There are action drives of floating, flicking and wringing appearing in movement. The dancers occupy a large kinesphere. Turnings in the pair happen with strong vertical axis feeling. When pair-turning, the dancers are very close to each other. Otherwise, partners dance individually; they return to the pair formation in a slower pace to recuperate after the individual output.

Podpoľanie woman

In the body category, we see alternating of homolateral and contralateral movements with leaning forwards and back. The upper body compensates by tilting the movement of the legs, with the accent on the tilt to one side. There is a lot of hand work with a scarf with active wrists and a lot of closing and opening. Ongoing horizontal hip movement happens. The vertical plane is also present through the eyes, with sight alternating up and down. Yielding and grounding is almost absent. The upper body is activated through the linkage of chest and head while opening and closing in the upper space.

In the category of effort, direct relationship to space, light weight and quick time with free flow dominates. In space we see direct paths, sagittal movement forwards and backwards and circle space formation. In the movement motif of the "mill" we see shape-flow in the hands.

Myjava pair dance

While the upper body holds the vertical axis, the lower body half moves in the sagittal while stepping out. Just the front part of the soles is in use – lack of grounding is compensated through the tension in the upper body. The action of arms and hands is limited to holding and pushing when lifting the partner and being lifted. Contralaterality is absent. In the effort category, a new type of action drive appears – pushing, especially when kneeling. Otherwise, there is direct relationship to space, light to neutral weight, neutral flow. Highlighting the weight and relation to space categories directs one to a stable inner state. Minimum work in the time category indicates transformation of the passion drive in movement changes. Holding hands while kicking legs defines the space between the partners. Legs work in sagittal pathways, the upper body is vertical. There is almost no horizontal plane. The upper kinesphere is not used in any way. In the category of shape that maps relations in movement, there is an exceptional appearance of precise mutual mirroring in the pair interrupted by lifting the woman dancer.

Myjava man

In the male solo we see hip rotation and strong upper body movement downwards with a palm hitting the ground. In the effort category light weight and direct relationship to the space in the lower limbs, the regular alternation of acceleration and deceleration associated with alternating of bound and free flow appears.

Shifts: from authentic folklore to the dance on a stage

What in Slovak folk dance has changed over the last 60 years? From being performed in pubs, courtyards and small rooms, the dance arrived on the large stage of theatres. And this changed the dance itself.

Dynamics and relationships in movement: relationship between the dance pair and the audience

In the original dance expression, at the end of the dance sequence, the dance pair was using strong weight downwards; while opening, the closed pair formation happened there, where the movement brought the dancers into the concrete situation. When the dance shifted to the stage, it brought the need to end the dance sequence by always facing the viewer. Thereby, the final opening of the pair formation lost grounding and changed the direction and relation to the space. The full stop after the dance, which was originally about the two who were dancing, changed into a final smile into the theatre spotlight.

Body and flow in movement: tiptoes and boots

The free swing of the leg in the men's solo dance transformed under the influence of classical scenic dance into stretched limb with strained tiptoe – which is hardly realizable in an authentic setting of dancing in a pub while wearing heavy working boots.

Gender and movement repertoire: male motifs in the female movement repertoire

Compared with authentic video recordings, in the contemporary folk dance the range of motifs in women's dancing is richer and more varied. Many elements are taken from the vocabulary of male motifs.

Lifts: from the hint of play to a physical power game

Lifts in Myjava dances were originally a rare movement element, usually appearing in a simple and accessible form at the end of a dance sequence. On the stage, the lifts have been multiplied, become physically demanding and acrobatic – which requires such concentration and muscle deployment that it excludes improvisation.

References

Capello, P. (2007). Dance as our source in dance/movement therapy education and practice. *American Journal of Dance Therapy, 29*(1).

Chatterjee, A. (2013). The therapeutic value of Indian classical, folk and innovative dance forms, Barasat College, West Bengal State University, India, Rupkatha. *Journal on Interdisciplinary Studies in Humanities, 5*(1).

Chodorow, J. (1995). Body, psyche and the emotions. *American Journal of Dance Therapy, 17*(2).

Davis, M. (1981). Movement characteristics of hospitalized psychiatric patients. *American Journal of Dance Therapy, 4*(1), 52–71.

Malchiodi, C. A. (2005). *Expressive therapies: History, theory and practice*. New York: Guilford Publications.

Serlin, I. (1993). Root images of healing in dance therapy. *American Journal of Dance Therapy, 15*(2).

Vasičáková Očenášová, Z. (2012). *Come on, Mr. Laban!: Laban movement analyses of the folk dances from the five regions of Slovakia* [DVD/publication]. Bratislava: Laban Atelier.

Chapter 10

Assessing negative symptoms of schizophrenia by the use of Aristotle's "Poetics" during a dramatherapy performance process

Lambros Yotis

Introduction

Psychological approaches tend to enhance the effect of medical treatment for clients with psychoses and propose a better quality of life for the suffering individuals and their families (Martindale et al., 2000). In addition, the stigma of individuals with psychoses, regarded both as social distance and as an internal process of self-stigmatization, can be effectively confronted by methods that target contact and education (Corrigan & Bink, 2016; Corrigan, Morris, Michaels, Rafacz & Rüsch, 2012; Rössler, 2016). Qualitative and quantitative research studies have shown that the use of dramatherapy in psychiatric settings for individuals with schizophrenia is an effective therapeutic approach aiming at the reduction of the clients' symptoms, as well as the improvement of their creativity and communication skills (Yotis, 2006). Considering clients with schizophrenia, dramatherapy takes place mostly within the closed boundaries of a group process; keeping the work within the group offers creative transformations and preserves safety, group cohesion and confidentiality, avoiding the stress of social exposure (Casson, 2004; Cox, 1992; Gersie, 1996; Jones, 1996, 2010; Landy, 1995; Langley & Langley, 1983; Reisman, 2016; Whitelock, 1987). Nevertheless, showing the creative outcome as a performance to an invited audience can empower, build social networks, improve social inclusion and decrease the stigma of people living with psychiatric disabilities (Bosco et al., 2014; Faigin & Stein, 2015; Yotis, Kravariti, Theodoridou & Megaloeconomou, 2003; Yotis, Theohari, Katan & Mantonakis, 2002). Therapeutic and community theatre methods have various outlines, phases and techniques, as a number of therapists using drama have shown in the relevant literature during the last century (Andersen-Warren, 1996; Bielanska, Cechnicki & Budzyna-Dawidowski, 1991; Emunah, 1994; Grainger, 1990; Johnson, 1980, 1981, 1982; Jones, 1996; Mitchell, 1998; Moran & Alon, 2011; Yotis, 2014). Therefore, there is a need to define therapeutic performance for an audience within the context of dramatherapy and to assess it both as a therapeutic and as a dramatic phenomenon.

A "dramatherapy performance" is a term that defines a performance event which is created by and contained within a therapeutic process and which is based on the group members' personal material that is evoked, worked through, reconstructed, combined and projected into a dramatic form, in order to be presented to an invited audience (Yotis, 2002). This definition implies the following aspects:

a A "dramatherapy performance" is a performance production, which is devised by a dramatherapy process, a drama process that has a healing intention.
b It differentiates "dramatherapy performance" from other dramatherapy group practices, which do not aim for a final product to be witnessed by an invited audience.
c Among the group members' personal material evoked during the "dramatherapy performance" process, only the parts that are worked through therapeutically and are ready to be exposed will reach the final performance, with the mutual consent of clients and therapists.
d Relating both the process and the final product to the group members' lives is the aim of this therapeutic intervention.
e Achievement or non-achievement of the intended final performance may both be options, the significance of which belongs to the therapeutic process.
f It differentiates between a "dramatherapy performance" and the processes of "ordinary" theatre performances or "para-theatrical" happenings, whose aim is the final theatrical outcome, the intrinsic healing quality of which, if apparent, is not subject to validation.

This chapter aims to show how this method can be assessed and how the clients' performance can be evaluated throughout the therapeutic process.

Within mental health services, individuals with schizophrenia live out their own life "roles", moving in their own dramatic bodies with specific symptoms and behaviours and particular expressive skills (Crisp, Gelder, Rix, Meltzer & Rowlands, 2000; Goffman, 1961). A changing image of their dramatic bodies becomes apparent when a performance takes place with "actors-patients" and an "audience". When such a process takes place in a psychiatric ward, the change has two basic observable parameters: the change in the clients' deficiencies and the creativity they develop. Within such a frame the "actors" can be seen as bearing a conflict between two opposite forces: the inertia, due to the biology of their psychiatric disorder, as opposed to a vital force to reach out to the world, participate and create. Symbolically, this conflict can be conceived as the lifelong struggle between two "bio-psycho-social" forces.

Theoretical concepts: tragedy, catharsis and Aristotle's "Poetics"

In the ancient Greek world, Tragedy occurred when a hero faced two opposing "rights". It revealed the tragic stories of human beings in front of their destiny and it served a social function within the democracy of Athens (Georgopapadakos, 1968). Furthermore, tragedian modes of practice, such as chorus enactments in open-air amphitheatres, were applied for therapeutic reasons for people who suffered (Aravantinos, 1907). Inspired by those ancient documents, similar methods of practice have been applied in mental health care during the last century (Lyketsos, 1980). Of course, the structure and hierarchy in ancient Greek society was very different from our contemporary world. However, having in mind the limitations of using the tragedian paradigm within a contemporary Western European culture, we may observe a "dramatherapy performance" as having the properties of a Tragedy. A person with schizophrenia playing a role in front of an audience within a mental health setting can be seen metaphorically as a "tragic hero". Therefore, the presented play of a "dramatherapy performance" project, regardless of its specific theme, can be assessed by the use of the tragedian aesthetics.

It is crucial here to explore how a "dramatherapy performance" can acquire a cathartic quality. Catharsis is the core concept in Aristotle's (384–322 BC) definition of Tragedy, which he gives in his "Poetics":

> Tragedy is an imitation of an action that is serious, complete, and of a certain magnitude; in language embellished with each kind of artistic ornament, the several kinds being found in separate parts of the play; in the form of action, not of narrative; through pity and fear effecting the proper *Katharsis*, or purgation, of these emotion.
>
> (Butcher, 1920, p. 240)

Since Aristotle's "Poetics", a number of interpretations have been given to the term catharsis (Chronopoulos, 2000; Kouretas, 1963; Ramphos, 1993), which are grouped into four basic views: the medical (physiological) view of catharsis as a physical cleansing function; the moral view of purification; the intellectual view of clarification and pedagogic development; and the aesthetic view which refers to the intrinsic structure of a tragic action. Else (1967), in his work *The Argument*, presents the aesthetic view that catharsis refers to the fatal or painful action, the tragic "passion". For Else, catharsis lies within the play. He argues that the spectator or reader does not perform the purification. He views catharsis as a functional and transitional component of the tragic structure. It is not the end in a Tragedy, but it is followed by letting off pity and by tragic pleasure. From this point of view, catharsis encompasses structure and containment and, under this consideration, it can be useful and meaningful to dramatherapy (Yotis, 2002).

A main concern for a dramatherapist is to construe the plot of the session so that it can act as a vehicle for the projection and containment of the group members' feelings. The idea of catharsis within a therapeutic process can be seen as initiated by the therapist's plan, as a plot to start with, a sequence of guided events throughout the sessions and, finally, a closure. A cathartic structure also includes the point of resolution and provides safety without strangling spontaneity. This can be related to the importance Aristotle places on the gradual construction of the plot of a drama, by acknowledging probability and necessity in order to provide not only a spectacle, but also a meeting of light with shadow within a respectful democratic situation; a place where differences can intermingle meaningfully. Working through various mediums – plays, stories, roles, bodywork, masks or puppets – catharsis in dramatherapy is a potential resolution and can promote transformation (Holmwood, 2016; Jennings, 1995). A play itself, according to contemporary dramatherapists, can be the container of human feelings in therapy (Jenkyns, 1996). Catharsis does not appear after the dramatic mediums have been applied in therapy; it is their own intrinsic properties that are cathartic.

Aristotle's "Poetics" is the first described sign system for theatre semiotics (Elam, 1980), analysing how catharsis is realized in an ancient Greek tragedy and which are its components. The "Poetics" include two kinds of components of a tragic form:

- poetic elements related to quantity: the offer of a structure with a beginning, middle and end, including episodes (scenes of action) and chorus parts;
- poetic elements related to quality: plot, character, ideology, diction, music and design. These elements will be examined next in relation to dramatherapy.

1 *Mythos* (Plot): As Butcher explains in his fundamental study on Aristotle (1920, p. 334):

> Of the six elements into which Aristotle analyses a tragedy, plot holds the first place. Plot in the drama, in its fullest sense, is the artistic equivalence of "action" in real life. [...] "Action" in Aristotle is not a purely external act, but an inward process, which works outward, the expression of a man's rational personality. [...] It must include outward fortune and misfortune, processes of the mental life.

Within a dramatherapy process, the storytelling and story-making models of work are often used. Also, stories appear in other models of dramatherapy work. The story in a group offers its plot, which guides the therapeutic work. This fictional plot affects the group and shapes the plot of the group's life.

2 *Ethos* (Character): As described in Aristotle's "Poetics", Ethos and Dianoia are each one side of character:

> They are two distinct factors which unite to constitute the concrete and living person. [...] Ethos is the moral element in character. It is an expression of moral purpose, of the permanent disposition and tendencies, the tone and sentiment of the individual. [...] Ethos reveals itself both in speeches and in the actions of the dramatic characters. Wherever moral choice or a determination of the will is manifested there ethos appears.
>
> (Butcher, 1920, pp. 340–343)

From a dramatherapy angle, Ethos relates to character creation in role-playing. It encompasses the characteristics, tendencies and behaviours of a character evoked and developed during role-playing.

3 *Dianoia* (Ideology):

> Dianoia is the thought, the intellectual element, which is implied in all rational conduct, through which alone ethos can find outward expression. Under Dianoia are included the intellectual reflections of a speaker; the proof of his own statements, the disproof of those of his opponents, his general maxims concerning life and conduct, as elicited by the action and forming part of a train of Reasoning.
>
> (Butcher, 1920, p. 343)

Within a dramatherapy context it refers to the cognitive part of a character, conveying ideas and beliefs, which are formed during role-playing.

4 *Lexis* (Diction): Diction refers to all kinds of verbal expression. However, from a dramatic point of view, silence can be considered as a dramatic diction. As Heimonas states (1987, p. 33): "diction includes many events of silence; the function of speech, the symbolic drama of wit enters within a wide zone of silence, which can be considered as anything but an absence of speech". Considering clients with schizophrenia, the poverty of verbal use and, often, muteness are part of the clients' negative symptoms, namely "alogia". Silence within a group of clients could be also conceived of as expressing the clients' inner existential void, still unable to be symbolized by words and to form meanings. It could reflect the clients' regression, a return to the self after ineffective attempts at communicating with others.

5 *Melos* (Music): Music was thought to be, according to the ancient Greeks, the most imitative or representative of the arts. But for Aristotle, music expressed the image and reflection of a character. Butcher (1920, p. 131) interprets this issue in relation to the Greek tradition of the role of music to which Aristotle adheres:

> We must bear in mind that the dominant element in Greek music was the rhythm; the spirit and meaning of any given composition was felt to reside especially here; and the doctrine which asserted the unique imitative capacity of music had for Aristotle its theoretic basis in this, that the external movements of rhythmical sound bear a close resemblance to the movements of the soul. Each single note is felt as a unique agitation. The regular succession of musical sounds, governed by the laws of melody and rhythm, are allied to those dramatic actions or outward activities which are the expression of a mental state.

The role of music and rhythm in dramatherapy sessions are vital. Singing, especially, offers a chance for clients with verbal difficulties to connect to each other.

6 *Opsis* (Design): According to Aristotle the design is the least important element of the Tragedy, however much it might contribute to the overall impression. Butcher (1920, p. 135), interpreting Aristotle, reminds us:

> Color and form too have a similar capacity though in an inferior degree. The instinctive movements of the limbs, the changes of color produced on the surface of the body, are something more than arbitrary symbols; they imply that the body is of itself responsive to the animating soul, which leaves its trace on the visible organism.

Considering "design" from a dramatherapy angle, not only the set and costumes are included, but also any real or symbolic use of props and objects, the position and status of the persons in space, their use and transformation of space, the light they transmit or absorb as energetic presences.

Creating a new evaluation tool

"Dramatherapy Performance Evaluation", a tool inspired by Aristotle's "Poetics", is devised in order to assess a dramatherapy process, including the performance event, as well as the individual performance of each client within this process. The development of the six elements of the "Poetics" can be followed in all the phases of a dramatherapy process in order to lead to a qualitative analysis in the form of a narrative. Usually, the method of creating and presenting a dramatherapy performance includes the following stages:

a *The first phase: projection and emotional bonding.* Acquaintance of group members takes place in this initial phase, followed by projections of their personal material on different dramatic mediums. The clients' dramatic involvement is facilitated by techniques aiming at their emotional bonding.

b *The second phase: working through personal material.* The clients' projective material from the first phase is combined into basic scenes, which constitute the themes of therapeutic work during this phase. Dramatic material is worked through according to the clients' needs and shaped into a containing structure.

c *The third phase: the performance event.* This phase consists of the opening of the group to an external audience, initially the ward, and finally an invited audience of the clients' "significant others". For this reason, both group members and therapists decide which pieces of work are ready to be "safely" presented. Rehearsals of those pieces of work take place during this phase.

d *The final phase: the closure.* The last phase deals with the post-performance effect on the clients, the gained insights from all the previous preparations, the experience of an ending and the future prospects after the group's closure.

In each of these phases the six poetic elements follow a parallel constructive process. In relation to the different phases of group work, the following questions need to be answered.

Has and to what extent the client group been able to:

a Structure a story with a beginning, a middle part and an end?
b Display characters within this story?
c Convey the ideas of these characters?
d Utter the characters' speech?
c Express themselves in relation to music and sounds?
f Express themselves in relation to the design (props, scenery and costumes)?

Table 10.1 offers a shape for the analysis of the group work as well as helping to observe changes in specific dramatic dimensions within each of the four phases of the therapeutic process, as they are described above.

Table 10.1 Grid for analysis of group work

Qualitative analysis	*Projection bonding*	*Work through structure*	*Role-playing performance*	*De-roling sharing*
Mythos				
Ethos				
Dianoia				
Lexis				
Melos				
Opsis				

"Dramatherapy Performance Evaluation" offers a new model of describing and analysing the therapeutic process, as the narrative based on the intrinsic poetic elements that are developed throughout this process. Furthermore, changes of the individual clients' psychopathology can be assessed by a combination of existing validated scales of psychopathology to the six poetic elements. For example, a researcher might focus on the effect of the process to the clients' negative schizophrenic symptoms or to a particular symptom included in this category. Andreasen's rating of negative symptoms for schizophrenia, the "SANS" (1982), includes specific symptoms, grouped into subcategories, one of which is "affective flattening". This cluster of symptoms includes: unchanging facial expression, paucity of expressive gestures, decreased spontaneous movements, lack of vocal inflections, poor eye contact, affective non-responsivity and inappropriate affect. The above symptoms can be assessed in dramatherapy by an adaptation of the SANS scale in relation to the clients' contribution to the poetic elements of the process. The example illustrated in Table 10.2 demonstrates such an assessment, focusing on "unchanging facial expression", one of the items of "affective flattening". Observations can be marked after each session, at certain moments of the group process, or after watching the recorded sessions. The marking can follow a scale from 1 to 5 (1: Not at all; 2: Mildly; 3: Moderately; 4: Marked; 5: Severely), so that a scale with 48 (8 × 6) items rated from 1 to 5 is constructed. Low scores of affective flattening (range from 1 to 5) indicate a better affective functioning of the clients.

Example

Client X has an "*unchanging facial expression*" at the following performance items:

- a During the plot of the scene (1–5)
- b During the display of a character(s) (1–5)
- c During the flow of the character's ideas (1–5)
- d During the flow of the play's diction (1–5)
- e In relation to music or sound effects (1–5)
- f In relation to his/her use of props and scenery (1–5)

In this way the ratings of the clients' symptoms provide objective measurements for further research as well as data for further discussion and interpretations. A paradigm of a client's presentation of affective flattening in relation to the different poetic elements is shown in Table 10.2. The client, named "Leto", has been assessed according to her contribution to the performance project, as illustrated by the following commentary.

> Comments: Leto's blunt affect influenced all the poetic elements of this performance noticeably. Her contribution was mainly through her

Table 10.2 Affective flattening components in relation to Aristotle's Poetic elements

Subject: Leto	*Unchanging facial expression*	*Paucity of expressive gestures*	*Decreased spontaneous movements*	*Lack of vocal inflections*	*Poor eye contact*	*Affective non-responsivity*	*Inappropriate affect*	*Global affective flattening*	*Total score*
Mythos	5	4	4	4	3	2	2	3	27
Ethos	5	4	4	5	4	3	4	4	33
Dianoia	5	3	3	3	3	2	2	3	24
Lexis	5	4	4	4	4	2	3	4	30
Melos	5	4	4	3	3	2	2	3	26
Opsis	5	4	4	4	4	3	3	4	31
Total score	30	23	23	23	21	14	16	21	171

participation in the Ideology (Dianoia) of the play. Her comments were thoughtful, sincere and important for the group. Her attempts to create Character (Ethos) were sparse (Character score is the highest) and she only held an almost mute part (high score in Diction) on stage, playing the role of a company member, as she sang with the others in the chorus. Her contribution to the Music (Melos) of the play was better than the rest of her performance, since she made a genuine effort to be tuned in harmonically with the rest of the members, even if not in a particularly animated manner. Her contribution to Design (Opsis) was restricted, with a limited use of space and props, as she was often hiding behind others on stage. Among her expressive components the most severely affected was her "facial expression", which was almost unchanging throughout the whole play. Much less influenced (moderately) were her "appropriate affect" and "affective responses", which indicated her positive intentions towards the groupwork and established her as a sympathetic presence within the group.

The Eginition project

The "dramatherapy performance" project as it was implemented at the Eginition Day Hospital of the National and Kapodistrian University of Athens, Medical School, Department of Psychiatry, will be presented next. Its aim was to measure the impact of a performance process with clients with schizophrenia on their creativity, decrease of symptoms and relationship with their significant others. This randomized controlled clinical trial took place comparing a dramatherapy group to a control group – the former containing 15 and the latter 16 clients with schizophrenia – during a four-month therapeutic period and a three-month follow-up. The Dramatherapy Group took place twice a week, in 90-minute sessions. The clients were young adults, aged between 18 and 35, both men and women, with duration of illness up to 15 years, without any established organic reason for their mental state or any mental retardation and without any drug or alcohol dependency. The clients were on anti-psychotic medication, prescribed by the psychiatrists of the unit and administered by the Day Hospital. For the needs of this research it was arranged that the clients' medication would remain standard for the months of the therapeutic project unless an important reason for an alteration of medication occurred, such as a relapse. An hour of group supervision took place once a week with all the therapists of the Day Hospital in which the group dynamics and the group process were discussed. Once a month, supervision by the head psychiatrist of the Day Hospital took place, during which the relation of the group to the functioning of the whole Day Hospital was discussed. The research project took place in real-life conditions, as the Day Hospital kept its ongoing service, and had the informed consent of the clients. The participation of the clients was continual, as they were informed about the strategy at every stage of the project, provided their points of view over the whole process and were interested in the outcome. Besides, the whole performance was based on their autobiographical material. In this way, this research project could be considered within the framework of "real world research" (Robson, 1993).

Methodology

This research followed a mixed methodology, combining qualitative and quantitative and art-based data. *Qualitative research* was based on the analysis of the group process, including the performance event, as a narrative of a case study, by using "Dramatherapy Performance Evaluation". Systematic observation of the clients' individual creativity throughout the whole process added to the research outcomes. Additionally, the performance's after-effect on the clients' "significant others" was analysed through semi-structured interviews. Moreover, a *quantitative evaluation* was undertaken, analysing the impact of this project on the clients' schizophrenic symptoms and their relationships with self and others. This part of the research investigated the impact of the "dramatherapy performance" on the clients' general psychopathology (Overall & Gorham, 1962), their level of depression (Zung, 1965), self-esteem (Robson, 1989), negative symptoms (Andreasen, 1982) and their perceived support from their "significant others" (Power, Champion & Aris, 1988). The analysis of the gathered data involved:

a a content analysis of the videotaped dramatherapy process (Waltrip et al., 1988), evaluating the sessions as well as the performance as an independent event;
b the analysis of qualitative data acquired from interviews; and
c the statistical analysis of the quantitative data provided by scales and questionnaires. The statistical approach for analysing this kind of longitudinal data, where the average response over time is the chosen target, involves three different approaches:

    1 "post" – an analysis that ignores the pre-treatment scores available and analyses the mean of each subject's post-treatment responses
    2 "change" – an analysis that uses the differences between the means of each subject's post- and pre-treatment responses
    3 "ANCOVA" – an analysis that takes into account the variation between subjects in the baseline measurements, by using the mean of the baseline values for each subject as a covariate in a linear model for the comparison of post-treatment means.

Statistical analysis was performed using the Statistical Package of Social Sciences (SPSS 10.0).

Qualitative results

Concerning the four phases of this dramatherapy procedure, which was based on the clients' autobiographical material, all six poetic elements (Plot, Character, Ideology, Diction, Music and Design), analysed separately, marked out a parallel development. Within this parallel analysis, a number of therapeutic interventions took place, concerning more or less each of the six poetic elements of the performance project. While gradually constructing the performance Plot, the clients' stories emerged, were linked to each other and were completed, until they became the Plot of the dramatherapy group. Character formation expanded the clients' repertoire and gave the opportunity of relating to each other through role, at an "as if" symbolic level. The final characters of the performance, being the "clients in role" within a clinical setting, rendered them the tragic heroes of their everyday life. The characters' Ideology, as it was developed, coincided gradually with the ideology of the dramatherapy group, giving the opportunity of a cognitive construing. At the same time it enhanced the clients' process of character formation with insight and rationale. The Diction of the project, developed in dialogues and lyrics, clarified diffused meanings and dressed the clients' verbalization with sentiment. Music, created either from sounds and primitive instruments or from existing musical pieces or songs familiar to the group, fostered a common affective springboard for the group members' verbal and nonverbal communication. Design set the marks of boundaries – sparse and diffuse in the beginning – and led to a whole stage of signifiers for the performance event, as well for the clients' lives thereafter. The whole process illuminated both the clients' abilities and difficulties relating emotionally to each other, to create affective bonds and to be able to separate from each other without experiencing chaos, after having worked together.

Regarding the performance event, the clients managed to perform on stage their own myth in front of an invited audience, through the presentation of a group autobiographical play. The structure of this myth was completed with an awareness of time and space, following a pre-structured sequence of the scenes with a flow of "*episodes*" and "*chorus parts*" that indicated a high level of collaboration and group cohesion. Most of the clients were able to interact in the large group as well as in subgroups and individually. All 15 clients were able to take part in the group as a whole and to form the chorus of the play, while nine clients were able to enact one or more individual roles and four clients held supporting roles in the episodes of the play.

The issues the clients brought to the group moved around three basic themes: suppression, stigmatization due to the psychiatric disorder and the need to connect with others. Initially in the clients' stories the disorder was experienced as conquering their lives. Through the metaphor of the story of Spartacus the clients had the opportunity to play both victims and perpetrators and to experience revolution and the feeling of fighting towards victory. The stigma of schizophrenia came in the group through the story of a member who was bullied in school after undressing himself in public. The role of support by friends in this awkward situation was explored and guided the group to the third theme: companionship. Accepting others despite their disorder and focusing on the advantages of a relationship was the common theme of the group, which gave the group members the opportunity to experience building real relationships within the group boundaries. Desire, pleasure and enjoyment arose and formed the last scene of the play, with the company singing and dancing together at a fictional beach party. "Sweet Automobile", the title of the performance, which was proposed by a group member, was the vehicle of this group, which moved towards human connection and intimacy despite the obstacle of the disorder.

The moving effect of the performance rested on the ability of the clients to create collectively and to form relationships. This encompassed hope and romance and provided the performance with an atmosphere of optimism and support. Together with the emotional material, conveyed by the chorus songs, it facilitated identification of the audience members with the performers. Witnessing the clients' emotional disposition during the performance was the most moving factor of the whole event, for emotional exchange, poor or inappropriate for a long time, had been a forgotten area in the clients' lives. What ran contrary to expectations was the clients' capability to stand up and perform on stage and to be able to express dramatically and convey meaning despite their disorder. Within the stress-provoking situation of a stage presentation, in front of an audience of family members and friends, the clients demonstrated what they had achieved. Despite the fact that not all performers were charismatic, the activity as a whole had appreciable artistic merit, and was an authentic moment in the clients' lives. For all participants this stage performance was a rehearsal for life.

Furthermore, the development of the six poetic elements throughout the therapeutic process was evaluated. First, the individual contribution of each group member was assessed (as shown earlier in Table 10.2) by a quantification of qualitative data gathered from observation of videotapes by two independent raters. Second, considering the average of these measurements, the development of the poetic elements by the group as a whole became evident. In addition, the ratings showed which elements had a statistically significant positive correlation ($r > 0.5$, $p < 0.01$) and which were influenced independently of each other (their distributions differed significantly, $p < 0.01$):

a The clients managed to create a united and coherent performance, all the particular poetic elements of which showed a statistically significant positive correlation ($0.759 < r < 0.981$, $p < 0.001$).
b The *Plot*, the *Ideology* and the *Diction* of the performance were created more through verbal processes. These elements showed a significant interconnection, influencing the clients' affective flattening in the same way.

c *Music* and *Design* had an interconnection, as they were created mainly through nonverbal processes. The clients' affective flattening was less apparent in these two poetic elements than in the other elements that were mostly based on verbal processes.

d *Character* included verbal as well as nonverbal processes and was positively correlated to all of the above elements, indicating that the common unifying element was character creation, manifested as individual role-playing.

e The *Ideology* was conveyed in a similar way through both character and chorus representations, although the more functional clients (whose flat affect scored lower) were keener to present individual characters than the others, and the more dysfunctional ones were better at participating in the performance chorus.

In general, clients whose negative symptoms were manifested through affective flattening were helped more when the "dramatherapy performance" project focused on the nonverbal processes as being important for enhancing the verbal ones.

Quantitative results

a There was no significant difference between the dramatherapy group and the control group in terms of the change in the clients' *general psychopathology*, as measured by the BPRS scale ($p=0.354$), and their *depression* level, as measured by the Zung scale ($p=0.187$).

b The clients' change in their overall *self-esteem*, as measured by Robson's self-esteem scale, did not show any significant difference between the two groups ($p=0.907$). However, among the self-esteem components the only significant difference between the two groups was in the change of the clients' feeling of "*competence and efficacy*" ($p=0.049$). Adjusted for the initial values of this subscale before the group work (linear regression analysis), this difference between the two groups was confirmed ($p=0.005$).

c The most important result was the difference in the decrease of the clients' *negative symptoms*, as measured by the SANS scale. This change differed significantly between the dramatherapy group and the control group after the four-month period of group work ($p<0.001$) and can be attributed to the therapeutic process of the dramatherapy group. For the dramatherapy group, there was a significant decrease in the total negative symptoms' score ($p<0.001$), as well as in all the negative symptoms subcategories after the four-month period of group work. After a seven-month period (which included the four-month group-work period and a three-month follow-up), the total SANS score change differed significantly between the two groups in relation to the initial scores ($p=0.027$), while among the SANS subscales, the changes in "*affective flattening*", "*anhedonia – asociality*" and "*inattentiveness*" still remained significant within the dramatherapy group ($p<0.05$). Adjusted for the initial values of the SANS scale (regression analysis), the difference of the SANS change between the two groups was confirmed for both the period of the group work ($p<0.001$) and the follow-up period ($p<0.029$) (Figures 10.1 and 10.2). As far as the dramatherapy group was concerned, the above results imply that the reduction of the clients' negative symptoms and especially their "affective flattening", "anhedonia-asociality" and "inattentiveness", as well as their improved sense of "competence and efficacy", occurred through a gradual involvement in the dramatic activities of the dramatherapy process.

d In the clients' perceived *support from their significant others*, as measured by Power's "Significant Others' Scale", there was no significant change between the two groups after the group work. However, the discrepancy between the ideal and the actual support the clients perceived from their significant others changed significantly only within the dramatherapy group ($p=0.039$), while this was not the case with the control group ($p=0.333$). This was possibly because the clients in the dramatherapy group, after having created strong supportive relationships with each other, were no longer satisfied by the actual level of support they perceived from their significant others and wished to enhance their

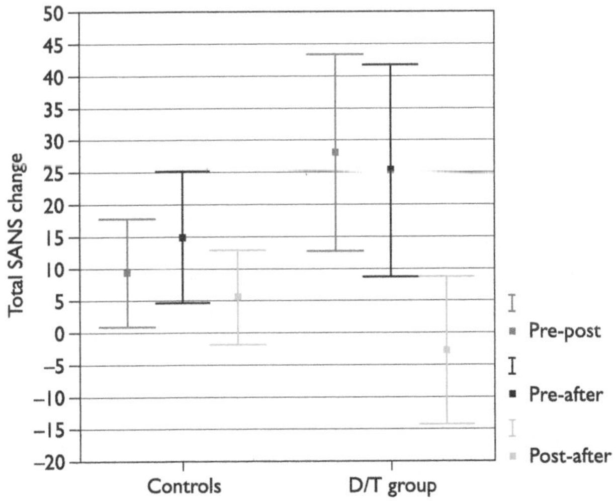

Figure 10.1 Comparison of the SANS subscales before, after the group work and after the follow-up period ("pre", "post" and "after" measurement) within the dramatherapy and within the control group as well as between the two groups. Pre-post shows the change before and after the group work. Post-after measurement shows the change lasting up to the follow-up. Pre-after shows the change of symptoms before the group work up to the follow-up.

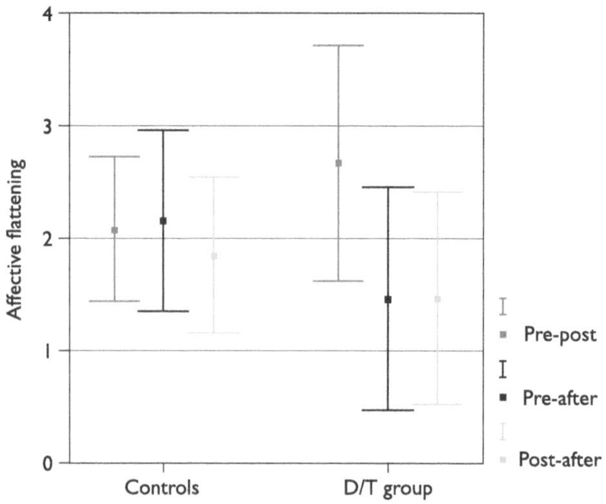

Figure 10.2 Comparison of the change in SANS' subscale "affective flattening" within the dramatherapy and within the control group as well as between the two groups. Pre-post, post-after and pre-after changes are indicated.

relationships with them. They perceived their relationships with their significant others from a more idealistic perspective (i.e. with higher expectations). In addition to the clients' and therapists' views, the spectators' views were also taken into consideration. The clients' significant others, invited as audience members for the final performance event, were interviewed one month after the performance. Qualitative data from semi-structured interviews with the clients' significant others confirmed the positive impact of the performance event. The clients' participation in the performance was considered the most important issue within the whole process. As a significant factor in this performance event, the clients' spontaneity stands out: a "vital force" not at all obvious in their previous everyday life. The significant others observed the following changes in the clients due to this project: spontaneity, acceptance from others, increased ability to socialize in and out of the therapeutic community, improvement in emotional response, confrontation of the fear of body contact, improvements in cognitive functions such as memory and concentration, and increase in their interests and motivation at home during the rehearsal period. Meeting the other relatives and friends of the clients during the performance instilled courage, provided an occasion of a social coming out for the significant others and a springboard for better relationships in the future. The staff's supportive but non-directive presence during the performance acted as a model towards this goal.

Discussion

The performance did not "cure" the clients' schizophrenic disorder nor did it represent a moment "free of symptoms" in the clients' lives. On the contrary, their difficulties with regard to the realization of the performance were definitely observable, through the motor, vocal or expressive inadequacies of the clients' communication skills. The effort demanded against the inertia of their psychopathology could be observed in their getting easily tired and dehydrated, losing concentration, forgetting some tasks, reacting more slowly than expected or with a smaller affective range and variety of responses. However, the clients showed that despite their schizophrenic symptoms, they are able to function in stressful situations if they can get the right level of support and they can create meaningful events and relate to each other with affection. Their inner vital force grew stronger and enabled them to present an integrated event that respected and incorporated social norms in a way that was vital for this client group; an event which was proved to be enlivening and not grotesque.

This project showed how research could be carried out within the conditions of an ongoing therapeutic programme, as in a Day Hospital, without disturbing its overall therapeutic functioning. This was made possible by designing a research strategy based on questions that arose from observations within this particular setting, rather than formulating questions beforehand and trying to investigate them within a clinical setting. This strategy furthers the existing dialectics between clinical practice and research within a day hospital by formulating research hypotheses, which can be investigated using the available clinical evidence. The results highlight features of interest that can become areas of further research. It can also permit practitioners and researchers in the same clinical setting to exchange views, collaborate and re-evaluate their work. Moreover, the participation of the clients in the project gives them a sense of their own unique contribution to scientific research and empowers them as active participants within the research process. Even if the clients do not design the research, the process of its construction is chiefly determined by their issues and developed through their material on which the research questions focus in order to find answers. In this sense, this research design, which combines quantitative methods of clinical trials with qualitative and art-based research methods, can be considered within the broader frame of "real-world research".

Hopefully, this project opens up future pathways for dramatherapy research. First, the role of performance within dramatherapy practice may be reassessed and new ways of evaluating of dramatherapy practice, deriving from Theatre Semiotics, may be developed. The creation of a "dramatherapy performance" involving clients with schizophrenia was based theoretically on the concept of a tragedian conflict as a metaphor for the schizophrenic condition. "Dramatherapy Performance Evaluation", inspired by Aristotle's "Poetics", was applied to measure, out of the various clusters of negative symptoms of the schizophrenic psychopathology, the subcategory of "*affective flattening*". It may also be used to measure the other subcategories as well, such as "*anhedonia–asociality*" or "*inattentiveness*", on which dramatherapy has a significant impact.

This instrument, based on the six poetic elements of Aristotle, may be used further to measure the efficacy of specific creative elements within dramatherapy practice for clients with schizophrenia, such as working on myth and characterization, cognitive work on ideology, work on poetic diction and verbalization, nonverbal involvement through music, and symbolic use of space, objects and design. Thus, it may help to formulate different areas of practice in relation to different clients' needs, strengths and weaknesses. Further research on similar and comparable client groups with schizophrenia may compare its results to this study and lead to a meta-analysis of this therapeutic practice. The standardization of the "Dramatherapy Performance Evaluation" as a valid and reliable instrument is also a future target.

"Dramatherapy performance" involving clients with schizophrenia is an area of dramatherapy practice that encompasses notions of Psychotherapy, Social Drama and Theatre Performance and provides by its definition a mutative metaphor for the clients' symptoms, relationships, social image and creativity. Research in all these areas may provide evidence for the therapeutic field and broaden our horizons so that the schizophrenic condition may be approached with understanding, as well as with a respect for the individuals suffering from it as "heroes" struggling to overcome their "tragic" fate.

Conclusion

"Dramatherapy Performance Evaluation", inspired by Aristotle's "Poetics", is a tool created for the qualitative assessment and evaluation of both the performance process and event in dramatherapy. It also provides quantitative measurements of symptoms of clients participating in a dramatherapy performance project, such as the "negative symptoms" of schizophrenia. This tool has been effectively used to measure the changes in the negative symptoms of outpatients with schizophrenia during a clinical trial conducted in a day hospital for young adult clients with schizophrenia, after a four-month dramatherapy project as well as after a three-month follow-up period. The results showed a reduction of the clients' overall negative symptoms and, specifically, of their "affective flattening", "anhedonia–asociality" and "inattentiveness". They also indicated the clients' improved sense of "competence and efficacy" and a change in their perceived support from their significant others, which occurred through a gradual involvement in the dramatic activities of the therapeutic process. "Dramatherapy Performance Evaluation" emphasized the performance's unifying cathartic structure and demonstrated how nonverbal therapeutic processes reinforced the impact of verbal processes. It also distinguished the usefulness of collective techniques – such as participation in a chorus – for the less functional clients, as opposed to character work for the more functional clients.

Acknowledgements

This research project was realized with the assistance of the scientific team of the Eginition Day Hospital (National and Kapodistrian University of Athens, Greece): Professor J. Mantonakis, K. Katan, E. Gyra and K. Theochari, and was supervised by Professors J. Dubowski, J. Done, P. Jones and A. Gersie (University of Hertfordshire, UK).

References

Andersen-Warren, M. (1996). Therapeutic theatre. In S. Mitchell (Ed.), *Dramatherapy clinical studies*. London: Jessica Kingsley Publishers.

Andreasen, C. N. (1982). Negative versus positive schizophrenia. *Arch. Gen. Psychiatry, 39*, 789–794.

Aravantinos, A. (1907). *Asklepios and Asklepieia [Ασκληπιός και Ασκληπιεία]*. Leipzig: Drougoulinos.

Bielanska, A., Cechnicki, A. & Budzyna-Dawidowski, P. (1991). Drama therapy as a means of rehabilitation for schizophrenic patients: Our impressions, *Am. J Psychotherapy, 45*(4), 566–575.

Bosco, N., Petrini, F., Giaccherini, S. & Meringolo, P. (2014). Theater as instrument to promote inclusion of mental health patients: An innovative experience in a local community. In C. Pracana (Ed.), *Psychology applications & developments: Advances in psychology and psychological trends series* (pp. 55–66). Lisbon: In Science Press.

Butcher, S. H. (1920). *Aristotle's Theory of Poetry and Fine Art with a critical text and translation of the Poetics*. London: Macmillan.

Casson, J. W. (2004). *Drama, psychotherapy and psychosis*. London: Routledge.

Corrigan, P. W. & Bink, A. B. (2016). The stigma of mental illness. In H. S. Friedman (Ed.), *Encyclopedia of mental health* (2nd ed., pp. 230–234). Oxford: Elsevier.

Corrigan, P. W., Morris, S. B., Michaels, P. J., Rafacz, J. D. & Rüsch, N. (2012). Challenging the public stigma of mental illness: A meta-analysis of outcome studies. *Psychiatric Services, 63*(10), 963–973.

Chronopoulos, C. (2000). *I Aristoteliki Tragiki Katharsis [Η Αριστοτελική Τραγική Κάθαρσις]*. Athens: Kardamitsas.

Cox, M. (1992). *Shakespeare comes to Broadmoor: The performance of tragedy in a secure psychiatric hospital*. London: Jessica Kingsley Publishers.

Crisp, A. H., Gelder, M. G., Rix, S., Meltzer, H. I. & Rowlands, O. J. (2000). Stigmatisation of people with mental illnesses. *Br. J. Psychiatry, 177*, 4–7.

Elam, K. (1980). *The semiotics of theatre and drama*. London: Routledge.

Else, G. (1967). *Aristotle's Poetics: The argument*. Leiden: E. J. Brill, published in cooperation with the State University of Iowa.
Emunah, R. (1994). *Acting for real*. New York: Brunner & Mazel Publishers.
Evreinov, N. (1927). *The theatre in life*. New York: Harrap.
Faigin, D. A. & Stein, C. H. (2015). Community-based theater and adults with psychiatric disabilities: Social activism, performance and community engagement. *American Journal of Community Psychology, 55*, 148–163.
Georgopapadakos, A. (1968). *Greek literature [Ελληνική Γραμματολογία]*. Thessaloniki: Mohlos.
Gersie, A. (Ed.). (1996). *Dramatic approaches to brief therapy*. London: Jessica Kingsley Publishers.
Grainger, R. (1990). *Dramatherapy and ritual in drama and healing: The roots of dramatherapy*. London: Jessica Kingsley Publishers.
Goffman, E. (1961). *Asylums: Essays on the social situation of mental patients and other inmates*. New York: Doubleday.
Heimonas, G. (1987). *I Dysthymi Anagennisi [Η Δύσθυμη Αναγέννηση]*. Athens: Hypsilon.
Holmwood, C. (2016). Dramatherapy and theatre: Current interdisciplinary discourses. In S. Jennings & C. Holmwood (Eds.), *The Routledge international handbook of dramatherapy* (pp. 160–169). New York: Routledge.
Jenkyns, M. (1996). *The play's the thing*. London: Routledge.
Jennings, S. (1995). *Theatre, ritual and transformation*. London: Routledge.
Johnson, D. R. (1980). Effects of a theatre experience on hospitalized psychiatric patients. *The Arts in Psychotherapy, 7*, 265–272.
Johnson, D. R. (1981). Drama therapy and the schizophrenic condition. In G. Schattner & R. Courtney (Eds), *Drama in therapy, Vol. 2: Adults* (pp. 47–66). New York: Drama Book Specialists.
Johnson, D. R. (1982). Developmental approaches to dramatherapy. *The Arts in Psychotherapy, 9*, 183–190.
Jones, P. (1996). *Drama as therapy*. London: Routledge.
Jones, P. (2010). *Drama as therapy* (Vol. 2). London: Routledge.
Kouretas, D. (1963). How the psychocathartic effect of tragedy is produced [*Πώς παράγεται η ψυχοκαθαρτική επίδρασις της τραγωδίας*]. In T. Mouzenidis (Ed.), *Twelve lectures – third series* (p. 23). Athens: National Theatre Organization.
Landy, R. (1995). *Drama therapy theory: Concepts and practices*. Springfield, IL: C. C. Thomas.
Langley, D. & Langley, G. (1983). *Dramatherapy and psychiatry*. London: Croom Helm.
Lyketsos, G. (1980). The Ancient Greek tragedy as a means of psychotherapy for mental patients. *Psychotherapy Psychosomatics, 34*, 241–247.
Martindale, B., Bateman, A., Crowe, M. & Margison, F. (Eds.). (2000). *Psychosis: Psychological approaches and their effectiveness*. London: Gaskell.
Moran, G. S. & Alon, U. (2011). Playback theatre and recovery in mental health: Preliminary evidence. *The Arts in Psychotherapy, 38*(5), 318–324.
Mitchell, S. (1998). The theatre of self-expression. *Dramatherapy: Journal of the British Association for Dramatherapists, 20*(1).
Overall, J. E. & Gorham, D. R. (1962). The Brief Psychiatric Rating Scale (BPRS). *Psychol. Rep., 10*, 799–812.
Power, M. J., Champion, L. A. & Aris, S. J. (1988). The development of a measure of social support: The Significant Others Scale. *British Journal of Clinical Psychology, 27*, 349–358.

Ramphos, S. (1993). *Mimesis against form [Μίμησις εναντίον Μορφής]*. Athens: Armos.

Reisman, D. M. (2016). Drama therapy to empower patients with schizophrenia: Is justice possible? *The Arts in Psychotherapy, 50*, 91–100.

Rössler, W. (2016). The stigma of mental disorders. *EMBO reports, 17*(9), 1250–1253.

Robson, C. (1993). *Real world research*. Oxford: Blackwell.

Robson, P. (1989). Development of the new self-report questionnaire to measure "self-esteem". *Psychol. Medicine, 19*, 513–518.

Waltrip, R. W., II, Strauss, M. E., Summerfelt, A., Heinrichs, D., Kirkpatrick, B., Jauch, D. & Oltmanns, T. F. (1988). Rating affective flattening from videotaped interviews. *Psychiatry Research, 27*(2), 199–205.

Whitelock, J. (1987). Dramatherapy in a psychiatric day centre. In S. Jennings (Ed.), *Dramatherapy: Theory and practice for teachers and clinicians* (Vol. 1, pp. 209–232). London: Croom Helm.

Yotis, L. (2002). *Dramatherapy performance and schizophrenia*. Doctoral thesis, University of Hertfordshire.

Yotis, L. (2006). A review of dramatherapy research in schizophrenia: Methodologies and outcomes. *Psychotherapy Research, 16*(2), 190–200.

Yotis, L. (2014). Playback Theatre: A theatre of reflection [*Θέατρο* Playback: *ένα θέατρο αναστοχασμού*]. *Epilogos*, 1–8.

Yotis, L., Kravariti, C., Theodoridou, D. & Megaloeconomou, T. (2003). The role of dramatherapy in the psychiatric reform: The paradigm of Leros. *Tetradia Psychiatrikis (Τετράδια Ψυχιατρικής), 81*, 48–58.

Yotis, L., Theohari, K., Katan, K. & Mantonakis, J. (2002). Communicating drama between clients with schizophrenia and their "significant others": How is the stigma affected? In L. Schiltz (Ed.), *Epistemology and practice of research in the arts therapies* (pp. 59–74). Luxembourg: CRP-Santé, Fonds National de la Recherche.

Zung, W. K. (1965). A self-rating depression scale. *Arch. Gen. Psychiatry, 12*, 63–70.

Index

Page numbers in *italics* denote tables, those in **bold** denote figures.

For Product Safety Concerns and Information please contact our EU representative GPSR@taylorandfrancis.com Taylor & Francis Verlag GmbH, Kaufingerstraße 24, 80331 München, Germany